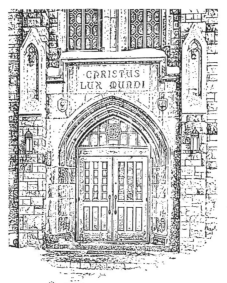

THE PSYCHOLOGY OF HUMOR

Theoretical Perspectives and Empirical Issues

CONTRIBUTORS

SUSAN ANTHONY

DANIEL E. BERLYNE

H. I. DAY

MICHAEL GODKEWITSCH

JEFFREY H. GOLDSTEIN

JACQUELINE D. GOODCHILDS

PATRICIA KEITH-SPIEGEL

LAWRENCE LA FAVE

RONALD LANGEVIN

WILLIAM LUCCHESI

PAUL E. McGHEE

WILLIAM H. MARTINEAU

RODNEY MERS

HOWARD R. POLLIO

JERRY M. SULS

THE PSYCHOLOGY OF HUMOR

Theoretical Perspectives and Empirical Issues

Edited by

JEFFREY H. GOLDSTEIN

Department of Psychology
Temple University
Philadelphia, Pennsylvania

PAUL E. McGHEE

Department of Psychology
State University of New York
Albany, New York

With a Foreword by H. J. Eysenck

ACADEMIC PRESS   New York and London   1972

ACADEMIC PRESS, INC.
111 Fifth Avenue, New York, New York 10003

United Kingdom Edition published by
ACADEMIC PRESS, INC. (LONDON) LTD.
24/28 Oval Road, London NW1

LIBRARY OF CONGRESS CATALOG CARD NUMBER: 71-187246

PRINTED IN THE UNITED STATES OF AMERICA

Contents

Part I INTRODUCTION

Chapter 1. Early Conceptions of Humor: Varieties and Issues

Patricia Keith-Spiegel

Part II THEORETICAL PERSPECTIVES

Chapter 2. Humor and Its Kin

Daniel E. Berlyne

Chapter 3. On the Cognitive Origins of Incongruity Humor: Fantasy Assimilation versus Reality Assimilation

Paul E. McGhee

v

92059

Chapter 4.   A Two-Stage Model for the Appreciation of Jokes and Cartoons: An Information-Processing Analysis

Jerry M. Suls

Chapter 5.   A Model of the Social Functions of Humor

William H. Martineau

Part III   EMPIRICAL ISSUES

Chapter 6.   Physiological Correlates of Humor

Ronald Langevin and H. I. Day

Chapter 11. Humor, Laughter, and Smiling: Some Preliminary Observations of Funny Behaviors

Howard R. Pollio, Rodney Mers, and William Lucchesi

Part IV   OVERVIEW AND CONCLUSIONS

Chapter 12. Advances toward an Understanding of Humor: Implications for the Future

Paul E. McGhee and Jeffrey H. Goldstein

APPENDIX

Chapter 13. An Annotated Bibliography of Published Papers on Humor in the Research Literature and an Analysis of Trends: 1900–1971

Jeffrey H. Goldstein and Paul E. McGhee

List of Contributors

Numbers in parentheses indicate the pages on which the authors' contributions begin.

SUSAN ANTHONY, Department of Psychology, Temple University, Philadelphia, Pennsylvania (159)

DANIEL E. BERLYNE, Department of Psychology, University of Toronto, Toronto, Ontario, Canada (43)

H. I. DAY, Department of Psychology, York University, Toronto, Ontario, Canada (129)

MICHAEL GODKEWITSCH, Department of Psychology, University of Toronto, Toronto, Ontario, Canada (143)

JEFFREY H. GOLDSTEIN, Department of Psychology, Temple University, Philadelphia, Pennsylvania (159, 243, 263)

JACQUELINE D. GOODCHILDS, Department of Psychology, University of California, Los Angeles, California (173)

PATRICIA KEITH-SPIEGEL, Department of Psychology, San Fernando Valley State College, Northridge, California (3)

LAWRENCE LA FAVE, Department of Psychology, University of Windsor, Windsor, Ontario, Canada (195)

RONALD LANGEVIN, Clarke Institute of Psychiatry, Toronto, Ontario, Canada (129)

WILLIAM LUCCHESI, Department of Psychology, The University of Tennessee, Knoxville, Tennessee (211)

PAUL E. McGHEE, Department of Psychology, State University of New York, Albany, New York (61, 243, 263)

WILLIAM H. MARTINEAU, Department of Sociology and Anthropology, Ohio Wesleyan University, Delaware, Ohio (101)

RODNEY MERS, Department of Psychology, The University of Tennessee, Knoxville, Tennessee (211)

HOWARD R. POLLIO, Department of Psychology, The University of Tennessee, Knoxville, Tennessee (211)

JERRY M. SULS, Department of Psychology, Temple University, Philadelphia, Pennsylvania (81, 159)

Foreword

"Life is a comedy to those who think and a tragedy to those who feel." True or false, this old saying embodies a widespread belief in the importance of humor: Without humor, life would be unbearable; hence its perennial attraction to writers of a philosophical, literary, or psychological cast. Contributions over the past 2000 years have been well reviewed in the first chapter of this book. The outcome, as far as any theory of humor is concerned, is of course nugatory; contradictions abound, and agreed conclusions are noticeable by their absence. This is hardly surprising; as the great Faraday said, "They reason theoretically, without demonstration experimentally, and errors are the result." Not until this century have psychologists attempted to tackle the problem of humor and its appreciation by experimental means, and little work in fact was done until just a few years ago. This book reviews the evidence and adds to it. To many people the very notion of catching this butterfly on the wing smacks of hubris. Only a man entirely lacking in humor would attempt to develop a scientific theory of humor or carry out experiments in this field! Such man-in-the-street objurgations we may safely dismiss; they have been encountered by every scientist who has attempted to extend the scope of his inquiries into new fields. But are there perhaps special difficulties in the study of humor which we do not encounter, or encounter only to a lesser degree in the study of other psychological topics?

I have always maintained that experimental psychologists tend to neglect a very important variable in their work, namely, personality; this neglect becomes much more important in experimental aesthetics, of which the study of humor is an important part. Consider the almost universal functional approach of the experimental psychologist. He seeks for equations of the kind $a = (f)b$, where a is the dependent variable and b is the independent variable. Thus what he is trying to find is a universal law, covering all subjects (humans, or rats, or dogs) with whom his experiment is concerned. This approach would make sense if only all humans, or rats, or dogs were as alike as uniovular twins; unfortunately they are not. Consider such a simple question as whether alcoholic fumes (the independent variable b) increase or decrease the activity of rats exposed to them (the dependent variable a). This sounds as if it should have an unequivocal answer, but in fact when six different strains of rats were tested, it was found that two strains increased in activity, two decreased, and two remained unaffected! Similarly, one might ask whether in humans a lengthy rest after learning paired associates to some criterion produces forgetting or reminiscence; this too sounds like a reasonable question. In fact, extroverts show forgetting, introverts reminiscence (and ambiverts presumably no change!). Thus the experimental paradigm which looks so pretty in its functional equation clearly lacks an important element.

We might with advantage look at physics for an answer. Consider Hooke's law of elasticity: Stress = k × Strain. Here, in addition to the dependent and independent variables, we have the constant k, which depends upon the nature of the material and the type of stress used to produce strain. No physicist would throw together all types of material and attempt to derive some universal law predicting what such a mixture would do; why should psychologists do otherwise? Our subjects differ from each other along many dimensions; some of these are implicated directly in most psychological experiments and require to be introduced directly into our functional equation, which now reads $a = (f)b, T$: in this equation T refers to the concept of type, i.e., the degree of extroversion–introversion, stability–neuroticism, or what not of the subject in question. Without the k Hooke's law would not make sense and could not be used for prediction; without T psychological laws do not make sense and cannot be used for prediction. This truth applies to all of experimental psychology; it applies with particular force to the study of complex, mediational phenomena such as sense of humor. One might have thought that a stimulus such as "alcoholic fumes" or "paired associates" would be sufficiently removed from contamination by past associations in a person's mind, or a rat's nervous system, to be acceptable as relatively uniform in meaning. If this is not so, then what hope have we when we use jokes, cartoons, and other materials which depend for their very meaning on past history, associations, verbal knowledge, and other background factors?

During my experimental work in this field, which took place in the early forties, I spent a good deal of time on something which no good behaviorist would dream of doing—something so scandalous that I am only now willing to admit it: I actually asked my subjects what they thought was funny about the cartoons they were asked to rate! Introspection was and is of course anathema to modern psychologists, but the results of this simple procedure were rather interesting. Take a cartoon showing a witch in full regalia, black pointed hat and all, riding along—not on a broomstick, but on a vacuum cleaner; there was no need of a caption. I asked one of my subjects what she thought was funny about this cartoon—she was a highly intelligent student of psychology and very pretty into the bargain. "Well," she said, after considering the problem for a while, "the price tag on the vacuum cleaner says £2.10s. and you obviously couldn't get a vacuum cleaner for two pounds ten shillings!" In spite of much further questioning she could not see anything else funny about the cartoon. In what sense could she and some other subject, who answered correctly that the humor in the cartoon derived from the substitution of the modern vacuum cleaner for the traditional broomstick, in a context of witchcraft which was obviously inappropriate to these modern inventions, be considered to be rating the same cartoon? How many different interpretations were there of each cartoon? I soon found that one's almost instinctive belief that everyone interprets cartoons and jokes similarly is quite mistaken; even among intelligent people different interpretations can be found, and among dull ones the number increases rapidly.

I attempted to make this observation into a test by cutting off the captions of a series of cartoons and getting subjects to write their own captions; the cartoons were selected in such a way that the nature of the caption was pretty firmly determined by the nature of the cartoon. One cartoon, for instance, showed a woman sitting in front of her dressing table, holding a telephone in her hand; her face was just an empty oval, without any features in it. "Hello," she was saying in the caption, "is this the Acme Vanishing Cream Company?" Clearly anyone writing a new caption would start with the observation that in an otherwise conventional picture this one feature was standing out asking for an explanation. One of my subjects, a highly intelligent psychiatrist who had written several well-received books, confessed himself unable to suggest any kind of caption. The first step of a series of "helps" was the suggestion to look for something unusual in the picture. He looked for a while and then said, "I see what you mean—the telephone is not properly connected!" Indeed, the artist had, with the usual artistic license of the cartoonist, drawn just a few squiggles connecting the telephone with the wall socket! The same psychiatrist did not like going to the cinema because he could never understand what was going on; he simply missed all the obvious cues which people much less intelligent than himself would have picked up without any trouble.

Finally, I had people rate cartoons, some of which had their captions cut off and substituted by some quite irrelevant and unconnected caption. Several raters judged these pseudocartoons quite highly; clearly they saw something in them no one else could discover. Again, questioning them on their introspections brought to light a lot of interesting material demonstrating the manifold individual differences that exist in different people's interpretation of comic material.

In my later work, *Dimensions of Personality,* I tried to bring personality types into the picture by making certain predictions, such as that extroverts would prefer sexual and aggressive types of jokes and cartoons, while introverts would prefer nonsense jokes, puns, and similar material. Freud had made exactly the opposite prediction, although not of course in those terms, and we did in fact discover that extroverts, i.e., people who are sexually more forthcoming, as well as being more aggressive, did in fact prefer jokes and cartoons of this type. This means that a person's "typical" behavior extends to his preferences in the humor field, instead of "repressed" trends finding an escape through humor, as Freud had maintained. Here then, it seemed to me, was one way out of the impasse which threatened an experimental psychology of humor; apparently there are groups or "types" of people whose reactions to humor are similar within the group and dissimilar from those of other groups. Later work has shown that experimental manipulation follows a similar paradigm: If you make your subjects more aggressive or more sexually aroused, then they will react to suitable jokes and cartoons embodying such content with greater approval. This too goes against Freud's hypothesis.

Sense of humor then should always be studied with proper reference to typological differences. Without such attention averaged scores may fail to reveal the most important and relevant facts. But can we even speak of such a thing as "sense of humor," or are there several different senses involved? When we refer to a person's sense of humor, we may mean one of several quite distinct and different things. We may mean that a person with a good sense of humor laughs at the same things we do; this is the *conformist* meaning of the term. Or we may mean that he laughs a great deal and is easily amused; this is the *quantitative* meaning of the term. Or we may mean that he is the life and soul of the party, telling funny stories and amusing other people; this is the *productive* meaning of the term. Are these three "senses of humor" usually found together in the same person? The answer seems to be NO; in some unpublished work one of my students found little correlation between these different ways of expressing "sense of humor." Most empirical work has concentrated on the first meaning, either by correlational studies or by observing the effects on ratings of manipulating environmental variables; the other two ways of expression have not been studied much. This is unfortunate: From the social point of view they are probably at least equally important, if not more so. Perhaps the future will remedy this omission.

The contents of this book are too varied to permit discussion—in any case, Chapter 12 provides an overview. However, it is probably true to say that this book marks a milestone in the development of the experimental study of humor, both by its review of past work and by the contribution made to theoretical and empirical advances in the present. It is curious that hitherto no such vade mecum has been in existence; students had to collect their data from widely scattered sources. Perhaps the bringing together of so much knowledge and expertise in one place will encourage others to try their hand at research into one of the most difficult, as well as one of the most fascinating, fields of psychological study. Such a consummation would be the most suitable reward for editors and contributors to this volume alike. A milestone merely marks out the beginning of a long journey!

H. J. EYSENCK

University of London

Preface

In recent years psychology has produced more than its share of edited treatises. Why, then, another? The topic with which we are concerned has long generated popular interest as well as efforts by scholars in many disciplines to understand and describe its essential nature. However, these efforts have typically been of a strictly speculative nature, with little empirical grounding. Over the past 70 years, this state of affairs has undergone some change, due primarily to the increased application of empirical methods by behavioral scientists. But our understanding remains in a highly fragmentary state, due to a continuing lack of any *systematic* empirical and theoretical attack on humor. While psychoanalytic theory has made significant contributions, both theoretically and empirically, to our slowly increasing understanding of the humor process, it is our firm belief that psychoanalytic theory is limited in its capacity to stimulate further advancement along many important humor dimensions. Thus, the primary aim of this book is to stimulate increased empirical interest in an old and troublesome topic. To achieve this aim, we have asked a number of investigators currently engaged in research on different aspects of humor to summarize their theoretical and/or empirical achievements to this point. While we might have accomplished this same end by merely summarizing these efforts ourselves, such a summary would undoubtedly reflect our own biases and inhibit, rather than facilitate, renewed attention to the multidimensional facets of humor.

Theoretical views of humor range from the physiological to the sociological and anthropological. The student interested in humor must be cognizant of this multiplicity of levels in order to attempt to come to grips with the issue of what humor is and how it can be explained. Any attempt to understand the many facets of humor requires the student to go beyond traditional disciplinary boundaries, a step which we view favorably. We also see the diversity of viewpoints contained in this book as a positive sign—an indication of a newly awakened interest in the psychology of humor by representatives of several behavioral sciences.

The research and theory presented in these pages certainly raise many more questions than they answer, yet unlike much previous work, they go far in raising *answerable* questions. So much remains to be done that the student of humor has a real opportunity to make a significant contribution to the field, and partly because of this, we expect future generations of psychologists to devote much more attention to humor than they have in the past. There is also a trend toward exploration of those positive aspects of behavior too long neglected, such as love, play, aesthetics—and humor. The day has not yet arrived, however, when students of psychology are actually encouraged to study such traits; in fact, many of the contributors to this volume have undertaken their studies of humor "on the side."

The chapters presented in this book were written by behavioral scientists, whose training lays emphasis on quantitative research and empirically verifiable theory, and all have agreed that progress toward understanding humor will sooner come about by these means than by any other. So, although there are disagreements in how to attack theory building, there is a more basic agreement that only through theoretical development will we come to grips with the formidable task of understanding humor.

The book is divided into five sections: (1) an introductory section in which the history of thought and major theoretical issues on humor are presented; (2) a theoretical section in which new models of different aspects of humor are advanced; (3) a section on empirical issues in which selected research areas are given detailed attention; (4) an overview and conclusions chapter which discusses the advancements made in the present volume and suggests directions for future research and theory development; and (5) an annotated bibliography from 1900 to 1971, including an analysis of research trends over the past two decades. All of these sections, and most particularly the last two, are designed to provide direction to those who would pursue the field of humor in their own laboratories.

The empirical and theoretical papers cover a broad spectrum of orientations toward humor, ranging from Langevin and Day's research on physiological correlates to La Fave's research on reference groups in the empirical realm, and from Berlyne's arousal theory to Martineau's discussion of the social functions of humor in the theoretical sphere. McGhee and Suls advance models of the nature of cognitive processing involved in humor, McGhee's views being concerned with children and those of Suls with adults. Berlyne deals with humor on a fairly broad theoretical level, discussing the relationships which humor bears to other phenomena, such as play, exploratory behavior, games, and aesthetics. The chapters by Langevin and Day and by Godkewitsch provide data to supplement Berlyne's views. The research of Goldstein, Suls, and Anthony was undertaken to provide an alternative theoretical account of appreciation for specific kinds of humor, and also serves to provide corroborative data for the information processing model of humor presented by Suls. The papers by Pollio, Mers, and Lucchesi, Goodchilds, and La Fave are all concerned with instances of humor in broad social settings.

Note that we have not, in this preface, attempted to define precisely what humor is. As Berlyne indicates in Chapter 2, we all know it when we see it, but it becomes difficult to specify *a priori* what it is. We have not attempted a definition here for the simple reason that there is no single definition of humor acceptable to all investigators in the area. Furthermore, too much energy has been expended in psychology attempting to define phenomena *in the absence of a theoretical framework,* only to conclude that there are multiple definitions, only operational definitions, or no definition at all. Since the precise meaning of the term varies from one psychologist to another, depending upon his theoretical orientation, we have opted to let each contributor define what it is that he is dealing with.

A variety of people have contributed to this volume in a number of ways, and while most will remain unacknowledged for lack of space, special appreciation should be extended to the people in Avalon for providing us with a place to work, to Barbara Baish for typing the manuscript, and to Academic Press for wise and skillful editorial assistance. Ted Huston kindly commented on the manuscript.

Part I

INTRODUCTION

Chapter 1

Early Conceptions of Humor: Varieties and Issues

Patricia Keith-Spiegel

Department of Psychology
San Fernando Valley State College, Northridge, California

I. Introduction

What does laughter mean? The greatest of thinkers, from Aristotle downwards, have tackled this little problem which has a knack of baffling every effort, of slipping away and escaping only to bob up again, a pert challenge flung at philosophic speculation.

—*Henri Bergson [1911, p. 1]*

The curious and somewhat rare breed of behavioral scientist who has entered in on the chase would have to agree with Bergson that humor is, indeed, a spirited challenge. But assigning humor the puny status of "little problem" seems little warranted. The element of humor, which is so much a part of people's daily lives, must surely be an important and legitimate area of inquiry.

The purpose of this chapter is to present the background of the current humor study scene. And though not wishing to be as disagreeable as McDougall (1922) when he stated that philosophers have given us many ludicrous theories of the ludicrous, we suggest that some of the theoretical notions put forth seem to complicate rather than unravel this Gordian knot (with McDougall's theory itself being one of them!). However, humor is a complicated subject, and the early writers have given us a variety of possibilities as to its nature and a host of theoretical issues with which to wrestle.

II. Varieties of Early Humor Theory

In this section some of the major types of early assumptions about the nature of humor are presented. The divisional headings utilized are only one set of possibilities and, like classification schemes used by others, remain imperfect since many theories can fall into more than one category, whereas others seem inappropriate for classification. For the most part, only writings produced during the "heyday" of humor theorizing—the nineteenth and first half of the twentieth century—are cited. There will be occasion to refer to authors of earlier periods, but only rarely to those more recent, since the remainder of the book is devoted to contemporary theory and research.

Throughout the chapter the term *theory* is used to refer to the notions writers have put forth, but this designation is for convenience only and is not to be taken strictly. Many statements are actually *descriptions* of conditions under which humor may be experienced rather than attempts to *explain* humor. Furthermore, many statements involve assumptions or concepts that defy operationalizing thereby precluding empirical testing. Sometimes we find that the explanations offered leave us perched atop a "black box" (e.g., humor as an instinct). Still others are speculations on the functions humor and laughter perform for the individual or the group but remain incomplete or unsatisfactory as adequate theory. Many of the early writings about humor are by philosophers and literary critics, and as Berlyne (1960) pointed out, there have been relatively few attempts to relate laughter to general psychological and biological principles.

Other overviews of early conceptions of humor appear in Sully (1902), Gregory (1923, 1924), Diserens (1926), Kimmins (1928), Diserens and Bonifield (1930), Piddington (1933), Monro (1951), Flugel (1954), and Berlyne (1969). A particularly useful summary of very early theories is found in the Appendix of Greig's (1923) book. Excerpts from many original writings on humor and comedy have been compiled and edited by Lauter (1964).

A. BIOLOGICAL, INSTINCT, AND EVOLUTION THEORIES

The rather loosely grouped theories illustrated in this section hold as common ground that laughter and humor potentials are "built-in" to the nervous mechanism of the organism and serve some adaptive function. That laughter appears early in life, before any complex cognitive processes have been formed, and that laughter and humor are universal phenomena are often used as points to support the hypothesis that we are dealing with behaviors that have survived for some utilitarian purpose.

Laughter and humor have been hailed as "good for the body" because they restore homeostasis, stabilize blood pressure, oxygenate the blood, massage the vital organs, stimulate circulation, facilitate digestion, relax the system, and produce a feeling of well-being

(Spencer, 1860; Darwin, 1872; Hecker, 1873; Dearborn, 1900; McDougall, 1922; Menon, 1931).

McDougall (1903, 1922, 1923) believed laughter to be an instinct. According to him, it was evolved as a necessary corrective of the effects of sympathy. Without a sense of the ludicrous, nature's antidote for the minor depressing and disagreeable spectacles confronting men, the species might not have survived. Others who have proposed instinct theories of humor include Drever (1917), Eastman (1921), McComas (1923), Gregory (1924), and Menon (1931).

A number of theorists have taken the stand that what we regard today as laughter and humor are but *vestiges* of archaic adaptive behaviors. Theories as to the nature and function of the original behavior that turned into humor, over the millennia, vary among those adopting this viewpoint. According to McComas (1923) and Hayworth (1928), laughter served communication functions in prelingual times. It signaled good news and indicated that the group could relax in safety. Wallis (1922) suggested that social laughter was expressive of unity in group opinion. The concept of laughter as a relic of struggling, biting, and physical attack and ultimate conquest was advanced by Kallen (1911), Crile (1916), Delage (1919), Ludovici (1932), and Rapp (1947, 1949, 1951). Gradually laughter and humor became a substitute for actual assault. The similarity of bodily stance (exposed teeth, contorted face, sprawling movements of the limbs, etc.) in both fighting and laughing is pointed to as evidence. Ludovici called the audible aspect of laughter a spiritualized snarl. Rapp shows in detail how present-day ridicule can be traced to the primitive thrashing of enemies. Laughter has also been viewed as the means of maintaining group standards in primitive times (Wallis, 1922).

Laughter gradually became pleasurable as it blended with sympathy and affection. Its "humanization" in the course of time has been discussed in detail by Gregory (1924) and Rapp (1949).

B. SUPERIORITY THEORIES

The roots of laughter in triumph over other people (or circumstances) supplies the basis for superiority theories. Elation is engendered when we compare ourselves favorably to others as being less stupid, less ugly, less unfortunate, or less weak. According to the principle of superiority, mockery, ridicule, and laughter at the foolish actions of others are central to the humor experience.

Aristotle's account of wit (in *The Poetics*)* holds that the ludicrous is to be found in some defect, deformity, or ugliness which is neither painful nor destructive. (For a thorough analysis of what has been salvaged of Aristotle's humor and comedy theory, see Cooper, 1922.) Hobbes (1651) defined laughter as a kind of "sudden glory" which we achieve primarily by observing the infirmities of others and comparing them with the "eminency" in ourselves. Bain (1888) extended Hobbes's theory by including ideas, political institutions, and inanimate objects as targets for ridicule. Bergson (1911) viewed humor as a punishment inflicted on unsocial persons. Thus humiliation becomes a social corrective. Bergson also stressed laughter at stupidity in habitual or stereotyped behavior when more intelligent action would have been more appropriate. Ludovici (1932) believed humor to be a case of superior adaptation whereby a person feels himself to be better adapted to a situation than someone else. The greater the dignity of the victim, the greater the resulting amusement.

Other theories incorporating superiority-related concepts as central to the nature of humor stress elation in triumph or victory (Carus, 1898; Leacock, 1935, 1937; Rapp, 1947, 1949); pleasure in outstripping one's competitors (Dunlap, 1925); joy of getting another at a disadvantage (Stanley, 1898); delight in the sufferings and misfortunes of others (Plato, in *Philebus*;† Beerbohm, 1921) or in the ugliness, deformity, or mental afflictions of others (Cicero, in *De Oratore*;‡ Knight, 1808; Meyerson, 1925, cited in Diserens & Bonifield, 1930); and amusement at the stupid actions of others (Sidis, 1913; Wallis, 1922).

Not all theorists who include the element of superiority as part of humor believe that laughter is always contemptuous or scornful. Sympathy, congeniality, empathy, and geniality may be combined with the laughter of superiority (Hunt, 1846; Bain, 1888; Carpenter, 1922; McDougall, 1922; Rapp, 1949).

C. INCONGRUITY THEORIES

Humor arising from disjointed, ill-suited pairings of ideas or situations or presentations of ideas or situations that are divergent from habitual customs form the bases of incongruity theories.

---

* Macmillan ed., 1895 (see References).
† Clarendon ed., 1871 (see References).
‡ Clarendon ed., 1881 (see References).

Early proponents of this viewpoint include Gerard (1759), who described the objects of humor as uncommon mixtures of relations and the contrariety in things; Beattie (1776), who believed that laughter arose when two or more inconsistent or unsuitable circumstances were united into one complex assemblage; and Priestley (1777), who viewed the cause of laughter to be the perception of contrast. More celebrated among the early incongruity theories are those of Kant (1790) and Schopenhauer (1819). According to Kant, laughter is "an affection arising from the sudden transformation of a strained expectation into nothing." Schopenhauer viewed the cause of laughter to be "simply the sudden perception of the incongruity between a concept and the real objects which have been thought through in some relation, and the laugh itself [to be] just the expression of this incongruity." When a conflict between a thought and a perception occurs, the perception is always correct. Thus, according to Schopenhauer, the realization of the accuracy of a perception over a thought leads to pleasure.

Spencer (1860) stated that laughter naturally occurs when "the conscious is unawares transferred from great things to small—only when there is a ... *descending* incongruity [p. 463]." Not all incongruities, then, cause laughter. For example, in ascending incongruity, when an insignificant entity develops unexpectedly into something great, the emotion resulting is "wonder."

Bergson (1911) viewed the underlying cause of humor as "something mechanical encrusted on the living [p. 27]." A person is laughable when he behaves in a stiff, rigid, or automatic manner—the more mechanistic the behavior, the greater the laughter. Furthermore, "a situation is invariably comic when it belongs simultaneously to two altogether independent series of events and is capable of being interpreted in two entirely different meanings at the same time [p. 96]."

A host of other theorists have utilized the basic tenets of incongruity theory in their conceptions of humor. Guthrie (1903) believed that amusement ensues in a disharmonious situation only if we are simultaneously assured that everything is "all right." Delage (1919) believed that incongruities which might be disagreeable to others are funny only if we are able to maintain a detached attitude. Leacock (1935) described humor as the contrast between a thing as it is or ought to be and a thing smashed out of shape, as it ought not to be. Willmann (1940) stated that humor is produced whenever a shocking idea is united with one which, in contrast, is playful, mild, or commonplace. Baillie (1921) asserted that we have the permanent conditions of laughter in a regulated society, since any departure from social standards is incongruous. Koestler (1964) described the pattern underlying humor as the perception of a situation or event in two habitually incompatible contexts. The abrupt transfer in the train of thought to different rules or logic cannot be followed quickly by certain emotions which work themselves off along the channel of least resistance—laughter. Other theorists utilizing incongruity as central to their conceptions of humor are Hazlitt (1819), Brown (1820), Hunt (1846), Everett (1888), Stanley (1898), Lipps (1898), Kallen (1911), Eastman (1921), Carpenter (1922), Kimmins (1928), and Menon (1931).

D. Surprise Theories

The elements of "surprise," "shock," "suddenness," or "unexpectedness" have been regarded by many theorists as *necessary* (though not necessarily *sufficient*) conditions for the humor experience. There is some similarity between the concepts of surprise and incongruity in that both involve an instantaneous breaking up of the routine course of thought or action. It is, therefore, not unusual to find many theorists utilizing a blend of surprise and incongruity in explanatory concepts.

Stanley (1898) traced surprise back to the method of attack which has been the most successful and thus the most pleasurable in the struggle for survival. The psychological counterpart is shock. Typical theories incorporating surprise as a major factor include Descartes' (1649) notion that laughter results from an admixture of not-too-intense joy and shock, and Willmann's (1940) theory that humor consists of surprise or alarm accompanied by an inducement to play. Other writers insisting on suddenness or surprise as at least one ingredient essential to the humor experience are Hobbes (1651), Quintilian (in *De Institutione Oratoria*),* Hartley (1749), Gerard (1759), Priestley (1777), Ramsay (1848), Darwin (1872), Courdaveaux (1875), Sully (1902), Carpenter (1922), Masson (1925), and Feibleman (1939).

One of the most striking aspects of reactions to humor is adaptation to a given stimulus. When novelty or surprise is eliminated, or if a joke is remembered, the reaction to a humorous situation is altered (Hollingworth, 1911). Thus writers incorporating surprise into their theories have the advantage of being able to

---

* Lamaire ed., 1821–1825 (see References).

account for the decline in appreciation level on repeated exposures to the same situation.

E. Ambivalence Theories

Ambivalence theories (or "conflict-mixture" and "oscillation," as Gregory, 1924, called them) hold that laughter results when the individual simultaneously experiences incompatible emotions or feelings. Monro (1951) described this viewpoint as follows: "We laugh whenever, on contemplating an object or a situation, we find opposite emotions struggling within us for mastery [p. 210]." Although there is obvious similarity between ambivalence and incongruity theories, incongruity theories tend to stress ideas or perceptions whereas ambivalence theories stress emotions or feelings.

In Plato's dialogue, *Philebus,* the prototype of ambivalence theory emerged when Socrates taught Protarchus that laughter arises from the simultaneity of pleasure and pain resulting from envy and malice. The concept of laughter as resulting from oscillation of the contrary physical movements in the expression of joy and sorrow was advanced by Joubert (1579, cited in Eastman, 1921). Descartes (1649) saw joys mixed with hate or shock or both as the cause of laughter. Other clashing feelings or emotions proposed as resolving themselves through laughter include love modified by hate (Greig, 1923), mania alternating with depression (Winterstein, 1934), superiority fused with limitation (Dessoir, 1923), playful chaos mixed with seriousness (Knox, 1951), sympathy and animosity (Gregory, 1924), and conflict engendered by blocking the behavior associated with an instinct drive (Menon, 1931). Willmann (1940), taking his cue from Pavlov's principle of positive induction, asserted that in tickling and humor the costimulation of the opposite responses of fear (or alarm) and playfulness *strengthens* rather than consolidates the response. "With adults the typical funny situation is one providing a playful appeal *plus* an antagonistic response to reinforce it [p. 85]." Hecker (1873), Höffding (1891), Eastman (1921), Hellyar (1927), and Lund (1930) also proposed duality of feeling as underlying laughter and humor.

F. Release and Relief Theories

The functions of humor as affording relief from strain or constraint, or releasing excess tension, are the bases of the theories illustrated in this section.

Spencer (1860) was the first to state clearly the excess-energy theory of humor. Purposeless nervous energy in search of an outlet takes the most yielding course. This is illustrated by the actions of the organs of speech and muscles of respiration with the resultant vocal–respiratory phenomenon known as laughter.

According to Kline (1907), the tension accompanying thought occasionally exceeds the capacity for controlled thinking causing a wave of emotion. Sometimes this leads to humorous experiences which serve the useful purpose of alleviating the strain involved in sustained attention. Gregory (1924) viewed relief as pervading all humor:

> Relief ... is written on the physical act of laughing and on the physiological accompaniments. It is written on the occasions of laughter and, more or less, plainly, on each of its varieties. A laughter of sheer relief may be the original source of all other laughters, which have spread from it like a sheaf. ... Relief is not the whole of laughter, though it is its root and fundamental plan. The discovery of sudden interruption through relaxation of effort merely begins the inquiry into laughter. But it does begin it, and no discussion of laughter that ignores relief or makes it of little account can hope to prosper [p. 40].*

Other theorists who have incorporated release or relief into their theories include Lipps (1898), Penjon (1893), Dewey (1894), Marshall (1894), Allin (1903), Bergson (1911), Sidis (1913), Bliss (1915), Patrick (1916), and Rapp (1947).

G. CONFIGURATIONAL THEORIES

That humor is experienced when elements originally perceived as unrelated suddenly fall into place is the basis of theories placed into this category. There is clearly some relationship between the notions behind both incongruity and configurational theories. Each stresses the cognitive and perceptual attributes of humor, but the main difference lies in the point at which humor emerges. As maintained in incongruity theories, it is the perception of "disjointedness" that somehow amuses. In configurational theories, it is the "falling into place" or sudden "insight" that leads to amusement. The configurational theories either anticipate or reflect the broader theoretical model of Gestalt psychology.

Foreshadowing the more fully elaborated configuration-based theories, Quintilian and Hegel (cited in Schiller, 1938) viewed the growing intelligibility of a situation, unintelligible at first sight, as a

---

* From J. C. Gregory. *The nature of laughter.* London: Routledge & Kegan Paul, 1924.

primary ingredient in the comic situation. According to Wallis (1922) the appreciation of a joke must be instantaneous regardless of how long it takes to prepare for that appreciation. A joke must be understood clearly and completely as opposed to dimly or in parts.

Maier (1932) was the first to utilize evidence based on Gestalt-oriented theories of reasoning which he felt also adequately explained the relevant mental processes of the humor experience. When material is presented, we start ordering it in a certain way. A humorous incident encourages a certain direction or point of view but concludes (that is, organizes the facts presented) differently than expected. The unexpected configuration is a surprise. What differentiates humor from other forms of thinking or reasoning is that the ridiculous is logical only within certain bounds, so we take it lightly. Maier summarizes his theory as follows:

> The thought-configurations which makes for a humorous experience must (1) be unprepared for; (2) appear suddenly and bring with it a change in the meaning of its elements; (3) be made up of elements which are experienced entirely objectively . . .; (4) contain as its elements the facts appearing in the story, and these facts must be harmonized, explained and unified; and (5) have the characteristics of the ridiculous in that its harmony and logic apply only to its own elements [pp. 73–74] .*

Schiller's (1938) "dynamic duality" theory proposed jokes to be a variety of problem solving. Jokes are analogous to ambiguous figures which can be seen in two different ways. "The comic feeling is a logical joy aroused by a sudden change in the configuration of a thought pattern of unstable structure, showing the double aspect of a moment in its dynamic duality [p. 234]." One moves from being embarrassed to understanding with the transition depending on a change in the configuration of the logic or thought pattern of the joke. Rejoicing results from the relief of embarrassment.

Later theories appropriate to this section were proposed by Scheerer (1948), who regarded humor as the playful realization of a multiplicity of coincidences in meaning, and Bateson (1953), who compared joke appreciation to figure–ground shifts in perception.

H. Psychoanalytic Theory

Freud presented his theory of humor in two publications. The first (1905) was a ponderous but highly influential work which dealt primarily with the distinctions among "the comic," "wit," and

---

* From N. R. F. Maier. A Gestalt theory of humour. *British Journal of Psychology,* 1932, **23**, 69–74.

"humor" and their processes. The second (1928) was a brief paper elaborating the third category of "humor." Numerous followers have restated, reworked, and modified Freud's theory, but this section will be primarily concerned with summarizing the original notions.

Freud contended that the ludicrous always represents a saving in the expenditure of psychic energy. When energy built up for occupation in certain psychic channels (cathexis) is not or cannot be utilized (owing to the censoring action of the superego), it may be pleasurably discharged in laughter. (Thus Freud could be characterized as the most eminent of the release theorists.) The pleasure in the *comic* is due to economy in the expenditure of thought. The comic may be found in many situations, and some contrast or deceived expectation is involved. In *wit,* the pleasure derives from economy in the expenditure of inhibition. Wit can be "harmless" as in the enjoyment of nonsense or childishness, or it can express inhibited tendencies. Social restrictions (introjected in the form of the superego) do not permit the acting out of regressive infantile sexual and aggressive behavior in a direct manner. The wit is a camouflage which functions to deceive the superego temporarily as repressions are being suddenly released. In *humor* there is an economy in the expenditure of feeling. Humor turns an event that would otherwise cause suffering into less significance. Energy is displaced onto the superego, and the ego is thereby allowed to return to an infantile state. Freud elaborated this "triumph of narcissism" in his later (1928) paper. Humor "signifies the triumph not only of the ego, but also of the pleasure-principle, which is strong enough to assert itself here in the face of the adverse real circumstances [p. 3]."

Other early theoretical statements take off on one or more of Freud's notions, sometimes elaborating, sometimes modifying. These include the postulates of Winterstein (1934), Dooley (1934, 1941), Bergler (1937, 1956), Kris (1938), Feldmann (1941), Eidelberg (1945), Tarachow (1949), Brody (1950), Lewin (1950), Wolfenstein (1951, 1953, 1954), Jekels (1952), Reik (1954), and Grotjahn (1957).

III. Issues Arising from Earlier Humor Theories

Grouping the earlier conceptions of humor according to central assumptions regarding its nature is useful for the purposes of illustration. However, this remains an incomplete, somewhat superficial, and deceptively clean categorization technique.

Another way of treating the earlier theories is to compare stands on specific issues or approaches. Such comparison vividly illustrates the varieties and disagreements apparent in the earlier conceptions of humor. And though some contemporary theories have managed to avoid or reconcile issues which confused earlier writers, many questions remain to be answered.

A. THE BRIER PATCH OF TERMINOLOGY

Regarding the term "humor," Sully (1902) observed that "hardly a word in the language—and it seems to be exclusively an English word—would be harder to define with scientific precision than this familiar one. It is often used with the greatest degree of looseness, as when a man is endowed with humour because he laughs readily [p. 297]." And though we continue to use the word "humor" as if we all understood its meaning, every contemporary student of this label knows the twinge following the question, "*Precisely* what is humor anyway?" The definitions offered are almost as many as the theories themselves, and still we are unsure of the complete dimensions of the concept.

Complicating the matter further is the myriad of other labels, often used interchangeably with "humor" and with each other. The following adjectives, gleaned from the theoretical papers, have been used to characterize humorous matters: *ludicrous, satiric, funny, absurd, mirthful, laughable, witty, silly, derisive, pleasurable, cheerful, amusing, comical, droll, fanciful, whimsical, jocose, facetious, waggish, nonsensical, ridiculous, merry, farcical, inane,* and *corny.*

Similarly numerous labels are used to characterize *people* according to their mode of humorous behavior or abilities (e.g., *comedian, wit, comic, practical joker, funny man, light-hearted optimist, merry maker, humorist*) or according to the absence of such behavior or abilities (e.g., *humorless, dullard, solemn, unemotional, serious, pious, reverent, sober, colorless*). And, perhaps the most difficult of all is understanding what it means to have, or *not* to have, a "sense of humor."

This hodgepodge of labels underscores, at every turn, the extreme difficulty encountered in comparing and contrasting various issues and topics related to humor. And though attempts have been made to classify types of "humor phenomena," the terminology situation in the area of humor remains perplexing.

B. VANTAGE POINTS OF THEORIZING

Another major problem encountered in attempting to compare, contrast, or integrate existent humor theories is that authors, all presumably talking about the same subject, approach it from different angles. Eysenck (1942) identified three approaches to theorizing: the "cognitive" (focus on the thinking processes), the "conative" (focus on the motivational aspects), and the "affective" (focus on the emotional aspects). Another way to demonstrate the approach problem is to note that some theorists focus on the specific thematic content of the humor-arousing event (e.g., misfortune of others), whereas others spell out characteristics of the humor process without regard to the theme (e.g., incongruity, shock). And, not mutually exclusive from the preceding, some speak of humor as an "intraindividual affair," motivated from within, whereas others apparently consider the crux of humor to be outside of the individual and acting upon him. And finally, the theories range from those presenting humor and laughter as physiological processes serving biological functions to those postulating these phenomena as meaningful only as they relate to interactions with others or the life of the group.

In short, the "what at?" "why?" "how?" "when?" "where?" and "with whom?" of humor have all been contemplated, but little has been done to set them all up together in one tidy theoretical household.

C. MONISTIC VERSUS PLURALISTIC BASES

Theories can be differentiated as to whether they put forward single or multiple principles as the bases of the humor experience. Examples of those advancing a single principle (with perhaps another supplementing it) have been presented in the theory overview section, so here we will be concerned only with those by theorists who outlined multiple dimensions of humor.

Perhaps the best known description of *situations* or *content* giving rise to laughter is by Sully (1902). His 12 classes of the laughter provoking are: novelties, physical deformities, moral deformities and vices, disorderliness, small misfortune, indecencies, pretenses, want of knowledge or skill, the incongruous and absurd, word play, the expression of a merry mood, and the outwitting or getting the better of a person. Others offering lists of categories of humor and laughter include Courdaveaux (1875), Hall and Allin (1897), Kline (1907), Dunlap (1925), and Valentine (1942).

Multiple categories of *humor* have also been set forth. Lilly (1896), for example, listed 21 varieties which included wit, irony, satire, sarcasm, parody, puns, banter, mimicry, and practical joking. Fowler (1926, cited in Berlyne, 1969) classified types of the ludicrous as humor, wit, satire, sarcasm, invective, irony, cynicism, and the sardonic and attempted to differentiate among them according to their motive, province, and methods of presentation and the type of receptive audience. Other theorists making distinctions between such concepts as wit, humor, and the comic include Hazlitt (1819), Freud (1905), Kris (1938), and Pearson (1938).

Hayworth (1928) held that no classifications of ludicrous situations are possible. To classify according to subject matter is inconceivable since all things in the universe would be included. Humor cannot be classified according to technique as this is done by creating tension and then suddenly bringing a relaxation. With universal subject matter and a limited technique, a classification on either of these bases is impossible.

D. THE RELATIONSHIP OF LAUGHTER TO HUMOR

Laughter usually accompanies the humor experience. For this reason the usage of the two terms (or their modifications, such as "laughable" and "humorous") are often difficult to distinguish.

Laughter is most often described as the overt expression of humor—an indicator that the person is in an "amused frame of mind" or experiencing something as "funny." The physical description of the laugh by Dearborn (1900) is one example of many attempts to describe its characteristic pattern:

> There occur in laughter and more or less in smiling, clonic spasms of the diaphragm in number ordinarily about eighteen perhaps, and contraction of most of the muscles of the face. The upper side of the mouth and its corners are drawn upward. The upper eyelid is elevated, as are also, to some extent, the brows, the skin over the glabella, and the upper lip, while the skin at the outer canthi of the eyes is characteristically puckered. The nostrils are moderately dilated and drawn upward, the tongue slightly extended, and the cheeks distended and drawn somewhat upward; in persons with the pinnal muscles largely developed, the pinnae tend to incline forwards. The lower jaw vibrates or is somewhat withdrawn (doubtless to afford all possible air to the distending lungs), and the head, in extreme laughter, is thrown backward; the trunk is straightened even to the beginning of bending backward, until (and this usually happens soon),

fatigue-pain in the diaphragm and accessory abdominal muscles causes a marked proper flexion of the trunk for its relief. The whole arterial vascular system is dilated, with consequent blushing from the effect on the dermal capillaries of the face and neck, and at times the scalp and hands. From this same cause in the main the eyes often slightly bulge forwards and the lachrymal gland becomes active, ordinarily to a degree only to cause a "brightening" of the eyes, but often to such an extent that the tears overflow entirely their proper channels [pp. 853–854] .*

Upon reading such an objective description of laughter and then adding to it the "series of incoherent and shocking noises" (as Armstrong, 1928, put it), one gets the feeling that a person engaging in this act must be critically ill rather than enjoying himself. It is here that Koestler (1964) finds it paradoxical that "humor is the only domain of creative activity where a stimulus on a high level of complexity produces a massive and sharply defined response on the level of physiological reflexes [p. 31] ."

However, if laughter were indeed an exact yardstick with which to measure humor experiences, we might have solved many of the riddles of humor long ago. Unfortunately, for science anyway, laughter is only a gross indicator which *may* accompany humor experiences. One can be amused and *not* laugh, especially if alone. Rapp (1947), among others, noted factors which condition laughter, such as deliberate self-restraint; certain emotional factors; and physical conditions, such as sleepiness and illness. Koestler (1964) contended that civilized laughter is rarely spontaneous and can be feigned or suppressed.

But perhaps the most important point to be made is that laughter may be forthcoming as a reaction to *any* sort of emotional state, not solely amusement (McDougall, 1903; Gregory, 1923, 1924; Burt, 1945; Flugel, 1954). And to attempt a listing of what can give rise to laughter is a hazardous undertaking, since man apparently laughs at just about everything. But from the listings of the sources of the laughable put forth by some writers, many conditions or situations are not very funny if viewed objectively; in fact, often they are quite disturbing or tragic.

Monro (1951) listed several "non-humorous" causes of laughter: (1) tickling, (2) laughing gas (nitrous oxide), (3) nervousness, (4) relief after a strain, (5) the defense mechanism of "laughing it off," (6) joy or the expression of high spirits, (7) play, (8) release from restraint, (9) make-believe, and (10) the victory expression of "ha ha!" after winning a game or contest. A few words about tickling

* From G. V. N. Dearborn. June 1, 1900, *Science*, 9, 851–856.

might be in order since the phenomenon of laughing, often with such intensity that it becomes an excruciating experience for the "ticklee," has been for many humor theorists a "sticky wicket" to explain. On the one hand, it appears to be a reflexive action in response to bodily stimulation. But tickling defies such a simplistic explanation for at least two reasons: (1) One cannot tickle oneself and elicit a laughter response or anything resembling the experience of being tickled by someone or something else; and (2) not just anyone or anything can do the tickling and elicit laughter. It must be administered by a "friendly" source and done in a playful manner lest the response be one of shock, fear, or anger. *Two* types of laughter have been proposed to handle the tickle–humor problem. Beattie (1776) differentiated an "animal" laugh aroused by tickling and a "sentimental" laugh aroused by ideas. Similarly, Lilly (1896) divided laughter into the physical, i.e., produced by purely physical means, and the "laugh of the soul." One may occur without the other, and only a gross and superficial analysis would confound the two. Yet Sully (1902) believed that all varieties of amusement grew out of the social act he called "play challenge," which is well illustrated in the game of reciprocal tickling. Other theorists who have discussed tickling in some detail include Hecker (1873), Tuke (1892), Hall and Allin (1897), Stanley (1898), McDougall (1903, 1922), Crile (1916), Greig (1923), Koestler (1964), and Giles and Oxford (1970).

At any rate, defining the essence of laughter is not nearly so simple as describing its behavioral components or linking it indiscriminately with humor. Diserens (1926) illustrated the many sides of laughter when he described it as "a complex form of behavior, unlearned yet highly susceptible to conditioning in the presence of psychic stimuli. It is at once a biological mechanism of adjustment, a physiological safety-valve, a psychological exhilarant and a regulator of social relations [p. 254]."

E. The Relationship between Laughing and Smiling

The relationship among the various expressive reactions, such as laughter and crying, has been discussed in the literature (Menon, 1931; Plessner, 1970). The question receiving the most attention applies to the connection, if any, between the laugh and the smile. Both have been viewed as manifestations of the same phenomenon with the smile often described as a "weak" laugh, an incipient laugh, or the aftermath of laughter as the person begins to relax (Darwin,

1872; Dearborn, 1900; Sully, 1902; Kallen, 1911; Beerbohm, 1921; Gregory, 1923; Greig, 1923; Hayworth, 1928; Rapp, 1949). The continuous gradations from a faint smile to full laughter have been noted (Darwin, 1872; Raulin, 1900) leaving Sully to wonder why "laugh" and "smile" came to be two different concepts. He suggested that this was due to paying more attention to the sounds accompanying laughter and the absence of sound in smiling than to the underlying process which, to Sully, was the same.

McDougall (1922), however, believed the equation of laughter and smiling to be in error. The laugh relieves us from depression, whereas the smile is the natural expression of the satisfaction that accompanies success in any striving. The laugh is ugly, but the smile is beautiful. Earlier, de la Mennais (1885) thought the laugh to be evil, while the smile could express opposite tendencies such as tenderness.

To complicate matters on this issue, it can be pointed out that there are "different" laughs (titter, giggle, belly laugh, chuckle, roar, etc.) just as there are different smiles (grin, smirk, sneer, the "Mona Lisa," etc.). Laughter and smiling may not only have "levels of intensity" within themselves, but the various types of each may also reflect entirely different purposes.

F. The Order of Pleasure and Laughter

A variation on the Lange–James versus Cannon theories of emotional reactions is encountered in the question, "which comes first, the pleasure or the laughter?" As we have seen, not all theorists contend that laughter is necessarily associated with pleasure; however the two are often discussed as belonging together somehow.

Laughter as the overt expression of an already existent pleasurable state is clearly the most prevalent stand (Hobbes, 1651; Spencer, 1860; Darwin, 1872; Stanley, 1898; Dearborn, 1900; Sully, 1902; Beerbohm, 1921; Drever, 1921; McComas, 1923; Grandgent, 1924; Hellyar, 1927; Willmann, 1940). Koestler (1964) spoke directly to the Cannon position by concluding that "the grain of salt which must be present in the narrative to make us laugh turns out to be a drop of adrenaline [p. 58]."

McDougall (1922) vigorously declared that things were the other way around. Laughter is not an expression of pleasure at all—rather a generator of pleasure. We laugh because we are miserable, and laughing makes us feel good. Laughter can also evoke pleasure when it represents appreciation and approval by the group (Wallis, 1922).

G. Expression of Pleasure versus Expression of Displeasure
Disguised

When we laugh or joke, it seems as though we are having a good time. And as discussed in the previous section, numerous writers have viewed laughter and humor as expressions of pleasure.

Yet it is interesting to note that many of the early theories on humor hold that what *appears* to be pleasurable, or what is *experienced* as pleasure, is actually displeasure converted somehow by the humor process. According to Nietzsche (cited in Brody, 1950), "Man alone suffers so excruciatingly in the world that he was compelled to invent laughter." Winterstein (1934) stated: "Humor laughs among tears [p. 307]." And the distressing, annoying, disagreeable, and tragic foundations of the amusing have been discussed by Guthrie (1903), McDougall (1922), Wilson (1927), and Bergler (1937, 1956). Wilson (1927) and Brody (1950) proposed that humor results from a sublimation of our unwanted impulses. But Freud (1905), who made much of the disturbing dynamics behind humor, believed that along with this "tendency wit" there is "harmless wit." However, most subsequent psychoanalytic writers have emphasized the more "displeasing" motivation behind humor and have either ignored or renounced a benign type of humor.

H. The Role of Nervous Energy Release

Whatever it is that seemingly builds up and is released explosively in laughter has been widely discussed. Whereas many writers make no reference to "nervous energy" or "tension," others find its discussion essential. Tension reduction through laughter has been described as arising from (1) repressed energy or "pent-up emotion" suddenly liberated in humor (Dugas, 1902; Angell, 1904; Freud, 1905; Patrick, 1916; Drever, 1921; Menon, 1931; Brody, 1950); (2) the escape of excess energy for which the body has no serious use (Spencer, 1860; Lipps, 1898; Marshall, 1894; Allin, 1903; Sidis, 1913; Crile, 1916); (3) released tension caused by mental blocking or interruption (Greig, 1923).

The concept of laughter as serving an energy-release function, for whatever reason, has come under criticism. Stanley (1898) wondered why, in the process of evolution, a superabundance of energy would be generated, as this is contrary to the "law of economy." Furthermore, a superfluity-of-energy theory cannot explain why an activity should be performed in a "playful" manner, e.g., playing at fighting rather than actually fighting. (Freud, remember, offered an explanation as to why this is so.) McDougall (1922) also believed that nature had no need to construct a complex nervous mechanism for the service of releasing an overflow of energy, since this could be effected through any of the other motor mechanisms. Hayworth (1928) noted that the amount of energy released through laughter is ridiculously small for such a complicated, highly developed process. The release model further fails to explain why the *audible* aspect of laughter has been developed to such an extent.

Brody (1950) theorized the possibility of laughter functioning to "take in" rather than to "release out," when he refers to the mouth, as the most archaic prehensile organ, trying to catch joy *into* it by laughing rather than flushing anything *out*.

So far, we have been considering laughter alone. When the reason for laughter is included, such as the presentation of a good joke, it becomes plausible to consider the humor–laughter process as both tension producing and tension releasing—a closed system unto itself. Energy builds as the story proceeds, and if successful (that is, if sufficient tension has been generated and abruptly released by the punch line), the story teller gets his laugh. (Of course, it may be possible that the "wrong kind" of tension, or excessive tension, has been generated in the listener and is released through anger or disgust.) The contemporary theory of Berlyne (1960, 1969) [see Chapter 2] emphasizes both the arousal and reduction in arousal factors involved in humor.

I. ANIMALS VERSUS HUMANS

Whether laughter and/or humor are strictly human affairs, or shared with at least the higher mammals, has been pondered. There is apparently no disagreement that men alone *tell* jokes and engage in the more subtle witticisms inextricably bound up with our advanced intellectual capacity (though the data on porpoises are not in!). But for more basic nonlinguistic humor-related behaviors (such as practical joking, tickling, playing, and laughing) the distinction becomes less clear-cut.

The reasons for contending that *only* humans possess the ability to laugh and engage in humor are quite varied. Whereas Koestler (1964) contended that laughter can only arise in a biologically secure species with intellectual autonomy, Walsh (1928) saw laughter as essential to the "upright" human because he is so poorly engineered that he needs the accompanying diaphragm movement to massage the vital organs. McDougall (1922) labeled laughter an instinct peculiar to the human species, but Bliss (1915) and Shaw (1960) held that it is because man has *no* instincts that humor arises to assist him in coping with the complexities and contradictions which constantly present themselves. Animals have no sense of the ludicrous, according to Lilly (1896), because they have neither reason nor the ability to engage in abstract knowledge.

Those who attribute what they consider to be humor-related behaviors to infrahuman species range from confining the phenomena to primates (Crile, 1916) to including even microscopic organisms (Stanley, 1898). Similarities between the laughter-like emissions and smile contortions of primates to the human laugh and smile have been described (Darwin, 1872; Köhler, 1921; Yerkes & Learned, 1925). Eastman (1921) contended that the canine equivalent of human laughter is tail-wagging. "Humor" in mammals was illustrated by Sully (1902).

Play is a part of both human and animal life, especially during the immature phase of the life span. The tricky task is specifying how, if at all, humor and play relate to each other. Like humor, opportunities for play are sought after, seem to be lacking in seriousness, are engaged in with much gusto, and afford satisfaction or pleasure. But much is lacking in the knowledge we need for adequately understanding whether play and humor are single, related, or distinct phenomena. (For a review of play in animals and humans, see Berlyne, 1969.)

J. INBORN VERSUS ACQUIRED ASPECTS

The nature-nurture controversy looms in many areas of psychology, and includes the problem of the extent to which humor-related behaviors are unlearned or learned. Yet perhaps for this area, more than for any other, it is useful to make the distinction between laughter and humor production, understanding, or appreciation.

Laughter has been observed by a substantial number of developmental psychologists to emerge from the human infant somewhere around the fourth month, preceded several weeks by the smile. We can probably safely assume laughter to be a maturational process even though, as with other maturational behaviors, there are individual differences in time of onset and frequency. Hence, laughter has been labeled an instinct (McDougall, 1922; Greig, 1923; McComas, 1923), an unconditioned mechanism (Mones, 1939), and a reflex (Koestler, 1964) and has been linked with the "strong native impulse of mastery" (Gates, 1925).

That laughter becomes increasingly conditioned as the person matures has been noted (McComas, 1923; Washburn, 1929; Justin, 1932). Moreover, numerous writers have resolved the relationship between laughter and the content of humorous expression and appreciation by accepting the inborn nature of the laughter response but claiming that what is laughed at is increasingly extended through experience, learning, and habit (Woodworth, 1921; F. H. Allport, 1924; Mones, 1939; Koestler, 1964). However, even laughter itself has been proposed to be a *learned* behavior (Hartley, 1749). Guthrie (1903) believed the smile to be inborn but the art of laughter to be learned, and Vasey (1875) asserted that the infant would probably not learn to laugh at all unless he had been tickled.

Regarding "humor sense," Hellyar (1927) stated that it can be strengthened through intellectual effort but cannot be achieved at all unless the appropriate inborn temperament is there. What is laughable has also been discussed in terms of an interaction of biological and experiential determinants as, for example, accounting for great sex differences in humor potential (Winterstein, 1934; Zippen, 1966). (Yes, Virginia, the fact that you don't have a penis also determines your sense of humor!)

Eastman (1936) offered "the ten commandments of the comic arts," and though he stated they would be difficult to implement, he does attempt to *teach* the reader how to make a good joke. To the author's knowledge, no theoretical paper has yet been published which fits humor into an established learning model, but at least three unpublished doctoral dissertations (Byrne, 1957; Fisher, 1964; Keith-Spiegel, 1968) have applied the Hullian model to humor appreciation expectancies.

K. UNIVERSALITY VERSUS SELECTIVITY

Related to the question of whether humor capacity is learned or innate is the issue of its universality. Many writers have stated, in an offhanded manner, that humor is prevalent worldwide. Those viewing humor as rooted in the evolution of mankind would agree. However, when we consider humor as a selective characteristic among men, the ever-present difficulties of defining it are confronted. Certainly every human being is not a skilled comic or clever wit. And we all know someone who could be characterized as having "no sense of humor." Such factors as age, sex, nationality, race, and breeding have been considered as affecting humor sense differentially (Diserens, 1926).

Even if all men have the potential for laughter and some sense of the humorous, the degree to which it exists in different individuals has been a subject for debate. Hellyar (1927) expected to find a larger proportion of men of humor among the optimists and the good-natured. For Menon (1931) the man of great humor is one with a keen and reflecting mind, a mind richly stored with experiences and capable of alertness. Freud (1928) saw humor as a rare and precious gift. A person *without* humor may be regarded with serious concern. As Wallis (1922) stated: "He is largely on a par with the man who cannot render military service to the group [p. 345]."

A few writers have strongly asserted that laughter and humor are *not* universal. Lilly (1896) stated that there are whole races of men without a sense of the ludicrous. Many savages are too stoic to laugh at all, while, on the other hand, the "true gentleman" may smile but not indulge in the habitual laughter characteristic of the shallow, the ignorant, and the vulgar! (Vasey, 1875).

L. NOMOTHETIC VERSUS IDIOGRAPHIC ASPECTS

What might seem a variation with a twist on the universal—selective issue is the question of whether humor is as distinctive among individual persons as fingerprints, or whether the underlying processes of humor are similar for everybody. Too many theorists to enumerate have ignored the question of individual differences altogether. It is often stated that "laughter occurs when X. . . ." with the focus on the stimulus material or situation and not on the person. This sausage-maker approach to the study of humor has been vigorously condemned by Hellyar (1927), as it does not take into account the fact that it is a man who laughs, not a laughing machine.

For the *organization* of content grasped as humorous, Scheerer (1948) sought a unifying principle which would allow for wide variation in the nature of the content itself. Others have addressed themselves to the person engaging in humor and have proposed individual differences, or at least types of individual patterns, leading to diverse "humor senses." Again, Hellyar (1927) stated that both the emotional and perceptual elements of mind combine to make laughter a completely individual affair. Wilson (1927) presented different types such as tragic characters with narrow senses of humor, "unemotional unimpressionables" devoid of humor, "merry irresponsibles" who do not convert their impulses to humor, and those with genuine humor who have successfully converted their unsocial impulses to something which is both delightful and manageable.

Some of the early research studies (e.g., Barry, 1928; Murray, 1934) demonstrated individual differences in humor appreciation, and it has generally remained the province of research to tackle this problem.

M. Good versus Evil

Is humor a gift handed down from the gods or a scourge delivered up from the devils? Whether laughter is representative of the best in man, reflective of goodness and love, or a manifestation of his selfish, ruthless, and cruel nature concerned many of the earlier writers.

According to McComas (1923), no nobler attribute has ever been given to a living creature than that of "laughing animal." Theories emphasizing the "good" indicate that humor and laughter bear witness to the positive direction in which man is evolving (Bliss, 1915; Gregory, 1924; Shaw, 1960); view laughter as one of mankind's most valuable assets which should be cultivated and applied since it is superior to logic (Armstrong, 1928); and describe laughter as a weapon against evil (Guthrie, 1903) with its essence as love (Carlyle, 1840).

The writers viewing humor and laughter as reflective of man's most undesirable qualities include Plato (in *Philebus*), Dryden (1668), Hartley (1749), Rousseau (1758),* and de la Mennais (1885). Those holding that humor and laughter have their roots in derision, ridicule, and the misfortunes of others (Hobbes, 1651; Dunlap, 1925; Rapp, 1947) or drunkenness and obscenity (Read, 1920) would apparently not classify humor as benevolent or worthy of any praise. Beerbohm (1921) ventured that 90% of the world's best laughter is *at* others, not with them. The never-failing merriment engendered at the expense of those afflicted with mental illness was disdainfully noted by Meyerson (1925, cited in Diserens & Bonifeld, 1930). Ludovici (1932) believed humor to be one of the main *causes* of modern decadence.

Though Armstrong (1928) is among the major advocates of the virtues of humor, he noted that, like all stimulants, it can be abused. The possibilities of laughter's being used for good or evil purposes

---

* Garnier frères ed., 1926 (see References).

serving as a manifestation of love or hate, or as a social blessing or social calamity have come under discussion (Plato, in *Philebus*; Wallis, 1922; Greig, 1923; Rapp, 1947). Kallen (1911) described comedy as composed of evil and discord which comes to us powerless to harm, thus turning an evil situation into a good one. But perhaps it is as Gregory (1923) stated: "The ills that laughter inflicts can be endured for the sake of the grace it bestows [p. 336]."

N. BASIS IN REALITY VERSUS BASIS IN UNREALITY

How does humor relate to *truth* (or "the real world") and *falsehood* (or unreality)? When humor is described as a reflection of "man's condition," we can assume that it functions as a means of enabling us to understand and cope with reality as we perceive it. Genuine humor must be true according to Masson (1925), and Meerloo (1966) contended that when man surrenders to reality, laughter (or crying) results. Jonson (1578), Hartley (1749), and Knox (1951) discussed how laughter and comedy took their cues from the situations of everyday life. Most of the evolutionary humor theorists held that humor is a vestige of direct attempts to cope with the real world. However, it has also been suggested that an important function of humor is to relieve us from the burdens of reality (Flugel, 1954).

Unreality as an inherent quality of humor has been put forth by several theorists. These include Freud (1928), who considered a denial of the claim of reality as being characteristic of humor. In bringing about a humorous attitude, the superego repudiates reality and serves as an illusion. We do not take the ridiculous situation seriously because it is not meant to be a part of reality (Maier, 1932). Carpenter (1922) gave the example of the "comic fall" as an illustration of the delusive aspect of a catastrophe; i.e., we recognize it as unreal and delight in our own judgment of that fact. Everett (1888) viewed the comic as purely subjective, whereas tragedy is objective. Similarly, Winterstein (1934) contrasted humor, which he said belongs among the regressive processes that protect the ego from reality, to active pity, which is in harmony with reality. Finally, Dugas (1902) described laughter as a sense of freedom from limitations of the real world.

Some theorists have ascribed the basis of humor to some interaction between the perception of the real and the unreal. Stanley (1898) characterized play as "reality putting on appearance"—a type of feigning where delight arises from contrasting the real and the unreal. According to Lilly (1898), the incorrectness and abnormality of the ludicrous provokes one to affirm what is correct and normal, whereas for Feibleman (1949) comedy is the indirect affirmation of the ideal logical order through derogation of the limited nature of actuality.

O. LEVEL OF CONTROL OR AWARENESS

A difficult issue to come to grips with is the question of how much conscious control or awareness the individual has of his humor sense. And if "something else" is in the driver's seat, is it the unconscious segment of the individual's *own* mind or the environmental circumstances?

Those proposing unconscious determination of humor are the easiest to identify because they speak directly to the issue. These include Freud (1905), Bliss (1915), Drever (1921), Gilver (1922), Wilson (1927), and Bergler (1956).

A great many theorists, particularly those writing before Freud, make no reference one way or the other to whether humor production and appreciation are consciously controlled or deliberately calculated reactions. Those viewing humor as a completely "emotional" affair, or positing its basis in instinct, would undoubtedly insist that we have little control over ourselves when the appropriate triggering stimuli are present. Others who spell out the circumstances or situations which call forth laughter and amusement apparently give us little choice in the matter, as it is "man's nature" to laugh in such instances.

It has been noted that humor production and appreciation become less spontaneous and proceed with more awareness and control as the person matures. Also, the intellectual element in humor becomes more apparent as one moves from childhood to maturity (McComas, 1923).

Environmental circumstances have been set forth as strong determinants of humor. We laugh in spite of ourselves when held in the grip of the group standard (Wallis, 1922). And casual observation attests to the futility of holding back a "pre-roar" of hilarity once it has gathered up steam inside. Forcing ourselves to laugh, when the circumstances are not conducive to an "honest" response, may be difficult to do convincingly. Certainly culture determines, in great measure, what is and what is *not* amusing. Greig (1923) notes that "it is only people with the same social heritage who laugh easily at the same kind of jokes [p. 71]."

P. Healthy versus Unhealthy Attributes

Does a laughing, joking person indicate that (1) he is revealing the fact that he is physically healthy and/or mentally well balanced; (2) he is divulging his innermost hangups, and because he laughs and/or jokes so intensely, deep-seated and severe problems are present; or (3) his mental conflicts and worries are the driving force behind his laughter and joking, but since he *is* laughing and joking, he is handling his pain in a healthy manner by converting it to pleasure? What humor reveals on a healthy–disturbed dimension has proponents of all three of the above possibilities.

Walsh (1928) advanced the most vigorous assertion of the absolute necessity of laughter in maintaining good physical health and preventing disease; and Sully (1902) cited numerous physicians who viewed laughter as a hygienic measure. Others supporting the stand that physical benefit is to be derived from humor and laughter include Spencer (1860), Hall and Allin (1897), Gregory (1923), and McComas (1923). (It might be noted, however, that excessive or uncontrollable laughter has been likened to an epileptic seizure by Pines, 1964, and that Meerloo, 1966, has documented literal instances of "laughing to death.")

The writers who maintained the lofty and "good" nature of humor would, assumedly, have attested to its correlate of stable mental health had the question been put directly to them. Numerous writers mention that when a person is discovered who does not laugh or has no "sense of humor," a strange being has been located, and most probably an unhappy and disturbed one.

Linking humor expression with certain disturbance processes is also common. Humor has been directly tied to masochistic and compulsive dynamics (Dooley, 1941; Brody, 1950), depression (Winterstein, 1934), and to an antisocial nature and split personality (Berend, 1926, cited in Winterstein, 1934). Brody, in discussing the place of humor and laughter analysis during therapy, felt that this defense is best left undisturbed, since sadness, regret, anger, and hatred may overwhelm the patient if the thin cover of laughter is thrown off. He observed that when frequent laughter and smiling occurs, it is primarily in the sickest patients. Yet other analysts (Brill, 1940; Zwerling, 1955) suggested eliciting from patients their favorite jokes which can then be interpreted for the purpose of discovering areas of conflict and repression.

That humor has, at its motivational base, disturbances which, if left to surface directly, would probably be labeled as unhealthy, maladaptive, or guilt and anxiety producing is perhaps the most prevalent stand, and especially characteristic of psychoanalytic theory. In this sense, behavior expressed in a humorous manner (including laughing) becomes a "healthy" or socially adaptive way of handling one's problems. Humor has been described as the result of sublimating unwanted impulses (Wilson, 1927) and unconscious needs for destruction (Murray, 1934); a useful defense against anxiety (Freud, 1928); an antidote for depression (McDougall, 1922); a way of desexualizing and freeing from regression threatening instinctual drives (Dooley, 1934); an indispensable little shock absorber (Eastman, 1921); and a "healthy internal debunking process" (Bergler, 1956).

Some of the contradictions among these three points of view may be softened by looking at this matter in another way—one which is becoming a more popular theoretical concept underpinning research studies. The view that a person's sense of humor is in no way removed or independent from his total personality allows for healthy senses of humor in healthy people and unhealthy ones in unhealthy persons. According to Gregory (1924), "the ways men laugh and the things they laugh at are excellent indexes of their nature [p. 202]."

Q. CREATIVE EXPRESSION VERSUS DEFENSIVE REPRESSION

Humor productions have been elevated alongside other creative endeavors, and in early philosophical and literary treatments humor has sometimes been discussed under the heading of "aesthetics." The adept joke maker has been designated an artist with a rare and valuable talent. Among those characterizing humor as creative expression are Lowenthal (1919), Mones (1939), Feibleman (1939, 1949), and Koestler (1964).

On the other hand, humor has been classified as another defense process, apparently possessing no artistic redemption, though possibly having survival value. In this context, the humorist reveals the nature of his repressions through his joke content (Crile, 1916; Gopola-Swami, 1926; Wilson, 1927; Barry, 1928; Dooley, 1934; Brody, 1950).

Freud (1928), as would be expected, considered humor to be a defensive mechanism, albeit a very advanced one. Yet interestingly enough, Freud observed that humor is "a rare and precious gift, and there are many people who have not even the capacity for deriving pleasure from humour when it is presented to them by others [p. 6]."

R. A Reaction to a Good Mood versus a Curative for a Bad One

How laughter and humor appreciation are related to the general state of a person at a specific point in time has been largely ignored by most humor theorists. Though many writers have indicated, often somewhat indirectly, that laughter and humor are often extensions of a "light frame of mind," McComas (1923) built his entire theory around this proposition. Hellyar (1927) spoke directly to the importance of determining the threshold for laughter for a given mood state. He postulated that the mind is most receptive to humor when it is blank of definite ideas or emotions. Comic incidents which might ordinarily provoke laughter and enjoyment may simply go unnoticed by one who is harassed, irritable, actively engrossed in an idea, or in a mood or passion.

McDougall (1922), however, believed that humor is actively welcomed or even sought after when one is depressed since it alleviates, for the moment at least, brooding and gloomy thoughts. In fact, McDougall asserted that the happy man does not laugh, for he has no need of it! Relating to this side of the issue are the scores of theorists, mentioned elsewhere in the chapter, who describe humor as emanating from "states of mind" which are, for example, aggressive or spiteful, but hardly pleasant or even passive.

S. Effort versus Economy of Effort

Does humor involve mental (or physical) work, or is it a work-saving device? As we can observe, the throes of violent laughter appear to involve much physical exercise. Walsh (1928) would agree that laughter is bodily work necessary to maintain physical health. The excess-energy theory, postulating laughter as the channel whereby this energy releases itself, does not hold that laughter is work; rather, it is the safety valve that releases nervous energy allowing the body to return to a more relaxed state.

Considering the total humor process, rather than laughter alone, Freud (1905) contended that the ludicrous experience always involves some economy in the expenditure of mental energy. It will be remembered that wit pleasure is due to economy in the expenditure of inhibition; in the comic there is economy in the expenditure of thought; in humor, economy in the expenditure of feeling.

Writers whose notions revolve around the techniques involved in constructing and understanding humorous materials often allude to the consumption of mental energy involved in these processes. For example, Carpenter (1922) held that pleasure results from correctly judging a situation as false. The greater the effort it takes to perceive falsity, the greater the resulting pleasure. Others such as Baillie (1921), Wallis (1922), and Maier (1932) similarly have noted that the enjoyment of humor is, in large measure, due to the exertion of mental effort.

However, the *atmosphere* conducive to humor must be relaxed (McComas, 1923). Thus Shaw (1960) observed that the person making jokes cannot appear to be laboring or straining and arouse laughter, though, as Eastman (1936) pointed out, it may require 25 years of effort to appear effortless!

T. Intellectual versus Emotional Aspects

Eysenck (1942) distinguished *cognitive* theories (stressing elements such as incongruity and contrast between ideas, i.e., "thinking") from *conative* (stressing the satisfaction of desire for superiority, self-glory, etc.) and affective (stressing emotional components). The last two were paired together under the label *orectic* (i.e., involving "feeling"). Similarly, Scheerer (1948) divided the basic theoretical approaches in humor study into (1) those localizing the condition of humor in the objective content of the situation, and (2) those explaining humor subjectively in terms of emotional content or motive. Both Eysenck and Scheerer singled out Freud for managing to include both approaches.

Theoretical statements including concepts such as pleasure and expressions of merry moods, joy, or happiness; tension release or catharsis value; physiological changes associated with humor; or any *feeling* as paramount to the basic explanation of humor would be classified as "emotion-based" theory as the term is being applied here. There are, of course, numerous such theories, and the emotional aspects of humor have already been discussed. Therefore this section will be concerned primarily with the intellectual aspects of humor.

The "thinking-based" theories are most likely to be found in the incongruity or Gestalt camps. Thus, humor based on reconciling the possible with the impossible (Shaw, 1960), recognizing the unusual and unexpected (Wallis, 1922), matching true and pretended values leading to a revelation of the counterfeit (Mones, 1939), or playfully realizing the multiplicity of coincidence and meaning (Scherrer, 1948) all involve mental operations.

The relationship between humor and intellectual ability has also been a topic of interest to some theorists. We can expect to find the best humor in the most intelligent (Menon, 1931), while those who are lacking in humor reveal their mental poverty (Lilly, 1896). The sense of humor has been said to be dependent on the ability to perceive shades of meaning which might go unnoticed by a "clumsy mind" (Hellyar, 1927). Comedy has been described as an intellectual affair dealing chiefly with logic (Feibleman, 1949). Rapp (1947) defined riddles as staged contests of wits. However, Dearborn (1900) disagreed that laughter is related to intellectual ability in a positive linear fashion. He cited the nearly continual smiling or laughing of the mentally deficient, which he believed to be expressive of the constant tone of pleasantness that such persons must usually experience.

The *pleasure* that results from the exercise of the intellect has been described, though not adequately explained. Wallis (1922) stated that, "no one understands a joke by laughing at it. He laughs because he understands it [p. 343]." And, according to Wilson (1927), "Things are not funny in themselves, only as we think them so [p. 629]." Those describing humor as the "joy of reasoning" (Schiller, 1938), or the "triumph of reason" (Carpenter, 1922), or "intellectual gratification" (Koestler, 1964) are among those who are deliberately combining, or unwittingly confusing, the emotional and intellectual elements in humor. Scheerer (1948) believed that cognitive functions were undoubtedly involved in the emotional reaction we have to humor. The contemporary theory of Berlyne (1960, 1969) [see Chapter 2] handles this combination adequately by explaining how arousal may be engendered through intellectual maneuvers and then abruptly reduced. (Kline, 1907, who viewed humor as affording relief after a mental strain, was a possible precursor of Berlyne.)

It has, however, been asserted that laughter and humor are *incompatible* with emotion. Bergson (1911) believed laughter to have no greater foe than emotion, for if the comic arouses feelings of sympathy, fear or pity will ensue. Others have contended that strong emotional *and* intellectual involvement must be absent in order for humor to be appreciated. In other words, the person should be in a relatively "detached frame of mind" (Stanley, 1898; Lowenthal, 1919; Hellyar, 1927).

U. SELF-SERVING VERSUS SOCIAL SERVING

Some early conceptions of humor stress its role in serving individual needs, whereas others stress its social functions. Theories proposing humor as a means of safeguarding physical health (Walsh, 1928), or keeping a person from getting too depressed (McDougall, 1922), or sublimating unwanted impulses (Wilson, 1927) or handling conflicts and repressions (Freud, 1905, 1928; Dooley, 1941) stress the importance of humor in sustaining the individual, though by doing so it may also assist him in coping with his social world. It has further been asserted that the *entire* humor process can be an intraindividual affair. Kris (1938), for example, discussed Freud's notion of humor play between the ego and superego and believed the humorist to be self-sufficient with no need of others in order to gain pleasure.

But it has also been insisted that humor and laughter are primarily social phenomena (Meredith, 1897; Dupreel, 1928). Laughter has also been described as a communication device (Wallis, 1922; McComas, 1923; Hayworth, 1928). Among those who view humor and laughter chiefly as social correctives, that is, as useful in maintaining group standards and values, are Shadwell (1671), Hazlitt (1890), Bergson (1911), Bliss (1915), Thomson (1927), Piddington (1933), Mones (1939), and Stephenson (1951). As Wallis (1922) stated, "Laughter is the jolly policeman who keeps the social traffic going after the approved manner [p. 344]." The potential of humor for solving many of the problems and conflicts facing mankind has been mentioned by Mace (1927), Wilson (1927), and Armstrong (1928). The contagion of laughter, the fact man rarely laughs when alone, and the audible sounds emitted calling attention to laughter have been points made to substantiate its social function.

V. CONFIDENCE LEVEL OF THEORISTS

A study of the original papers upon which this chapter is based revealed another dimension to humor theory. It deals *not* with the theoretical notions themselves, but rather with the *authors'* statements concerning how convinced they were of the validity of their own notions about humor. Such writers as Schopenhauer (1819), Carpenter (1922), McDougall (1923), and Mones (1939) simply announced that they had discovered the essence of humor and implied either indirectly or blatantly that previous conceptions of the nature of humor were incredibly narrow-minded, myopic, or foolish. Of course, an analysis of their systems reveals that they might have been better off standing aside with the angels than rushing in with the "ultimate explanation" of humor. McDougall's theory, for example, makes some common sense. Yet after lambasting those before him, he labels laughter an "instinct" which really does not *explain* much. But he did attempt to describe the process by which this instinct came into existence: Mother Nature was faced with a dilemma and had to make a choice—hardly a legitimate explanation in the framework of an acceptable philosophy of science!

Most others proceeded more on tippy-toes while traversing relatively unexplored area with theories in hand. This was often done by admitting at some point that the theory did not cover *all* situations (though it was usually felt to cover most). Others pay compliments to the theorists from opposing camps. And among the more admirable writers are those who actively attempt to indicate the dimensions of their theoretical umbrellas by comparing and contrasting their notions with those of others.

IV. Conclusion

To present a summary of the nature of humor by drawing together all of the scattered pieces rent apart over centuries of theorizing would be, to put it mildly, an impossibility. My goal was to line some of them up, or separate them into piles, in an attempt to familiarize the reader with the incredibly complex backdrop our contemporary humor researchers and theorists find draped across their stage. And as we continue to trek steadily after that which we call humor with hopes and spirits high, Armstrong's (1928) commentary causes us momentary pause and a thin, wry smile of concern.

> The learned and philosophic have given laughter their most serious consideration, and as they pore over the spritely and elusive thing, testing it with the dry and colourless terms of science and philosophy, the tables are frequently turned on them and the Ariel which they are anatomizing so absorbedly shakes himself free, straps them upon the operating table and sets about anatomizing them in turn, and the earnest analysts of laughter become themselves laughable [p. 28] .*

References

Allin, A. On laughter. *Psychological Review,* 1903, **10**, 306–315.
Allport, F. H. *Social psychology.* Boston, Massachusetts: Houghton, 1924.
Angell, J. R. *Psychology: An introductory study of the structure and function of human consciousness.* New York: Holt, 1904.

* From M. Armstrong. *Laughing.* London: Jarrolds, 1928.

Aristotle. The poetics. In S. H. Butcher (Ed. and Trans.), *Aristotle's theory of poetry and fine art*. New York: Macmillan, 1895.

Armstrong, M. *Laughing*. London: Jarrolds, 1928.

Baillie, J. Laughter and tears: The sense of incongruity. *Studies in Human Nature*, 1921, 9, 254–293.

Bain, A. *The emotions and the will*. (3rd ed.) New York: Longmans, Green, 1888.

Barry, H., Jr. The role of subject matter in individual differences in humor. *Journal of Genetic Psychology*, 1928, 35, 112–128.

Bateson, G. The role of humor in human communication. In H. von Foerster (Ed.), *Cybernetics*. New York: Macy Foundation, 1953.

Beattie, J. Essay on laughter and ludicrous composition. In *Essays*. Edinburgh: William Creech, 1776.

Beerbohm, M. Laughter. *North American Review*, 1921, 214, 39–49.

Bergler, E. A clinical contribution to the psychogenesis of humor. *Psychoanalytic Review*, 1937, 24, 34–53.

Bergler, E. *Laughter and the sense of humor*. New York: Intercontinental Medical Book Corp., 1956.

Bergson, H. *Laughter: An essay on the meaning of the comic*. New York: Macmillan, 1911.

Berlyne, D. E. *Conflict, arousal and curiosity*. New York: McGraw-Hill, 1960.

Berlyne, D. E. Laughter, humor and play. In G. Linszey & E. Aronson (Eds.), *Handbook of social psychology*. (2nd ed.) Vol. 3. Reading, Massachusetts: Addison-Wesley, 1969.

Bliss, S. H. The origin of laughter. *American Journal of Psychology*, 1915, 26, 236–246.

Brill, A. A. The mechanism of wit and humor in normal and psychopathic states. *Psychiatric Quarterly*, 1940, 14, 731–749.

Brody, M. W. The meaning of laughter. *Psychoanalytic Quarterly*, 1950, 19, 192–201.

Brown, T. *Lectures on the philosophy of the human mind*. Edinburgh: W. & C. Tait, 1820.

Burt, C. The psychology of laughter. *Health Education Journal*, 1945, 3, 101–105.

Byrne, D. Response to humor as a function of drive arousal and psychological defenses. Unpublished doctoral dissertation, Stanford Univ., 1957.

Carlyle, T. Jean Paul Friedrich Richter. In *Critical and miscellaneous essays*. (2nd. ed.) London: James Fraser, 1840.

Carpenter, R. Laughter, a glory in sanity. *American Journal of Psychology*, 1922, 33, 419–422.

Carus, P. On the philosophy of laughing. *Monist*, 1898, 8.

Cicero. *De Oratore* (55 B.C.) London and New York: Oxford Univ. Press (Clarendon), 1881.

Cooper, L. *An Aristotelian theory of comedy*. New York: Harcourt, 1922.

Courdaveaux, V. *Études sur le comique: Le rire dans la vie et dans l'art*. Paris, 1875.

Crile, J. W. *Man an adaptive mechanism*. New York: Macmillan, 1916.

Darwin, C. *The expression of the emotions in man and animals*. London: Murray, 1872.

Dearborn, G. V. N. The nature of the smile and the laugh. *Science*, June 1, 1900, 9, 851–856.

Delage, Y. Sur la nature du comique. *La Revue du Mois*, 1919, 20, 337–354.

Descartes, R. *Les passions de l'âme*. Paris, 1649.

Dessoir, M. *Ästhetik und allgemeine Kunstwissenschaft*. Stuttgart: Enke, 1923.

Dewey, J. The theory of emotion. *Psychological Review*, 1894, 1, 553–569.

Diserens, C. M. Recent theories of laughter. *Psychological Bulletin*, 1926, 23, 247–255.

Diserens, C. M., & Bonifield, M. Humor and the ludicrous. *Psychological Bulletin*, 1930, 27, 108–118.

Dooley, L. A note on humor. *Psychoanalytic Review*, 1934, 21, 50–57.

Dooley, L. Relation of humor to masochism. *Psychoanalytic Review*, 1941, 28, 37–46.

Drever, J. *Instinct in man*. London and New York: Cambridge Univ. Press, 1917.

Drever, J. *The psychology of everyday life*. London: Methuen, 1921.

Dryden, J. An essay of dramatic poesy (1668). In D. D. Arundell (Ed.), *The text of an essay of dramatic poesy and others*. London and New York: Cambridge Univ. Press, 1929.

Dugas, J. *Psychologie du rire*. Paris, 1902.

Dunlap, K. *Old and new viewpoints in psychology*. St. Louis, Missouri: C. V. Meaby, 1925.

Dupreel, E. Le probleme sociologique du rire. *Revue Philosophique*, 1928, 106, 213–260.

Eastman, M. *The sense of humor*. New York: Scribner, 1921.

Eastman, M. *Enjoyment of laughter*. New York: Simon and Schuster, 1936.

Eidelberg, L. A contribution to the study of wit. *Psychoanalytic Review*, 1945, 32, 33–61.

Everett, C. C. *Poetry, comedy, and duty*. Boston, Massachusetts: Houghton, 1888.

Eysenck, H. J. The appreciation of humor: An experimental and theoretical study. *British Journal of Psychology*, 1942, 32, 295–309.

Feibleman, J. K. *In praise of comedy*. New York: Macmillan, 1939.

Feibleman, J. K. The meaning of comedy. In J. Stolnitz (Ed.), *Aesthetics*. Chicago, Illinois: Meredith, 1949

Feldmann, S. A supplement to Freud's theory of wit. *Psychoanalytic Review*, 1941, 28, 201–217.

Fisher, G. M. Response to aggressive humor by depressive, sociopathic, and normal persons. Unpublished doctoral dissertation, Univ. of Utah, 1964.

Flugel, J. C. Humor and laughter. In G. Lindzey (Ed.), *Handbook of social psychology*. Vol. 2. Cambridge, Massachusetts: Addison-Wesley, 1954.

Fowler, H. W. *A dictionary of modern English usage*. London and New York: Oxford Univ. Press, 1926.

Freud, S. *Wit and its relation to the unconscious*. New York: Moffat Ward, 1916. (Originally: *Der Witz und seine Beziehung zum Unbewussten*, Leipzig and Vienna: Deuticke, 1905.)

Freud, S. Humour. *International Journal of Psychoanalysis*, 1928, 9, 1–6.

Gates, A. I. *Psychology for students of education*. New York: Macmillan, 1925.

Gerard, A. *An essay on taste*. London, 1759.

Giles, H., & Oxford, G. S. Towards a multidimensional theory of laughter causation and its social implications. *Bulletin of the British Psychological Society*, 1970, 23, 97–105.

Gilver, R. C. *Psychology: The science of human behavior*. New York: Harper, 1922.

Gopala-Swami, M. V. The genesis of the laughter instinct. *Psychological Studies*, Univ. of Misore, 1926, 1, 1–25.

Grandgent, C. H. *Getting a laugh and other essays*. Cambridge, Massachusetts: Harvard Univ. Press, 1924.

Gregory, J. C. Some theories of laughter. *Mind*, 1923, 32, 328–344.

Gregory, J. C. *The nature of laughter*. London: Kegan Paul, 1924.

Greig, J. Y. T. *The psychology of laughter and comedy*. New York: Dodd, Mead, 1923.

Grotjahn, M. *Beyond laughter*. New York: McGraw-Hill, 1957.

Guthrie, W. N. A theory of the comic. *International Quarterly*, 1903, 7, 254–264.

Hall, G. S., & Allin, A. The psychology of tickling, laughter, and the comic. *American Journal of Psychology*, 1897, 9, 1–42.

Hartley, D. *Observations on man, his frame, his duty, and his expectations*. London: S. Richardson for Leake & Frederick, 1749.

Hayworth, D. The social origin and function of laughter. *Psychological Review*, 1928, 35, 367–385.

Hazlitt, W. C. On wit and humour. In *Lectures on the English writers*. London: Taylor, 1819.

Hazlitt, W. C. *Studies in jocular literature*. London: Elliot Stock, 1890.

Hecker, E. *Die Physiologie und Psychologie des Lachens und des Komischen.* Leipzig, 1873.

Hellyar, R. H. Laughter and jollity. *Contemporary Review,* 1927, 132, 757–763.

Hobbes, T. *Leviathan.* London: Crooke, 1651.

Höffding, H. *Outlines of psychology.* New York: Macmillan, 1891.

Hollingworth, H. L. Experimental studies in judgment: Judgment of the comic. *Psychological Review,* 1911, 18, 132–156.

Hunt, L. *Wit and humour.* London: Smith, Elder & Co., 1846.

Jekels, L. On the psychology of comedy. In *Selected papers.* London: Imago, 1952.

Jonson, B. Dedication to Promos and Cassandra (1578). In G. Smith (Ed.), *Elizabethan critical essays.* London and New York; Oxford Univ. Press (Clarendon), 1904.

Justin, F. A genetic study of laughter provoking stimuli. *Child Development,* 1932, 3, 114–136.

Kallen, H. M. The aesthetic principle in comedy. *American Journal of Psychology,* 1911, 22, 137–157.

Kant, I. *Kritik der Urteilskraft.* Berlin: Lagarde, 1790.

Keith-Spiegel, P. The relationship between overtly aggressive behavioral modes and reactions to hostile humor. Unpublished doctoral dissertation, Claremont Graduate School and Univ. Center, 1968.

Kimmins, C. W. *The springs of laughter.* London: Methuen, 1928.

Kline, L. W. The psychology of humor. *American Journal of Psychology,* 1907, 18, 421–441.

Knight, R. P. *An analytical enquiry into the principles of taste.* (2nd. ed.) London: T. Payne, 1808.

Knox, I. Towards a philosophy of humor. *Journal of Philosophy,* 1951, 48, 541–548.

Koestler, A. *The act of creation.* London: Hutchinson, 1964.

Köhler, W. *Intelligenzprüfungen an Menschenaffen.* Berlin and New York: Springer-Verlag, 1921.

Kris, E. Ego development and the comic. *International Journal of Psychoanalysis,* 1938, 19, 77–90.

Lauter, P. *Theories of comedy.* Garden City, New York: Doubleday, 1964.

Leacock, S. B. *Humour: Its theory and technique.* London: John Lane, 1935. New York: Dodd, Mead, 1935.

Leacock, S. B. *Humour and humanity.* London: Butterworth, 1937.

Lewin, B. *The psychoanalysis of elation.* New York: Norton, 1950.

Lilly, W. S. The theory of the ludicrous. *Fortnightly Review,* 1896, 65, 724–737.

Lipps, T. *Komik und Humor.* Hamburg: L. Voss, 1898.

Lowenthal, M. M. The laughter of detachment. *Dial,* 1919, 66, 133–135.

Ludovici, A. M. *The secret of laughter.* London: Constable Press, 1932.

Lund, F. H. Why do we weep? *Journal of Social Psychology,* 1930, 1, 136–151.

Mace, C. A. *Sibylla: Or the revival of prophecy.* New York: Dutton, 1927.

Maier, N. R. F. A Gestalt theory of humour. *British Journal of Psychology,* 1932, 23, 69–74.

Marshall, H. R. *Pain, pleasure and aesthetics.* New York: Macmillan, 1894.

Masson, T. L. Humor and the comic journal. *Yale Review,* 1925, 15, 113–123.

McComas, H. C. The origin of laughter. *Psychological Review,* 1923, 30, 45–55.

McDougall, W. The theory of laughter. *Nature,* 1903, 67, 318–319.

McDougall, W. Why do we laugh? *Scribners,* 1922, 71, 359–363.

McDougall, W. *An outline of psychology.* London: Methuen, 1923.

Meerloo, J. A. M. The biology of laughter. *Psychoanalytic Review,* 1966, 53, 189–208.

Mennais, R. de la. *De l'art et du beau.* Paris, 1885.

Menon, V. K. *A theory of laughter.* London: Allen & Unwin, 1931.

Meredith, G. *An essay on comedy and the uses of the comic spirit.* London: Constable Press, 1897.

Meyerson, A. *Psychology of mental disorders.* New York, 1925.

Mones, L. Intelligence and a sense of humor. *Journal of Exceptional Child Psychology,* 1939, 5, 150–153.

Monro, D. H. *Argument of laughter.* Melbourne: Melbourne Univ. Press, 1951.

Murray, H. A. Mirth response to aggressive jokes as a manifestation of aggressive disposition. *Journal of Abnormal and Social Psychology,* 1934, 29, 66–81.

Patrick, G. T. W. *The psychology of relaxation.* New York: Houghton, 1916.

Pearson, H. Humour. In H. Kingsill (Ed.), *The English genius.* London: Eyre & Spottiswoode, 1938.

Penjon, A. Le rire et la liberte. *Revue Philosophique,* 1893, 36, 113–140.

Piddington, R. *The psychology of laughter: A study in social adaptation.* London: Figurehead, 1933.

Pines, L. N. Laughter as an equivalent of epilepsy. *Soviet Psychology and Psychiatry,* 1964, 2, 33–38.

Plato. *Philebus.* (c. 355 B.C.) In B. Jowett (Ed. and Trans.), *The dialogues of Plato.* London and New York: Oxford Univ. Press (Clarendon), 1871.

Plessner, H. *Laughing and crying.* Evanston, Illinois: Northwestern Univ. Press, 1970.

Priestley, J. *A course of lectures on oratory and criticism.* London: J. Johnson, 1777.

Quintilian, M. F. *De institutione oratoria.* Paris: N. E. Lamaire, 1821–1825.

Ramsay, G. *Analysis and theory of the emotions.* London, 1848.

Rapp, A. Toward an eclectic and multilateral theory of laughter and humor. *Journal of General Psychology,* 1947, 36, 207–219.

Rapp, A. A phylogenetic theory of wit and humor. *Journal of Social Psychology,* 1949, 30, 81–96.

Rapp, A. *The origins of wit and humor.* New York: Dutton, 1951.

Raulin, J. M. *Le rire et les exhilarants.* Paris, 1900.

Read, C. *The origin of man and of his superstitions.* London and New York: Cambridge Univ. Press, 1920.

Reik, T. Freud and Jewish wit. *Psychoanalysis,* 1954, 2, 12–20.

Rousseau, J. J. *Lettre á M. d'Alembert.* Paris: Garnier frères, 1926.

Scheerer, M. An aspect of the psychology of humor. Paper presented before the Graduate Faculty of the New School for Social Research, New York, May 19, 1948. (Published in *Bulletin of the Menninger Clinic,* 1966, 30, 86–97.)

Schiller, P. A configurational theory of puzzles and jokes. *Journal of Genetic Psychology,* 1938, 18, 217–234.

Schopenhauer, A. *Die Welt als Wille und Vorstellung.* Leipzig: Brockhaus, 1819.

Shadwell, T. *The humorists.* London: Herringman, 1671.

Shaw, F. J. Laughter: Paradigm of growth. *Journal of Individual Psychology,* 1960, 16, 151–157.

Sidis, B. *The psychology of laughter.* New York: Appleton, 1913.

Spencer, H. The physiology of laughter. *Macmillan's Magazine,* 1860, 1, 395–402.

Stanley, H. M. Remarks on tickling and laughing. *American Journal of Psychology,* 1898, 9, 235–240.

Stephenson, R. M. Conflict and control functions of humor. *American Journal of Sociology,* 1951, 56, 569–574.

Sully, J. *Essay on laughter.* New York: Longmans, Green, 1902.

Tarachow, S. Remarks on the comic process and beauty. *Psychoanalytic Quarterly,* 1949, 18, 215–226.

Thomson, M. C. *The springs of human action.* New York: Appleton, 1927.

Tuke, D. H. Ticklishness. In *A dictionary of psychological medicine.* Vol. 2. New York: McGraw-Hill (Blakiston), 1892.

Valentine, C. W. *The psychology of early childhood.* London: Methuen, 1942.

Vasey, G. *The philosophy of laughter and smiling.* London: J. Burns, 1875.

Wallis, W. D. Why do we laugh? *Scientific Monthly,* 1922, 15, 343–347.

Walsh, J. J. *Laughter and health.* New York: Appleton, 1928.

Washburn, R. W. A study of the smiling and laughing of infants in the first year of life. *Genetic Psychology Monographs,* 1929, 6(5 & 6), 397–535.

Willmann, J. M. An analysis of humor and laughter. *American Journal of Psychology,* 1940, 53, 70–85.

Wilson, K. M. Sense of Humor. *Contemporary Review,* 1927, 131, 628–633.

Winterstein, A. Contributions to the problem of humor. *Psychoanalytic Quarterly,* 1934, 3, 303–316.

Wolfenstein, M. A phase in the development of children's sense of humor. In *The psychoanalytic study of the child.* Vol. 6. New York: International Univ. Press, 1951.

Wolfenstein, M. Children's understanding of jokes. In *The psychoanalytic study of the child.* Vol. 8. New York: International Univ. Press, 1953.

Wolfenstein, M. *Children's humor: A psychological analysis.* Glencoe, Illinois: Free Press, 1954.

Woodworth, R. S. *Psychology: A study of mental life.* New York: Holt, 1921.

Yerkes, R. M. & Learned, B. W. *Chimpanzee intelligence and its vocal expression.* Baltimore, Maryland: Williams & Wilkins, 1925.

Zippin, D. Sex differences and the sense of humor. *Psychoanalytic Review,* 1966, 53, 209–219.

Zwerling, I. The favorite joke in diagnostic and therapeutic interviewing. *Psychoanalytic Quarterly,* 1955, 24, 104–114.

Part II

THEORETICAL PERSPECTIVES

Chapter 2

Humor and Its Kin

Daniel E. Berlyne

Department of Psychology
University of Toronto, Toronto, Ontario, Canada

I. Affinities of Humor

Humor has always stood out as a unique and puzzling psychological phenomenon, and the scant attention it has received from psychologists does them little credit. If any of the famous explorers of old had caught sight of a strange geological formation, seemingly unlike anything else within their territory, they would surely have made straight for it, ignoring everything else within sight until they had examined it and perhaps scaled it in the hope of surveying the whole country from a matchless vantage point. Compared with these adventurers, psychologists do not cut impressive figures. Our Freuds may equal their intrepidity and their sound sense of priorities but not their rigorous surveying techniques. Most others refuse to venture outside familiar cabbage patches of proven fertility. An increasing number, impatient of the restrictions imposed on the surveyor and the horticulturist alike, turn their eyes away from the landscape and toward the clouds.

Humor is unique in the sense that it can hardly be mistaken for anything else. Nobody is ever in any doubt about whether a joke is funny to him. Its humor can hardly be confused with any other quality. Anybody can usually pinpoint without hesitation what it is about a joke that amuses him, although it is often hard to explain why it is amusing. There is also generally little difficulty in deciding whether or not somebody else finds something humorous.

Yet humor possesses unmistakable affinities with other psychological phenomena, notably with curiosity and exploratory behavior (see Berlyne, 1960, 1963, 1966), play (see Berlyne, 1969), and art (see Berlyne, 1971). First, there is a common association with pleasure. Yet this association is much closer in the case of humor than in other cases. Some quests for information to satisfy curiosity can be exacting and stressful. So can some activities that are classed as "games" or "playing," such as those of the avid gambler or the professional football player. Even the play of the child is sometimes marked by a painful, compulsive intensity rather than light-hearted merriment, as his facial expression will show. Pleasure has been recognized as a defining hallmark of art by Plato, St. Thomas Aquinas, and many later writers. But there have been those who have denied that art must always be pleasurable (the latest being Coleman, 1971). It is, however, hard to imagine anybody finding something humorous and not enjoying it. He might very well be left indifferent by somebody's attempt at humor. But if he does not derive pleasure from it himself, it is certainly not humorous for him.

Second, all these phenomena are bound together by the sources of pleasure on which they draw. Humor can derive some of its appeal from virtually any kind of motivation. Sexual, scatological, and hostile content are, of course, frequent. It is not unusual for people to joke about things they have reason to fear, and hunger has been known to promote jocular remarks about food. Similarly, extrinsic content of these kinds can contribute savor to the stimulation resulting from exploratory behavior, play, and aesthetic activity. Nevertheless, in these phenomena as in humor, such ecological or semantic factors may play no part at all. Whether or not they are responsible for part of the pleasure, some pleasure invariably comes from structure, which means from comparison or, more generally, from collation or interrelation of stimulus elements, thoughts, and items of information. For example, in humor, it may be a matter of comparing two objects that are perceived side by side (e.g., a thin Laurel and a fat Hardy), two events that are perceived in close succession (e.g., a pompous person stalking arrogantly down the road and then falling on his face), or attributes of something perceived now and attributes of similar objects that have been perceived in the past (e.g., any familiar object that is unusually large or unusually small or somehow distorted out of its usual shape). Humor may, on the other hand, depend on the combination in one object or event of attributes or lines of thought that are normally unrelated— incongruous juxtapositions of sights or sounds (e.g., somebody well known in fancy dress or playing a role in a play that sharply contrasts with his normal character), discourse drawing attention to two normally unconnected meanings of a word or of two similar-sounding words (e.g., puns—"Try our cigars. You can't get better!" "I know. I tried one last week, and I am still not better!"), convergence of two normally unrelated lines of thought (e.g., paradoxical witticisms—"Nothing succeeds like excess." "The wages of gin is breath."). These instances, and many others that do not fit these particular categories, reveal the motivational importance of the "collative" variables, whose decisive role in exploratory behavior, aesthetics, and other spheres has become so evident (Berlyne, 1960, 1963). They include degree of novelty, surprisingness, complexity, rate of change, ambiguity, and incompatibility. They are closely related to the information theorist's concepts of "uncertainty," "information content," and "redundancy."

II. Collative Variables and Pleasure

Although related assumptions can be uncovered in the philosophical writings of earlier centuries and among the pioneers of experimental psychology, the Gestalt psychologists were the first to sense the far-ranging significance of the principle that certain structures, certain relations between elements of a perceived or conceived pattern, can be disharmonious and disturbing. Yet they confined their attention to circumscribed aspects of this significance. Essentially the same principle was propounded, in a form that made contact with motivation theory and with neurophysiological knowledge, by Hebb (1949). The experimental work on exploratory behavior that began in earnest in the 1950s documented the complementary principle that other structural relations can be rewarding and pleasurable. This work, in its turn, encouraged research and interest in aesthetics, play, and humor. The motivational effects of structure, i.e., of collative variables, were overlooked for a long time because they are not easy to account for and do not seem to follow immediately from the requirements of biological adaptation. However, two bodies of recent research findings help to make these motivational effects more understandable.

First, one experiment after another has shown, and newly reported experiments continue to show, that collative properties of stimulus patterns can affect the intensity of various indices of increased arousal (see Berlyne, 1960, 1967, 1971) [see Chapters 6 and 7].

Second, there is a substantial array of evidence, psychological, physiological, and anatomical, indicating close relations between shifts in arousal level and "hedonic value," a term that covers both pleasure (manifested through verbal reports or expressive behavior) and reward value (manifested through the reinforcement of learned responses) (see Berlyne, 1967). There is, in fact, a *prima facie* case for the view that pleasure and reward can depend on either of two mechanisms, both activated by changes in arousal but in different ways. One mechanism is brought into play by a moderate rise in arousal, an "arousal boost." The other operates when arousal is reduced after climbing to an uncomfortably high level. This succession of a rise followed by a fall in arousal has been called an "arousal jag" (Berlyne, 1960). In some circumstances, including many instances of humor, a rise in arousal may be moderate enough to fall within the scope of the arousal-boost mechanism, and a subsequent drop in arousal may add pleasure in its turn by activating the arousal-reduction mechanism. Then, both phases will be pleasurable (cf. Freud's "fore-pleasure" and "end pleasure"), and we may speak of an "arousal boost–jag."

This provisional theoretical scheme implies that the relation between hedonic value and "arousal potential" (a term covering all the stimulus properties that tend to drive arousal upward, including intensity, inherent or conditioned biological significance, and collative properties) will follow a curve of the shape shown in Figure 1. This is the shape of the curve introduced by Wundt (1874) to represent the function linking pleasure with stimulus intensity. But we are giving its coordinates a broader interpretation than he did. With this reinterpretation, the curve denotes that stimuli of moderate arousal potential will be maximally pleasurable and rewarding. If, however, arousal potential rises above a certain point (the point where the curve crosses the base line), hedonic value will become negative, and any condition that reduces arousal will then be a source of pleasure and reward. The curvilinear relation between hedonic

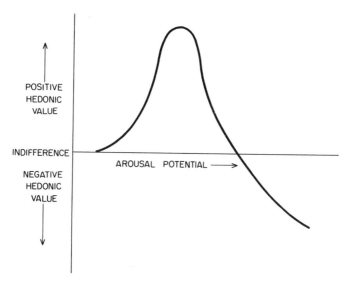

Figure 1. Hedonic value and arousal potential: A reinterpretation of the Wundt curve. (From: *Aesthetics and psychobiology,* D. E. Berlyne. Copyright © 1971. By permission from Appleton-Century-Crofts, Educational Division, Meredith Corporation.)

value and components of arousal potential, including stimulus intensity and collative properties, has abundant experimental support. This curvilinearity could result from an interaction between two opposing systems in the brain, one governing positive and the other negative hedonic value, such as several writers have been led to posit by both psychological and neurophysiological data (Berlyne, 1967, 1971). One has only to make the assumption, for which there is no lack of evidence in the experimental literature (Berlyne, 1967), that the system subserving negative hedonic value (aversive or punishing effects) requires a higher level of arousal potential to activate it than the system subserving reward and pleasure (see Figure 2). A third system—a "secondary reward system"—apparently comes into play when something occurs to relieve arousal after the hedonic value of a stimulus has become negative, thus accounting for the arousal-reduction or arousal-jag mechanism of reward and pleasure.

All this explains how collative variables, which are capable of driving arousal upward or downward and thus qualify as components of arousal potential, can generate either pleasure or its opposite. At the same time, drive conditions like anger, fear of injury, and sexual appetite, can also heighten arousal—as can stimuli that have taken over arousal-inducing power from them, by conditioning or by

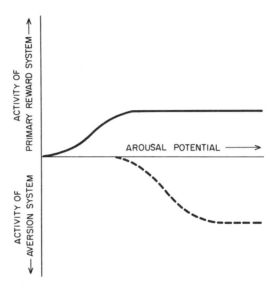

generalization. Similarly, stimuli associated with alleviation of these drives can contribute to pleasure, either by inducing an arousal boost or by bringing arousal down from uncomfortable heights. These "ecological factors" (Berlyne, 1967) collaborate with collative components of arousal potential in what Freud called "tendentious" jokes, as they do in much representational art and program music. The collative variables can, however, stand alone, as they do in Freud's "harmless" jokes and in nonrepresentational art (or, for that matter, in representational art in which the form of a depicted object is what matters) and absolute music. It is noteworthy, however, that while humor depends heavily, and at times exclusively, on the structure of a joke, the relations that constitute the structure are almost always those obtaining between recognizable perceived objects or verbal meanings. A structure bereft of content may suffice for art and mathematics, but rarely for humor. The nearest we come to finding exceptions to this rule is in musical humor (e.g., some of the abrupt contrasts in the works of Haydn and Beethoven).

III. Experiments on Collative Variables and Humor

Most of the rather meager experimental work on humor that has been carried out until recently (see Berlyne, 1969) has related various measures of appreciation to the personality of the appreciator, his social-group membership, his motivational condition, and the subject matter of the jokes to which he is exposed. In view of the foregoing discussion, it is encouraging and significant that experimenters are now examining the effects of collative variables.

Zigler, Levine, and Gould (1967) have presented cartoons to children aged 8 through 13, recording verbal expressed preferences, facial expressions of mirth, and degrees of comprehension. The degrees of comprehension shown by the subjects were used to divide the cartoons into "easy," "moderately difficult," "difficult," and "impossible" categories. Both facial expression and preferences showed the moderately difficult cartoons to be most appreciated. There is an immediate temptation to identify the inverted U-shaped curve that relates appreciation to degree of difficulty with a portion of the Wundt curve. But this would probably be a mistake. The Wundt curve represents the extent to which a stimulus generates pleasure through an arousal boost. Moderately difficult cartoons, on the other hand, presumably afford pleasure through the arousal-jag mechanism, i.e., through the sequence of initial challenge and incomprehension followed by resolution and enlightenment. Zigler *et al.* (1967) speak, in fact, of the "degree of cognitive congruence existing between the cognitive demand features of the humor stimulus and the cognitive resources of the individual [p. 335]." Easy jokes will offer no prospect of an arousal jag, because they make no demands on the subject's intellectual capacities and thus no rise of arousal into the uncomfortable range. Difficult jokes, we may suppose, produce bewilderment without any hope of prompt clarification.

This experiment used ready-made humorous material and measured some of its collative properties. It is often said, however, that nobody understands a phenomenon until he can produce it at will. Eventually, we must hope that our knowledge of the principles underlying humor will have advanced to the point where we can use them to construct jokes. Important strides toward this goal have been taken by means of two recent experiments, in which some semblance of humor was extracted from arbitrarily chosen elements by manipulation of collative variables. Ertel (1968) used Shannon and Weaver's (1949) method for generating approximations to normal discourse: An "nth-order approximation" is produced by presenting a subject with n consecutive words taken from a sentence and asking him to supply a word that could reasonably follow them. The lower the order of approximation, and therefore the greater the departure from the statistical structure of normal German prose, the more "absurd" the resulting passage was judged to be. However, judged humor was greatest at intermediate degrees of approximation: The fourth-order approximation was judged most "funny" *(komisch)* and the sixth-order most "witty" *(witzig).* In a later experiment Ertel gave subjects lists of nouns and adjectives, asking them to select adjective–noun pairs that would be "normal," "witty," "funny," and "absurd." The degree of incongruity between an adjective and a noun was calculated from other subjects' judgments of degree of "connection" *(Zusammenhang)* or "fitness" *(Stimmigkeit).* The most "witty" and "funny" adjective–noun pairs tended to be more incongruous than those judged "normal" but less incongruous than those judged "absurd." So once again, patterns representing intermediate degrees of deviation from the familiar harbored the most humor.

An experiment by Nerhardt (1970) was even more imaginative in conception and impressive in its findings. It used nonverbal stimulus events of a kind quite remote from the customary ingredients of jokes, and recorded laughter rather than verbal judgments. Subjects were required to lift weights in what purported to be a psychophysiological experiment. After a number of weights falling within a narrow range, one that was much heavier or much lighter was presented. Laughter after exposure to the final weight tended to be more frequent, the greater the discrepancy between it and the weights that had been experienced hitherto. Here, the relation between humor and incongruity was monotonic, rather than curvilinear, as it had been in the other experiments.

The experiments by Zigler *et al.* and Ertel used verbal material, which means that relief from incongruity must have come mainly through efforts to make sense of what was presented. These efforts will be of no avail once a certain level of incongruity has been exceeded, which can account for the turn-down. As far as Nerhardt's weights are concerned, relief must be a result simply of recovery from surprise, and this will be forthcoming whatever the degree of incongruity, so that the discomfiture and subsequent recovery will be more intense, the more surprising the experience.

IV. Laughter

More than anything else, what makes humor distinctive and enigmatic is its association with laughter, that strange and complicated pattern of behavior which warrants much more intensive study than it has received even from specialists in the psychology of humor. It is true that situations other than humor can provoke laughter. The laugh of triumph, of contempt, and of relief have often been noted, and the laughter that occurs in response to tickling has been discussed in particular. Furthermore, humor can be enjoyed without laughing, but laughter is always in the offing.

Laughter has several distinguishable components. First, there is the widening of the mouth and pulling up of its corners, which the laugh shares with the smile. Second, there is an unusual respiratory pattern, accompanied by vocalization. Darwin (1872) speaks of "short and broken" expirations "with the inspirations prolonged." A recent psychophysiological study by Fry (1969) indicates that the "primary component of laughter is an abrupt, strong expiration" at the beginning, followed by "a series of expiratory–inspiratory microcycles superimposed upon the larger expiratory movements." Third, there is the opening of the mouth and baring of the teeth, shared with the grin and the snarl. Fourth, there is a generalized tremor ("quaking with laughter"), amounting at times to a convulsion.

Some of these components, notably the smile and the snarl, can appear without others. Nevertheless, the laughter pattern usually occurs as an integrated whole. It emerges in full bloom during the first few months of life, although it is likely to be preceded by the smile. It can be evoked as a complete unit by stimulation of the anterior globus pallidus during neurosurgery (Hassler & Riechert, 1961).

The laugh is a conspicuous example of "expressive behavior." This label is attached to responses that correspond to motivational or emotional states but do not seem to exert effects of obvious biological utility on the external or internal environment. Expressive responses often play an important part in social interaction by providing cues that affect the behavior of other individuals. Tinbergen (1959) has suggested, for example, that laughter is comparable to the submissive "appeasement gestures" of lower animals. But the communicative function is often acquired later by behavior that originated for quite different reasons. Laughter is certainly remarkably amenable to social facilitation and influential in interpersonal relations. But it can occur in a solitary individual, so that it seems doubtful that its prime significance is a social one.

Attempts to account for expressive behavior (see Frijda, 1964) have invariably come close to one or another of Darwin's (1872) three "general principles of expression." The "principle of the direct action of the nervous system" states that "when the sensorium is strongly excited, nerve-force is generated in excess, and is transmitted in certain definite directions, depending on the connection of the nerve-cells and partly on habit." The conception of laughter as a safety valve for "surplus energy" was advanced by Spencer (1860). Similarly, Freud (1905) saw laughter as an outlet for discharging a "sum of psychic energy." This kind of hypothesis is not viewed very favorably nowadays, mainly because the underlying notion of a quantity of pent-up "nerve-force," "energy," "excitation," or "tension" that demands release receives little support from our present knowledge of how the nervous system works. Nevertheless, laughter seems clearly to be capable of a cathartic effect. People often feel better and more relaxed after it. It is, however, far from clear why the particular motor channels and specific and distinctive patterns of responses associated with laughter should be selected for a generalized discharge. The threshold for laughter does not seem especially low, except when there is social facilitation or in exceptionally giggly individuals.

Darwin himself connected laughter with his "Principle of Antithesis." Because laughter expresses a "state of mind" opposite to that expressed by "screams or cries of distress," it involves a pattern of respiration as different as possible from that of the latter. The principle of antithesis has not been taken very seriously by later writers. There is, however, some neurophysiological support for this kind of process. The central nervous system seems to contain many antagonistic and mutually counteracting centers, such that inhibition of one leads to activation of the other. Conditions that inhibit sympathetic discharge lead to an upsurge of parasympathetic activity; ablation of the satiation center in the hypothalamus leads to excess eating; and dogs that have been shocked after extending a paw do not merely refrain from this action but strongly contract the flexors of the same limb (Konorski, 1946, p. 227).

Nowadays, psychologists and ethologists are most partial to thinking in line with Darwin's "Principle of Serviceable Associated Habits." When acts occur in a situation where they are not plainly appropriate or useful, they are likely to be interpreted as "displacement" activities (explained today in terms of stimulus generalization, response generalization, and disinhibition, rather than hydraulic analogies); as "intention movements" or fragments of useful actions occurring when motivation is insufficiently strong or inhibiting factors are present; or, in human beings, as vestiges of reactions that had uses for our animal ancestors. The various components of laughter have been singled out and made the basis for explanations of this kind at one time or another. The baring of teeth has been related to the threatening snarls of animals in an aggressive mood or to the snigger of triumph or derision. The paroxysmic aspect of laughter has suggested analogies with epilepsy and other convulsive phenomena (Bateson, 1953; Pines, 1963).

Andrew (1963a, b), in the most thoroughgoing evolutionary interpretation of facial expression to have been worked out in recent times, traces the laugh back to the protective responses of the buccal area in lower mammals, which prepare for biting, for ejection of noxious substances from the mouth, as for blocking the ingestion of noxious substances. Andrew maintains that such responses tend to be evoked by all kinds of situations involving "contrast." He used this word in an extremely broad sense. Like "discrepancy" (McClelland, Atkinson, Clark, & Lowell, 1953; McCall & Kagan, 1967), "conflict" (Berlyne, 1954, 1960), "stimulus change" (Dember & Earl, 1957), "incongruity" (Hunt, 1963), and "inconsistency" (Abelson, Aronson, McGuire, Newcomb, Rosenberg, & Tannenbaum, 1968), it covers a variety of situations in which collative properties—novelty, surprise, change and movement, incongruity—conduce to a rise in arousal.

V. The Smile

The question of how the laugh and the smile are related has always been a contentious one. Many writers have assumed that they represent different intensities of the same response. On the other hand, McDougall (1923) insisted vehemently that they have quite different origins. A laugh may grow out of a smile, fade into a smile, or be replaced by a smile. There are, on the other hand, many situations in which smiles occur but laughter would be unusual and inappropriate. There seem to be few, if any, situations in which the opposite is the case. It seems safest to conclude that the smile and the laugh are distinct but not independent. Perhaps the smile can be regarded as one element of the laughter pattern that frequently appears by itself.

Naturally enough, much has been made of the importance of the smile as a social stimulus, especially in cementing the early affective bonds between mother and child. Wolff (1963) has carefully studied the smilelike grimaces that appear from the first day of life, antedating the first social smiles by a month or two. These are sometimes called "gas smiles," but, Wolff points out, without adequate justification. Such presocial smiles occur only when the infant is drowsy or sleepy, except that premature infants may produce them while awake. Wolff was able to elicit smiling with various mild auditory stimuli. Louder sounds would no doubt have occasioned distress instead. Other smiles occurred "without known external or systematically demonstrable internal causes." One can only surmise that transient internal events of some sort were responsible for them. All in all, these smiles seem to be responses to short-lasting stimuli of moderate intensity or arousal potential. The stimuli may well be such as give rise to an arousal boost or an orientation reaction rather than a defensive reaction (Sokolov, 1958). One might well wonder why the response takes this particular form. At the present time, Andrew's hypothesis seems as promising as any.

Zelazo (1970) has demonstrated the susceptibility of smiles of older infants (age about 13 weeks) to the influence of collative variables. Visual patterns, sound sequences, and sequences of visual stimuli were presented. On the whole, the frequency of smiling tended to rise and then fall over trials. Smiling also increased when a repeated, and therefore familiar, visual sequence was replaced by a variant. There was evidence, therefore, that the incidence of smiling is governed by degree of novelty. The effective stimuli could be those with just enough novelty for a pleasurable arousal boost. On the other hand, Zelazo, like Kagan, Hen-Tov, Levine, and Lewis (1966), favors the view that smiling corresponds to "effortful assimilation," which seems to imply a succession of arousal-raising disorientation, uncertainty, conflict, and arousal-relieving recognition, i.e., an arousal jag.

VI. How Does Humor Differ?

What has so far been argued about the relations between humor, laughter, and smiling, on the one hand, and collative variables and arousal, on the other, can hardly be held to constitute even the makings of a theory of humor. As we have observed, many other psychological phenomena, notably exploration, play, and aesthetic appreciation, similarly depend on hedonic effects of fluctuations in arousal due to collative and other factors. But the stimulus situations that give rise to them are, for the most part, not judged to be humorous. Nor do we laugh all the time we are engaged in them.

At this point, advocates of the various classical and recent theories of humor will feel called upon to step in. They comprise the exponents of the older superiority, conflict, and relief theories (see Berlyne, 1969), as well as those responsible for more recent "cognitive" theories (e.g., Maier, 1932; Bateson, 1953; Fry, 1963; Koestler, 1964), who see the essence of humor in some particular form of interplay among perceptual or intellectual processes [see Chapter 1]. What they have to say warrants the deepest respect and reflection. But, if our arguments so far have been too broad, their explanations are too narrow (see Berlyne, 1969). Apart from insufficiencies of definition with regard to the factors they invoke, these theorists show that their theories fit certain kinds of jokes, which they cite, quite admirably. They have, however, invariably failed to make sure that their theories can encompass all conceivable instances of humor. Furthermore, they usually fail to give us much inkling of why the mechanisms they describe should produce pleasure.

We must therefore aspire toward a theory that will be comprehensive enough to cover all humor but specific enough to cover nothing else (although it will, of course, have to illuminate the relations between humor and other psychological phenomena). We are still a long way from such a theory. So, for the time being, we have no recourse other than the most blatant speculation in facing the question of how humor differs from its nearest kin. A few incipient hypotheses may, however, be ventured.

1. Time Scale

Whatever processes produce humor, including any perceptual or intellectual processing and any shifts in arousal level, are generally abrupt and over within a few seconds. There may be a prolonged prelude leading up to an incident or "punch line" that is to be recognized as funny. And the prolonged anticipation may be enjoyed. But the humorous configuration itself appears suddenly and is over quickly. There may be virtually continuous laughter throughout the course of a comical film or play, but the laughs clearly correspond to transient episodes. In contrast, the succession of internal events underlying appreciation of a work of art may take minutes or hours to complete itself. And most forms of play, multifarious as they are, must last at least a few minutes to fulfill their functions.

2. Cues Precluding Seriousness

It is recognized that humorous events are somehow cut off from the main body of life, which has to be taken seriously. They call upon us to abandon our predominant roles, to set aside the habits and ways of thinking to which we are subject most of the time, and to go over temporarily to a quite different set of attitudes and behaviors. Humor takes place, it has been said more than once, within a frame. Humor is accompanied by discriminative cues, which indicate that what is happening, or is going to happen, should be taken as a joke. The ways in which we might react to the same events in the absence of these cues become inappropriate and must be withheld [see Chapter 3].

Much of the same applies to situations that bear the labels of "play" or "games" (see Huizinga, 1939; Berlyne, 1969). And similar points are made with reference to art (Berlyne, 1971, Chap. 10). Art, it is contended, requires "psychic distance." It always contains reminders that we are confronting a depiction or representation of objects rather than the objects themselves. When these reminders are missing or are ineffective as in *trompe-l'oeil* paintings, the result is not held to be artistic.

There is, however, an important distinction. Humor and most play are accompanied by cues that mark them as not "serious." Art and make-believe or role-playing games contain cues that mark them as not "real." The sets of responses that are inhibited in the two cases are not the same. When something is stamped as "lacking in seriousness," more responses are inhibited than when it is stamped as "unreal." When we see Hamlet and Laertes dueling on the stage, we refrain from many actions that would occur if we witnessed something similar in the street. We do not, for example, call the police or interpose our bodies between the combatants. But we can still indulge in pangs of fear for their safety, melancholy feelings, and solemn reflections on the human condition. When, however, we see two clowns battering each other in the circus, not only preventive action but even disquiet and sympathy are ruled out.

3. Arousal Boost, Arousal Jag, or Both?

Reference has been made to the tentative conclusion (Berlyne, 1967) that positive hedonic value can arise in either of two ways. It can result from some condition that raises arousal moderately (the arousal boost) or from a sequence of conditions generating an uncomfortable state of heightened arousal which is subsequently reversed (the arousal jag).

There are plenty of jokes that fit the arousal-jag paradigm. There is a phase of discomfiture, puzzlement, "tension," even fright, and then something happens to resolve all this rapidly. It may be that later stimulus material alleviates the confusion due to what came earlier, for example, by explaining it or indicating how it should be reinterpreted ["What's black and white and red (read) all over?" "A newspaper."]. Sometimes, following completion of the joke, some intellectual work is required to make everything clear ("Does this bus stop at the Waldorf Astoria?" "No, it's left in the garage at night."). It is often merely a matter of recovery from the disconcerting impact of a surprising event, possibly related to the homeostatic mechanisms that dampen the response of the reticular arousal system to alerting stimuli (Dell, 1963).

Cases of the latter kind are admittedly difficult to distinguish from cases of the arousal boost, in which an arousing, rather than dearousing, phase generates pleasure. So the question arises of whether humor can work through the arousal boost. We have seen that smiles can occur, especially in infants, in response to events that might be productive of arousal boosts. But what of the kinds of behavior in which the arousal boost is most likely to be operative, namely "diversive" exploratory behavior (Berlyne, 1960)? A child playing with a toy may smile or have a grim look on his face. He is unlikely to laugh unless something quite unexpected happens. Fechner (1876) mentions several kinds of stimulation that seem to provide just the right amount of "unity in multiplicity" and are therefore able to foster prolonged observation without fatigue, e.g., the flapping of flags in the wind, the veining of marble. We might add the sight of the sea's waves or a fireworks display. People do not usually laugh continuously while exposed to these.

Then, we must recall the clear signs that laughter functions as a discharge, as a means of relief. People may very well be extremely wrought up and uncomfortable before laughing, but they usually feel markedly better for at least a short while afterward. Freud (1905) equated the various forms of the ludicrous with "economy of psychic expenditure." Somebody is braced for a degree of effort or stress that turns out to be unnecessary, whereupon the excess energy that was held in reserve is vented through laughter. Freed from its dependence on an archaic conception of "psychic energy," this view can be reinterpreted in more modern terms of arousal (Berlyne, 1960). The behavior of a human being is not determined solely by the stimulus of the moment. It also depends on his anticipations of what is to come and on his recollections or reconstructions of what went before. Apart from considering the specific content of past and future events, he must make some estimate of the demands that will be made on him in the near future, how much information he will have to take in, how energetically he will have to act. This means that premonitory cues must set up an appropriate level of anticipatory arousal, preparing him to cope effectively with what is probably impending. There will, however, be occasions—and humor will supply many of them—when the estimate turns out to be wrong and the person in question finds that his degree of mobilization, of arousal, was too high. Laughter seems to have something to do with speedily remedying this state of affairs.

Finally, we must note that, whereas humor, exploration, play, and art all feed on novelty, surprise, incongruity, or departures from what is usual and expected, there are marked differences in degree. It seems that art (Berlyne, 1971), like most forms of exploration (Berlyne, 1960, 1966), requires either relatively mild deviations from the familiar and humdrum, or stimulus patterns that offer some degree of abnormality or contrast without straying too far from what is regular and understandable. This is implied by phrases like "uniformity and variety" and "order combined with complexity." However, the anomalies out of which humor grows can be quite extreme. As McDougall (1923) argued, many of the things that we find funny would be quite harrowing if they did not bear this label. As Byron wrote, "And if I laugh at any mortal thing, 'tis that I may not weep." Tendentious jokes often depict events that would normally be gruesome, terrifying, and shocking in the extreme. "Harmless" jokes, which rely exclusively on collative variables, present extraordinary happenings, illogicalities, and tricks of thought or language that, if they were characteristic of most of life, would leave us totally bewildered, stupefied, and incapacitated.

VII. Conclusion

We are still far from the day when we shall be able to detail the workings of humor with confidence. At present, we can only entertain some provisional conjectures. It seems plausible that the smile can be expressive of any kind of pleasure, whether it comes from the arousal boost or from arousal reduction. On the other hand, laughter (or, one might say, those parts of laughter that are added to the smile) seems restricted to situations in which a period or a moment of aversely high arousal is followed by sudden and pronounced arousal reduction. This is exemplified mainly by humorous situations in which the preliminary rise in arousal is due, at least partly, to collative variables. But the same may apply to situations in which laughter is precipitated by the abrupt removal of intense fear or anger.

In short, our speculation is that humor and laughter do not work through pure arousal boosts. They appear to require arousal jags or arousal boost-jags.

Acknowledgment

The preparation of this chapter was facilitated by Research Grant APA-73 from the National Research Council of Canada.

References

Abelson, R. P., Aronson, E., McGuire, W. J., Newcomb, T. M., Rosenberg, M. J., & Tannenbaum, P. H. (Eds.) *Theories of cognitive consistency.* Chicago, Illinois: Rand McNally, 1968.

Andrew, R. J. Evolution of facial expression. *Science,* 1963, 142, 1034–1041.   (a)

Andrew, R. J. The origin and evolution of the calls and facial expressions of the primates. *Behavior,* 1963, 20, 1–109.   (b)

Bateson, G. The role of humor in human communication. In H. von Foerster (Ed.), *Cybernetics.* New York: Macy Foundation, 1953.

Berlyne, D. E. A theory of human curiosity. *British Journal of Psychology,* 1954, 45, 180–191.

Berlyne, D. E. *Conflict, arousal and curiosity.* New York: McGraw-Hill, 1960.

Berlyne, D. E. Motivational problems raised by exploratory and epistemic behavior. In S. Koch (Ed.), *Psychology—A study of a science.* Vol. 5. New York: McGraw-Hill, 1963.

Berlyne, D. E. Curiosity and exploration. *Science,* 1966, 153, 25–33.

Berlyne, D. E. Arousal and reinforcement. In D. Levine (Ed.), *Nebraska Symposium on Motivation.* Lincoln, Nebraska: Univ. of Nebraska Press, 1967.

Berlyne, D. E. Laughter, humor and play. In G. Lindzey & E. Aronson (Eds.), *Handbook of Social Psychology.* (2nd ed.) Vol. 3. Reading, Massachusetts: Addison-Wesley, 1969.

Berlyne, D. E. *Aesthetics and psychobiology.* New York: Appleton, 1971.

Coleman, F. J. Is aesthetic pleasure a myth? *Journal of Aesthetics and Art Criticism,* 1971, 29, 319–332.

Darwin, C. *The expression of the emotions in man and animals.* London: Murray, 1872.

Dell, P. Reticular homeostasis and critical reactivity. In J. Moruzzi, A. Fessard, & H. H. Jasper (Eds.), *Brain mechanisms.* Amsterdam: Elsevier, 1963.

Dember, W. N., & Earl, R. W. Analysis of exploratory, manipulatory and curiosity behaviors. *Psychological Review,* 1957, 64, 91–96.

Ertel, S. *Eine psychologische Theorie des Komischen.* Habilitationsvortrag, Univ. of Münster, 1968.

Fechner, G. T. *Vorschule der Ästhetik.* Leipzig: Breitkopf & Härtel, 1876.

Freud, S. *Wit and its relation to the unconscious.* New York: Moffat Ward, 1916. (Originally: *Der Witz und seine Beziehung zum Unbewussten.* Leipzig and Vienna: Deuticke, 1905.)

Frijda, N. H. Mimik und Pantomimik. In R. Kirchoff (Ed.), *Handbuch der Psychologie.* Vol. 5. *Ausdruckspsychologie.* Göttingen: Hogrefe, 1964.

Fry, W. F., Jr., *Sweet madness: A study of humor*. Palo Alto, California: Pacific, 1963.

Fry, W. F., Jr., Instinctual and physiological bases of the humor experience. Paper presented before Western Psychological Association, Vancouver, 1969.

Hassler, R., & Riechert, T. Wirkungen der Reizungen und Koagulationen in den Stammganglien bei stereotaktischen Hirnoperationen. *Nervenarzt*, 1961, 32, 97–109.

Hebb, D. O. *The organization of behavior*. New York: Wiley, 1949.

Huizinga, J. *Homo ludens*. Amsterdam: Pantheon, 1939. (*Homo ludens*. London: Routledge, 1949.)

Hunt, J. M. Motivation inherent in information processing and action. In O. J. Harvey (Ed.), *Cognitive factors in motivation and social organization*. New York: Ronald Press, 1963.

Kagan, J., Henker, B. A., Hen-Tov, A., Levine, J., & Lewis, M. Infants' differential reactions to familiar and distorted faces. *Child Development*, 1966, 37, 519–532.

Koestler, A. *The act of creation*. London: Hutchinson, 1964.

Konorski, J. *Conditioned reflexes and neuron organization*. London and New York: Cambridge Univ. Press, 1946.

Maier, N. R. F. A Gestalt theory of humor. *British Journal of Psychology*, 1932, 23, 69–74.

McCall, R. B., & Kagan, J. Stimulus–schema discrepancy in the infant. *Journal of Experimental Child Psychology*, 1967, 5, 381–390.

McClelland, D. C., Atkinson, J. W., Clark, R. A., & Lowell, E. L. *The achievement motive*. New York: Appleton, 1953.

McDougall, W. *An outline of psychology*. London: Methuen, 1923.

Nerhardt, G. Humor and inclination to laugh: Emotional reactions to stimuli of different divergence from a range of expectancy. *Scandinavian Journal of Psychology*, 1970, 11, 185–195.

Pines, L. N. Laughter as an equivalent of epilepsy. *Soviet Psychology and Psychiatry*, 1964, 2, 22–38.

Shannon, C. E., & Weaver, W. *Mathematical theory of communication*. Urbana, Illinois: Univ. of Illinois Press, 1949.

Sokolov, E. N. *Vospriiatie i uslovny refleks*. Moscow: Univ. of Moscow Press, 1958. (*Perception and the conditioned reflex*. Oxford: Pergamon, 1964.)

Spencer, H. Physiology of laughter. *Macmillan's Magazine*, 1860, 1, 395. (Reprinted in *Essays, scientific, political and speculative*. Vol. 2. New York: Appleton, 1891.)

Tinbergen, N. Einige Gedanken über "Beschwichtigungsgebärden." *Zeitschrift für Tierpsychologie*, 1959, 16, 651–665.

Wolff, P. Observations on the early development of smiling. In B. M. Foss (Ed.), *Determinants of infant behavior*. Vol. II. New York: Wiley, 1963.

Wundt, W. *Grundzüge der physiologischen Psychologie*. Leipzig: Engelmann, 1874.

Zelazo, P. R. Smiling and vocalizing: A cognitive emphasis. Paper presented before American Psychological Association, Miami, 1970.

Zigler, E., Levine, J., & Gould, L. Cognitive challenge as a factor in children's humor appreciation. *Journal of Personality and Social Psychology*, 1967, 6, 332–336.

Chapter 3

On the Cognitive Origins of Incongruity Humor: Fantasy Assimilation versus Reality Assimilation

Paul E. McGhee

Department of Psychology
State University of New York, Albany, New York

I. Introduction

Although the past few years have witnessed a resurgence of empirical research on humor, research on children's humor has been relatively meager (see McGhee, 1971a). Furthermore, while numerous general theories or conceptions of humor have been advanced [see Chapter 1], developmental theories of humor have been rare. Thus the present chapter constitutes an effort to begin filling this void by advancing a theoretical model concerned with specifically developmental issues.

An important issue facing any theorist attempting to advance the scientific understanding of a given field is that of the relative merits of global versus more restricted theories. While the many theories reviewed by Keith-Spiegel [Chapter 1] vary widely along this dimension, the most typical approach has been to account for as wide a range of humor events as possible using the theoretical constructs advanced. While it is tempting to try to account for all aspects of humor in terms of a few basic principles, this approach has not been successful in either generating new research or satisfactorily explaining data already obtained. (Psychoanalytic theory stands as the exception.) In view of our present limited understanding of humor phenomena, global theories would seem to be of restricted usefulness since they discourage attention to important dimensions or mechanisms operating in the very situations they attempt to explain. While it is probably not a necessary consequence, it has been the case that global unidimensional theories have not achieved a sufficient level of differentiation to account for many important humor dimensions. Thus, a new approach is needed, one which will lead to more highly differentiated theoretical systems. Such systems will need to be more amenable to empirical testing and capable of stimulating a higher quality and quantity of research on humor.

In this writer's opinion, the greatest gains toward the goal of a more complete understanding of the many dimensions and influences on humor may be achieved by the development of alternative mini-theories designed to account for limited aspects of the total humor process. This would maximize the probability of identifying significant stimulus, social, personality, cognitive, physiological, developmental, etc., dimensions which play an important role in humor. Only with the development of a wide range of mini-models designed to account for limited ranges of data will we obtain a sufficiently differentiated and sophisticated set of theoretical constructs for ultimate integration and elaboration into broader theories with wide ranges of application. The mini-theory approach would more rapidly draw attention to salient humor dimensions and, consequently, stimulate a greater amount of research designed to test hypotheses related to those dimensions. As valid empirical relationships and reliable generalizations are established, the road to more global theoretical frameworks will be opened.

The developmental mini-theory advanced below deals with a type of cognitive processing hypothesized to characterize a single very restricted basis for humor, namely, incongruity or stimulus discrepancy. Thus, this category includes humor based on stimulus properties referred to by Berlyne [see Chapter 2] as "collative variables." It would seem desirable for initial explanatory models to be restricted to stimuli in which only one potential basis for humor exists. Since the affectively salient content of, e.g., sexual, aggressive, and superiority humor stimuli undoubtedly combines with any accompanying expectancy violations or incongruities to determine any resulting humor response, stimulus discrepancies containing some affectively neutral stimulus content would seem to afford the best means of isolating stimuli with only a single depicted basis for humor [see Chapter 7]. Specific attention is given by the model to the following points:

(1) the onset of the capacity to experience humor in stimulus discrepancy;

(2) the ontogenetic relationship between smiling and laughing as a sign of pleasure in assimilation and an index of humor;

(3) the role of conceptual thinking in the perception of humor;

(4) the role of the acquisition of logical thinking in developmental changes in the humor response;

(5) the role of stimulus, social, and cognitive cues in determining the probability of a humor response.

II. Stimulus Discrepancy and Affective Arousal

During the past decade or so, a growing body of theoretical and empirical evidence has pointed toward the importance of stimulus change in generating increases in general arousal or emotion. (See Berlyne, 1960, 1967; Chapter 2; Sokolov, 1964; and Pribram, 1967, for reviews of this evidence.) However, the question of how such general arousal fluctuations become translated into qualitatively different affective or emotional experiences must be resolved before progress can be made in identifying the process by which some novelty or incongruity situations are able to generate humor responses. Since it has long been apparent (Berlyne, 1960, 1967; Chapter 2) that arousal changes may be associated with a wide range of pleasurable and nonpleasurable stimulus events, it seems clear that neither stimulus nor arousal characteristics hold the answer to the basis for the differential reactions (e.g., fear, curiosity, or humor; see Berlyne, 1960) that have been found to occur in response to stimulus discrepancy.

The well-known studies of Schachter (1964) and his associates may provide the most promising suggestions concerning this issue. Schachter interprets his data as suggesting that "cognitions arising from the immediate situation as interpreted by past experience provide the framework within which one understands and labels his feelings [p. 51]." Schachter and Singer (1962) found that the injection of individuals with epinephrine served only to increase Ss' general arousal level. The specific form of emotion (euphoria or anger) in which the arousal was manifest was found to vary with Ss' cognitive evaluation of cues provided in the general stimulus environment. In a similar study designed to control for the possibility of self-generated arousal by placebo Ss in the previous study, Schachter and Wheeler (1962) found that while watching a brief humorous movie, both an epinephrine and placebo group showed a greater amount of smiling and laughter than a chlorpromazine (which serves to depress sympathetic activity) group. Thus these data strongly suggest that it is the way in which the subject processes information available at the time of arousal which determines the specific nature of the affective experience.

III. Fantasy Assimilation versus Reality Assimilation

Piaget (1952) has elaborated in great detail upon the way in which a child (or adult) behaves upon encountering a stimulus which is discrepant from previously formed relevant cognitive schemata. If the novel object or event cannot be assimilated into the appropriate schema, the child attempts to accommodate or change the structure so as to incorporate the new object or event. If the new stimulus is widely discrepant from those previously incorporated into that cognitive structure, the child may make repeated attempts to assimilate it, gradually modifying the appropriate structures until the new stimulus is able to be fully assimilated. We might refer to the child's assimilatory efforts in this case as a process of "reality assimilation." This is the standard equilibration process (described by Piaget), which occurs when the child encounters "real" discrepancies from already formed structures or concepts. It seems clear, however, that this process does not always occur upon encountering stimulus situations that are inconsistent with already established knowledge; the inconsistency does not in fact occur in the "real world." Thus, for example, when a child sees a cartoon drawing showing a mother elephant climing up a small tree to sit on a nest of eggs for a mother bird, he will undoubtedly find this to be inconsistent with previously established concepts and knowledge regarding elephants and their size, abilities, etc. However, the child does not reality-assimilate this event in the fashion described above. That is, he does not change those relevant conceptual categories to incorporate this new information about elephants. Rather, in a fashion which might be labeled "fantasy assimilation," he proceeds to assimilate the source of inconsistency or expectancy disconfirmation into existing relevant cognitive structures *without attempting to accommodate those structures* to fit the discrepant stimulus input. In this example the most important cue suggesting that a serious or realistic interpretation of the events depicted is not required is found in the fact that the information is presented in a drawing or diagrammatic fashion. If the same sequence of events had been experienced via a photograph or film, or in person, a reality mode of assimilation would be much more likely to occur. Encountering the information in a drawing, however, immediately informs the individual that the depicted events do not necessarily occur in real life and that the events may be interpreted or assimilated in a fantasy or pretend fashion. Because of the child's understanding that the situation only comprises an imaginatory event, there is no need for accommodation to occur. While this process is similar to the predominance of assimilation over accommodation which Piaget (1951) referred to as play, the operation of the fantasy-assimilation mechanism must include additional variables, which appear to play an important role in eliciting humor in response to expectancy violation. Since the specific variables involved and the nature of their operation are considered to depend on the child's age, the following section will deal with developmental factors influencing the nature of the operation of the fantasy-assimilation mechanism.

IV. The Development of Fantasy Assimilation

All infants begin to reality-assimilate their environment soon after birth. If Piaget (1952) is correct, this begins in most infants by the end of the first month. Of course the normal reality-assimilation process only occurs on a sensory–motor basis during infancy. By the end of infancy the child is beginning to reality-assimilate into symbolic schemata, and also shows the first signs of fantasy assimilation. This may take the familiar form of assimilation of inappropriate objects into various schemata (e.g., treating a block as an animal). This type of behavior marks the first appearance of imagination or fantasy and sets the stage for the onset of humor. While fantasy assimilation of objects into different symbolic schemata may be accompanied by various signs of pleasure in assimilation (e.g., smiling or joyous verbalizations during play) during the second and third year, the fantasy-assimilation mechanism does not serve to generate the experience of humor until the onset of conceptual thought capacities (this usually occurs some time during the third year according to Piaget, 1952).

A. The Onset of Humor

It is hypothesized here that conceptual thinking is a necessary cognitive prerequisite for the experience of humor based on violation of cognitive expectancies. The possession of concepts is essential to the development in a child of a sense of confidence or certainty regarding his growing knowledge of his environment; and a high level of cognitive mastery over different aspects of the environment is postulated here as being a necessary, but not sufficient, prerequisite for the identification of humor in the representation of the environment in a manner which is inconsistent with the child's prior experience and acquired concepts regarding it. In short, in order for the violation of cognitive expectancies to be perceived as funny, the child must be sufficiently certain of the way the depicted elements actually occur to assure himself that the events simply do not occur as depicted.

Translating this into the Piagetian terminology advanced earlier, three preliminary conditions must be met in the very young conceptual child before the fantasy assimilation of discrepant stimuli may be channeled into a humor response: (1) awareness of the normal criteria governing assimilation of salient stimulus elements into relevant cognitive structures (concepts); (2) comprehension of the way in which assimilation of the elements as depicted requires violation of those criteria; and (3) confidence in the impossibility or improbability of the stimulus elements occurring as depicted. This sequence of cognitive events allows the child to fantasy-assimilate the stimulus events and leads to the channeling of resulting arousal changes into the positive affect of laughter.

B. The Acquisition of Logical Thinking

For the first three or four years after the acquisition of conceptual thought capacities, the identification of humor in stimulus discrepancies is restricted to stimuli that are perceptually discrepant from the child's prior experience. The child is very perceptually oriented during this period and will find humor only in sights and sounds (or descriptions of the same) which are inconsistent with the conceptual expectancies formed through prior experience. The child at this time is unable to find humor in more abstract expectancy violations which are not physically represented in some way (either visually or by verbal description).

With the acquisition of concrete operational thinking (Piaget, 1952) some time around the seventh year, a new source of humor in expectancy violation becomes available to the child. The newly acquired capacity for logical thinking in concrete situations leads to a growing awareness of the behavioral inconsistencies an individual may show. The child may now find bases for humor in situations in which nothing is physically discrepant from his prior experience. Consider the following two jokes: (1) "Molly the elephant is very kindhearted. In yesterday's parade she stepped on a mother bird, and then went up to the bird's nest and sat on the baby bird to keep it warm." (2) "Well, I see you have a new dog. I thought you didn't like dogs." "Well, I don't, but my wife bought a lot of dog soap on sale, so we had to get a dog to use it up." In the first example, the knowledge that elephants cannot climb trees, that elephants do not sit on nests, or that the limb would break with an elephant on it is sufficient to generate a humor response in a 4- or 5-year-old child. Either this knowledge or prior awareness that the statement is a "joke" would lead the child to fantasy-assimilate the stimulus content. In the second example, on the other hand, as the child conjures up visual images of the depicted content, no inconsistency with prior knowledge occurs. It is only upon the identification of some logical inconsistency that a potential basis for humor occurs. Thus, either one or some combination of the following inconsistencies may generate humor: buying a dog when you do not like dogs; buying dog soap because of a sale when you do not have a dog; or buying an unwanted dog simply to use the dog soap.

McGhee (1971b) has obtained support for the view that concrete operational thinking plays an important role in the identification of bases for humor in cartoons and jokes of the second type just described, but not of the first (the two examples cited in the preceding paragraph were used in this study). Among 7-year-old boys, those who were further along in the acquisition of concrete operational thinking showed greater comprehension of humor stimuli in which only behavioral inconsistencies occurred than did *S*s who were still primarily at a preoperational level. For stimuli involving some perceptual expectancy violation, acquisition of operational thinking was not significantly related to comprehension.

Thus by the age of 7 or 8, a new form of humor appears to become available to the child, one in which newly acquired cognitive capacities play a central role in generating humor in response to stimulus discrepancy or expectancy violation. This development allows the child to begin to experience different levels of humor. The level of humor depicted, in turn, begins to play an important role in determining the relationship between comprehension and appreciation of humor stimuli.

With the development of logical thought capacities, fantasy assimilation, in combination with the three criteria for humor listed earlier, ceases to operate as the only mode of assimilation capable of generating humor in response to stimulus incongruity or inconsistency. In the realm of behavior people cannot reach the same level of certainty about behavioral expectancies as they can about the occurrence of natural events, behavior of infrahumans, or relationships among objects. That is, people do in fact behave in ways which an observer may judge to be illogical or inconsistent. It would appear that in many incongruity jokes (such as the dog-soap joke) part of the humor experienced lies in the fact that some people behave exactly as described in the joke. Thus, both reality assimilation and fantasy assimilation should contribute to the comprehension and appreciation of such humor stimuli. The greater the extent to which reality assimilation plays a role in eliciting humor, the more clearly motivational (rather than purely cognitive, as described earlier) factors may be seen as the major determinants of the affect expressed. Instead of being based on the purely cognitive pleasure of identifying as impossible some event depicted as actually occurring, humor based on reality assimilation of some content area may be primarily based on the partial satisfaction (in the psychoanalytic sense) of salient need areas. Thus, in the dog-soap joke, the greatest source of humor pleasure may lie not in the fantasy assimilation of the inconsistent behavior depicted, but in acknowledgment of the reputed weakness of many women of being unable to pass up a "bargain," even if the item is not needed or cannot be used. A sense of superiority may also be experienced by the hearer of the joke, since he "would never engage in such absurd behavior."

In "incongruity" cartoons and jokes, therefore, either mode of information processing may be involved in the production of any ensuing humor response. While different humor stimuli may rely on these two modes to widely varying degrees, the main concern of the present discussion is not to suggest a means of evaluating the differential contribution of each to different stimuli, but rather to establish that these two different modes of processing may occur in incongruity stimuli. A later section will consider the operation of fantasy and reality assimilation in tendential or need-related humor.

Along with the new basis for humor in behavioral inconsistencies and the new role played by reality assimilation upon the development of operational thinking, the child's new logical thought capacity also generates the capacity for a higher level of appreciation of certain types of humor based on incongruity. Many incongruity jokes and cartoons can be fully understood only upon the identification of some other general principle or rule that is alluded to by the incongruity depicted. As suggested by Suls [see Chapter 4] in the presentation of his "information-processing model" of humor, it is the retrieval of this principle or rule which allows the perceiver to make sense out of the incongruity and consequently to understand the basis for the humor depicted. Suls uses the following joke to exemplify his model:

> Fat Ethel sat down at the lunch counter and ordered a whole fruit cake.
> "Shall I cut it into four or eight pieces?" asked the waitress.
> "Four," said Ethel, "I'm on a diet."

Suls notes that in the process of following "the heuristic rule that an increase in number frequently means an increase in total amount," Ethel ignores the rule of conservation of quantity. Thus, as soon as the recipient of the joke realizes both the accepted principle violated in the joke (conservation) and the errant principle on which Ethel based her statement, the intended humor has been understood. For our present concerns, the point to be emphasized is that it is only upon the acquisition of a concrete operational level of thinking that the child is able to bring the logical principle of conservation to bear on Ethel's behavior. Thus, comprehension of the intended humor in this joke should not occur before age 7 or 8.

Similarly, in the dog-soap joke, comprehension depends on two realizations: (1) It is thrifty and wise to purchase goods on sale instead of at the regular price, and it is wasteful not to use goods you have paid for. (2) It is logically inconsistent to buy something you do not want simply because it is a good buy, or to buy a second unwanted or unneeded item in order to dispose of the first. As noted earlier, McGhee (1971b) found that operational thinking does play a central role in comprehension of this and other similar humor stimuli.

C. MASTERY AND SOCIAL DIMENSIONS OF HUMOR

Several psychoanalytic writers have also emphasized the role of mastery in much of young children's humor. Kris (1938) argued that to experience the comic, "a preliminary condition is complete control over the function in question. An absurd movement on the part of another person will seem funny to a child *only* when it has itself mastered the movement [p. 83]." Similarly, Grotjahn (1957) argues that children first discover comic situations when they begin to master and enjoy bodily movements. When they begin to feel superior to other children in this respect, they are likely to see their mistakes or weaknesses as funny. Wolfenstein (1954) stresses the importance of whether the absurdity or nonsense of a joke is set forth by the child himself or by an adult. "While they can easily break away from the demands of reason on their own initiative and enjoy fantasy or nonsense, it is not always clear to them when others, especially their elders, make this shift [p. 196]." In terms of the formulations advanced above, it seems clear that children are more likely to reality-assimilate some absurdity or unlikely event if initiated by adults, but fantasy-assimilate it if initiated by themselves or a peer. Cues provided by the source of the improbable event are likely to determine which mode of assimilation will be adopted. While children usually rely on adults for serious communications, undoubtedly a smile on the face of the adult issuing the expectancy violation would suffice to switch the child from reality assimilation to fantasy assimilation of the event.

The emphasis of these psychoanalytic writers suggests that mastery may be an important dimension not only for humor based on discrepancies from acquired knowledge of the physical environment, but for tendential and interpersonal aspects of humor as well. The basic question remains, however, of why the identification of an event as an inaccurate portrayal of the true occurrence of that event in the environment should be regarded as humorous. The writer has no suggestions for a solution here, except to direct attention to White's (1959) concept of competence or effectance motivation. Young children appear to show very early a need to master or deal competently with their environment, both cognitively and physically. Immense pleasure seems to be derived from the child's initial understanding of some previously confusing event or accomplishment of some previously unmastered physical task. The acknowledgment of the inaccurate depiction of that event may serve to remind S of his own high level of mastery of the event and consequently reinitiate the original pleasure in mastery. This pleasure is manifest in the form of a smile or laugh. Such pleasure in mastery may be broken down into two types, each of which forms the foundation for a different type of humor experience. While one basis for humor lies in the obviously inaccurate depiction of some nonsocial stimulus content, the other lies in the violation of expectations having social implications (e.g., a surprising failure to demonstrate a high level of understanding of some problem or mastery of a physical act, as when someone responds inaccurately or falls), as described by the psychoanalytic writers discussed above. While surprise and expectancy violation play an important role in both sources of humor, the type discussed by psychoanalytic writers appears to have important motivational components that straight cases of stimulus discrepancy do not have. In Western culture children acquire very early a sense of competition regarding physical and cognitive mastery of the environment. Since greater social rewards from both peers and adults are generally received by brighter and more physically able children, mastery-related stimulus content gradually achieves a high level of affective salience. Thus, any stimuli demonstrating mental or motor ineptness of other persons acquire a relatively high arousal potential, leading to a greater expression of affect due to the child's relief that, in comparison with the individuals depicted, he has achieved a superior level of competence. This basis for humor would appear to be the prototype for the mechanisms involved in the appreciation of sexual, aggressive, etc., types of humor as originally described by Freud (1916).

V. Humor in Infancy?

Since it is immediately apparent to any casual observer of infant behavior that even very young infants smile and laugh, the position that the capacity for the perception of humor in stimulus discrepancies depends on the acquisition of conceptual thinking deserves to be questioned. While smiling behavior has been observed in response to a wide range of social and nonsocial stimuli, in light of the "cognitive" emphasis of the present theory, attention will only be given here to smiling or laughing in response to stimulus discrepancy. The central issue lies in the range of meanings which may be attributed to the infant's smile. It is hypothesized here that in the preconceptual child, a smile in response to novelty or stimulus change is only a manifestation of the cognitive pleasure of being able to assimilate the new or unexpected stimulus content into existing structures where some accommodatory effort is required (see Kagan, 1969). This is a reality-assimilation process, and this pleasure in assimilation does not become transformed into the pleasure of humor until the level of cognitive mastery over the environment associated with conceptual thinking is achieved.

Since Piaget's (1951) early observations of expressions of pleasure in infants (i.e., smiling) upon successful accommodation of structures to permit assimilation of some new aspect of the environment, some data coming out of work on infant attention have lent support to Piaget's original theoretical framework. In line with the data cited in Section II, moderate levels of novelty or mismatch with established schemata have been found to increase arousal level in infants (Kagan, Henker, Hen-Tov, Levine, & Lewis, 1966; McCall & Kagan, 1967). Recently, Zelazo (1970) and his associates have argued that by experimentally manipulating the formation or elaboration of an infant's schemata, a curvilinear trend in pleasure (smiling) in assimilatory efforts should be observable. A novel or discrepant stimulus should initially produce no smiling, until the novelty of the stimulus is reduced and the content becomes capable of being assimilated. While pleasure (smiling) should accompany early successful assimilations, repeated exposures of the stimulus should make assimilation so easy and automatic that smiling should decline. Zelazo and Komer (1970) found this curvilinear trend in smiling for repeated presentations of auditory stimuli, and Zelazo and Kagan (in preparation) found the same for visual stimuli.

In an earlier study Kagan (1967) showed various patterns representative of the human face to the same group of infants at 4, 8, and 13 months of age. While 4-month-old infants showed significantly more frequent smiling to a photograph or sculpture of a regular face than to a schematic regular face or disarranged face, 8-month-olds showed equal amounts of smiling to the regular and distorted faces. By 13 months of age, most smiling occurred to such alterations of the human form as a three-headed man and a mule's head on a man's body. Kagan argues that these developmental trends are due to the increasing elaboration or development of schemata for the human face and body. While some effort is required for the young infant to assimilate a representation of a regular face (and later a disarranged face), assimilation is very easy for the 13-month-old, and more complex discrepant or novel stimuli are required to evoke a smile.

The demonstration of affect described by Piaget (1951) and Kagan (1967, 1969) appears to be similar to the pleasure (which may be manifest as a smile or laugh) experienced by adults upon making sense out of cognitive confusion or finding the solution to some originally insolvable problem. Clearly, humor plays no role in this process. As long as the infant or young child remains in a reality mode of assimilation of the novelty or discrepancy, a humor response cannot occur, although some other form of positive affect may occur. As soon as the child begins to fantasy-assimilate during the second year, however, his inability to experience humor becomes less clear. When a 2-year-old child imaginatively assimilates an inappropriate object into some schema (e.g., petting a large pillow as if it were a dog), he is fully aware that the object is not what he imagines it to be. He is simply exercising and gaining increased cognitive mastery over his schemata in the fashion referred to by Piaget (1951) as play. During the preconceptual period, fantasy assimilation tends to be engaged in only relative to self-initiated activities. The child has not yet achieved sufficient cognitive mastery over his environment to know when fantasy assimilation is appropriate in response to activities or stimuli introduced by others. Hence, reality assimilation is likely in the latter case. Therefore, for the preconceptual child, externally induced novelty or stimulus change is likely to meet with reality-assimilation efforts, which remove the opportunity for perception of the change as being funny. While the young child may demonstrate smiling and laughter as expressions of his pleasure in playing at fantasy assimilation, the pleasure is a manifestation of enjoyment in ongoing activity—not of humor.

VI. Factors Influencing Mode of Assimilation

If the probability of perceiving humor in stimulus discrepancy depends on whether a reality or fantasy mode of assimilation occurs, it becomes important to consider the process by which a child decides which mode of assimilation is appropriate for a given set of circumstances.

A. EXTERNAL CUES

Of course, in most humor situations (jokes, cartoons, interpersonal communications, etc.), various external cues are readily available, leaving no doubt that the situation is not to be construed in a serious manner. The schematic nature of a cartoon (or such statements as "look at this cartoon" or "have you heard this joke?"), for example, makes it clear even to a young child that the depicted content is only a caricature of events which do not necessarily occur in the real world. Thus, the child is likely to fantasy-assimilate the information, as described earlier. Very young children rely heavily on this type of cue for humor stimuli which they do not understand. Thus, a 5-year-old may report having laughed at a joke "because it's a joke," and jokes are "things that are funny." If these cues were eliminated, by presenting the cartoon material in a photograph or in person, or the joke material as a standard communication, the discrepant stimulus events might arouse curiosity, surprise, anxiety, or simply confusion, but the possibility of a genuine humor reaction would be eliminated since the child would remain in a reality mode of assimilation.

An important cue in interpersonal humor situations lies in the facial expression of the initiator of the communication. As long as the joketeller has a serious facial expression and, in general, leads the listener to believe that the communication is a serious one, the listener will be set to reality-assimilate the punch line and will likely fail to see any humor in the statements made. Rather, he is likely to report being unable to make any sense out of the communication until he perceives the smile on the face of the joketeller. This causes the listener to switch to a fantasy mode of assimilation, enabling him to make sense out of the discrepant communication in a humorous fashion.

B. INTERNAL CUES

As suggested earlier, the degree of certainty regarding the possibility of a potential event outcome plays an important role in determining whether reality assimilation or fantasy assimilation occurs. If the child is certain that the depicted events could not really occur, this in itself should be sufficient to lead the child to fantasy-assimilate them. However, many potential humor situations contain conflicting sets of cues. A child's prior experience and knowledge may suggest fantasy assimilation, while other cues (e.g., a photograph or straight face) suggest reality assimilation. While the final outcome will depend on the relative "strength" of the cues present, the child may vacillate between a humorous and nonhumorous interpretation of the events or—perhaps more likely—experience sufficient conflict to remove altogether any chance of seeing humor in the events.

We might speak of a "humor threshold" with respect to this internal cue, such that a child with a high level of cognitive mastery over the stimulus elements in question has a lower threshold for perceiving a discrepant or inaccurate depiction of those elements as humorous than does a child with less certain knowledge of them. A child who is very certain that the depicted events could not occur should have a sufficiently low fantasy-assimilation threshold so that even if a host of cues suggest that reality assimilation is appropriate, he is likely to look for some trick or catch (e.g., a fake photograph) and proceed to fantasy-assimilate. A child with little experience or certainty regarding the depicted events, on the other hand, is likely to have a much higher fantasy-assimilation threshold and should rely more on external cues in deciding how to process the information.

C. The Role of Early Experience

Given that the child's level of cognitive mastery over the environment plays a central role in determining whether he construes some depiction of the environment as being humorous, it follows that early experiences conducive to the development of such mastery should increase the number of opportunities for perceiving stimulus discrepancies as humorous. Thus, children growing up in a highly stimulating and diverse environment should acquire a broader range of knowledge and expectancies than a child growing up in a more deprived environment. This increased breadth and depth of knowledge should allow the child to fantasy-assimilate a greater number of the expectancy violations he might encounter. Assuming a positive relationship between degree of early environmental enrichment and rate of cognitive development, more cognitively advanced children should show greater comprehension of humor based on stimulus discrepancy than less bright children. Since other factors appear to be important in determining appreciation of humor (see McGhee, 1971a), more cognitively advanced children should not necessarily find such inconsistencies to be funnier than less advanced children.

In addition to breadth of environmental experience, regularity or consistency of experience with some aspect of the environment constitutes an important determinant of engagement in fantasy- or reality-assimilation upon encountering some stimulus discrepancy. Other things being equal, a greater degree of regularity should enhance the probability of fantasy-assimilating elements which deviate from that regularity. Thus, a child who has had relatively limited experience with some stimulus situation, but has consistently experienced it in precisely the same fashion, may be more likely to see a discrepant depiction of it as humorous than a child who has had a great deal more experience with it, but has experienced the combination of elements composing the stimulus context in a greater number of ways or levels. For the latter child, any new representation of the situation is less discrepant from his total prior experience and is consequently more likely to be perceived as within the range of potential outcomes for that situation.

D. EFFECTS OF MOOD OR STATE

While specific external and internal cues have been suggested as major determinants of engaging in fantasy assimilation of discrepant stimulus situations, the individual's general mood or frame of mind may modify the influence of both sets of cues. Many past writers (see Piddington, 1933; Flugel, 1954) have emphasized the importance of a playful or nonserious mood in most humor situations. Flugel concludes that "this lack of biological urgency or seriousness is found in every kind of humor." In terms of the present theoretical framework, it may be argued that when a person is in a playful or nonserious mood, his threshold for fantasy-assimilating events is lowered, leading him to perceive a wider range of events as humorous. In extreme cases the stimulus source of laughter may be entirely consistent with one's expectancy; yet the event is perceived as humorous.

Other things being equal, children are generally more play oriented than adults. Thus, although their level of cognitive mastery of the environment is vastly lower than that of adults, children have a generally lower threshold for fantasy assimilation and therefore find humor around them more frequently than adults. The fact that we associate this tendency with children leads us to perceive adults who frequently engage in fantasy assimilation (i.e., always clowning around or misconstruing communications) as being childish and immature. As suggested by Freud (1916), however, it may be that all adults need a temporary escape from the burdens of reality (and hence reality assimilation) once in a while. Humor offers an easy and socially acceptable means of accomplishing this, perhaps accounting for its frequency and importance in everyday behavior.

Since overly frequent engagement in fantasy assimilation does create the risk of generating the impression of immaturity, adults often seek out socially sanctioned changes of mood or state which allow a free rein to fantasy-assimilation behavior. Thus, we all have experienced the effect of alochol and other drugs in generating a state in which the humor threshold is greatly reduced, i.e., in which we may feel free to fantasy-assimilate at will. In general, any condition which reduces our perception of the situation to one requiring serious efforts at assimilating stimulus input is likely to lower the threshold for fantasy assimilation and increase the probability of perceiving that input as humorous.

VII. Mode of Assimilation and Affectively Salient Humor

While the theoretical view advanced here is designed to account for children's perception of humor in expectancy violations for which there is no prior investment of affect in the specific content used to convey the discrepancy, many occasions for humor clearly do not fall in this category. Sexual, aggressive, superiority, and other themes have received more attention from writers and researchers than this more purely cognitive basis for humor. While preschool children do laugh at jokes or other communications in which some taboo content is verbalized (e.g., "bathroom" jokes; see Wolfenstein, 1954), the fantasy-assimilation mechanism of humor described earlier does not appear to be operating (although fantasy or imagination is certainly involved in this type of humor). Rather, in a Freudian (1916) fashion, it seems to be the mere expression of the affect-laden *content* which plays the key role in evoking the child's laughter. Thus, of the two modes of information processing discussed here, reality assimilation seems to play a more important role in this type of humor; however, it is questionable whether its role in such humor is a central one. The research of Goldstein, Suls, and Anthony [see Chapter 8] has cast doubt on the traditional psychoanalytic emphasis on affective salience (due to repression of content areas with strong affect attached to them), suggesting rather that cognitive salience may be the important factor in determining humor potential. While some expectancy violation or incongruity may accompany the salient content, the latter would still appear to bring into play additional cognitive mechanisms which are not involved in the perception of humor in incongruity based on affectively or cognitively "neutral" content. At this time, perhaps the greatest need in humor research is for theoretical constructs delineating the nature of cognitive mechanisms playing the key role in this type of humor.

VIII. Summary

The aim of this chapter has been to draw attention to the premature efforts of many earlier humor theorists to develop broad or general theoretical frameworks. Little scientific progress has been made using this approach, partially because of the limited capacity of such theories to generate a sufficiently differentiated set of testable hypotheses to account satisfactorily for the multidimensional character of the humor process. While broad and highly differentiated theories should be our goal, it was argued in this chapter that the greatest progress toward this goal may be made by the development of various mini-theories designed to account for more restricted identifiable dimensions of the multidimensional humor process.

To exemplify this approach, a developmental mini-theory was presented in an effort to identify the origins of one very limited basis for humor: the perception of stimulus discrepancies or inconsistencies in the physical environment. By drawing on Schachter's (1964) data and other data demonstrating the capacity of stimulus discrepancy to generate general increases in arousal, it was concluded that a specific mode of cognitive processing should characterize such bases for humor. The notions of fantasy- and reality-assimilation were introduced, with the former designated as playing a central role in the young child's perception of humor in environmental discrepancies. A high level of cognitive mastery over the environment, coincident with the acquisition of conceptual thought capacities, was hypothesized to be a necessary prerequisite for the ability to experience this basis for humor. Thus, although pleasure in assimilating discrepancies may occur in infancy, this pleasure is not manifest in the form of humor. The influence of the acquisition of logical thinking upon the perception of humor in stimulus discrepancy was also considered. Finally, factors influencing the mode of assimilation of stimulus discrepancies were discussed, and the fantasy-assimilation mechanism was concluded to contribute minimally to appreciation of tendential humor.

Acknowledgment

The author wishes to express his appreciation to Shirley Brown, Ted Huston, Jeffrey Goldstein, and Charles Wenar for their comments and suggestions on earlier drafts of this paper.

References

Berlyne, D. E. *Conflict, arousal and curiosity.* New York: McGraw-Hill, 1960.

Berlyne, D. E. Arousal and reinforcement. In D. Levine (Ed.), *Nebraska symposium on motivation.* Lincoln, Nebraska: Univ. of Nebraska Press, 1967.

Flugel, J. C. Humor and laughter. In G. Lindzey (Ed.), *Handbook of social psychology.* Vol. 2. *Special fields and applications.* Reading, Massachusetts: Addison-Wesley, 1954.

Freud, S. *Wit and its relation to the unconscious.* New York: Moffat Ward, 1916. (Originally *Der Witz und seine Beziehung zum Unbewussten.* Leipzig and Vienna: Deuticke, 1905.)

Grotjahn, M. *Beyond laughter.* New York: McGraw-Hill, 1957.

Kagan, J. On the need for relativism. *American Psychologist,* 1967, 22, 131–143.

Kagan, J. On continuity: A demonstration from infancy. Paper presented at meeting of the Society for Research in Child Development, Santa Monica, March 1969.

Kagan, J., Henker, B. A., Hen-Tov, A., Levine, J., & Lewis, M. Infants' differential reactions to familiar and distorted faces. *Child Development,* 1966, 37, 519–532.

Kris, E. Ego development and the comic. *International Journal of Psychoanalysis,* 1938, 19, 77–90.

McCall, R. B., & Kagan, J. Stimulus-schema discrepancy and attention in the infant. *Journal of Experimental Child Psychology,* 1967, 5, 381–390.

McGhee, P. E. Development of the humor response: A review of the literature. *Psychological Bulletin,* 1971, 76, 328–348. (a)

McGhee, P. E. Cognitive development and children's comprehension of humor. *Child Development,* 1971, 42, 123–138. (b)

Piaget, J. *Play, dreams and imitation in childhood.* New York: Norton, 1951.

Piaget, J. *The origins of intelligence in children.* New York: International Press, 1952.

Piddington, R. *The psychology of laughter: A study in social adaptation.* London: Figurehead, 1933.

Pribram, K. H. The new neurology and the biology of emotion: A structural approach. *American Psychologist,* 1967, 22, 830–838.

Schachter, S. The interaction of cognitive and physiological determinants of emotional state. *Advances in Experimental Social Psychology,* 1964, 1, 49–81.

Schachter, S., & Singer, J. Cognitive, social and physiological determinants of emotional state. *Psychological Review,* 1962, 65, 379–399.

Schachter, S., & Wheeler, L. Epinephrine, chlorpromazine, and amusement. *Journal of Abnormal and Social Psychology,* 1962, 65, 121–128.

Sokolov, E. N. *Perception and the conditioned reflex.* S. W. Waydenfeld. (Trans.) New York: Pergamon, 1964.

White, R. W. Motivation reconsidered: The concept of competence. *Psychological Review,* 1959, 66, 297–333.

Wolfenstein, M. *Children's humor.* Glencoe, Illinois: Free Press, 1954.

Zelazo, P. Smiling and vocalizing: A cognitive emphasis. In M. Haith (Chm.), On the meaning of smiling and vocalizing in infancy. Symposium presented at the meeting of the American Psychological Association, Miami, September 1970.

Zelazo, P., & Kagan, J. Infant smiling to sequential visual stimuli: Trial and age effects. In preparation.

Zelazo, P., & Komer, M. J. Infant smiling to non-social stimuli and the recognition hypothesis. *Child Development,* in press.

Chapter 4

A Two-Stage Model for the Appreciation of Jokes and Cartoons: An Information-Processing Analysis

Jerry M. Suls

Department of Psychology
Temple University, Philadelphia, Pennsylvania

I. Introduction

The purpose of this chapter is to introduce a model of the humor-appreciation process based on an information-processing type of analysis. Although the model is decidedly cognitive and structural in nature, it also incorporates situational, motivational, and emotional factors which may play an active role in the appreciation of humor.

The model is an account of how recipients process and appreciate verbal jokes and captioned cartoons. Certain other forms of humor do not fit into the present paradigm, e.g., physical forms of slapstick, exaggerated gestures and facial expressions, cartoons without captions, and political caricatures. The forms of humor covered by the model may be characterized as narrative and elicit their humor from a sequence of ideas. The other forms of humor may be considered as nonnarrative and obtain their humor from a Gestalt configuration derived from a single exposure.

A. ASSUMPTIONS

In keeping with other information-processing models, the present model consists of a flow-chart analysis with a series of steps that include reading-in, storing, and comparing information. It is related to, and borrows from, the General Problem Solver (GPS) (Newell, Shaw, & Simon, 1958; Newell & Simon, 1956). The model involves some of the same psychological processes used in reading and listening since a person must obviously read or hear a joke to appreciate it. We emphasize this rather obvious point because some basic strategies of reading and listening are essential to the model proposed.

II. The Basis of Joke and Cartoon Humor

It is suggested here that a joke or cartoon is found to be funny as the result of a two-stage process. In the first stage, the perceiver finds his expectations about the text disconfirmed by the ending of the joke or, in the case of a cartoon, his expectations about the picture disconfirmed by the caption. In other words, the recipient encounters an incongruity—the punch line. In the second stage, the perceiver engages in a form of problem solving to find a cognitive rule which makes the punch line follow from the main part of the joke and reconciles the incongruous parts. A cognitive rule is defined as a logical proposition, a definition, or a fact of experience. The retrieval of such information makes it possible to reconcile the incongruous parts of the joke. Although it is difficult to assemble these cognitive rules into a system, they appear to be part and parcel of the cognitive apparatus.

The perceiver must proceed through these two stages to find the joke funny. More succinctly, humor derives from experiencing a sudden incongruity which is then made congruous. The joke that follows should illustrate these points:

Fat Ethel sat down at the lunch counter and ordered a whole fruit cake.

"Shall I cut it into four or eight pieces?" asked the waitress.

"Four," said Ethel, "I'm on a diet."

According to the present model, this joke derives its humor from the fact that the ending is incongruous with the preceding text but can be seen to follow from certain rules. Ethel, apparently, ignores the rule of conservation of quantity; that is, whether the cake is cut into four pieces or eight, it remains the same amount of cake. Ethel instead employs the heuristic rule that an increase in number frequently constitutes an increase in total amount. The ending can be conceived as congruous with the main part when one realizes that Ethel is using the heuristic to supplant the logical rule.*

This example can also be used to show that an incongruous ending is not a sufficient condition for humor, only a necessary one. If Ethel had answered, "Don't cut it. I'm on a diet," her answer would be unexpected and incongruous but not funny. Also answering, "Eight pieces. I'm on a diet," would not follow and would not be funny. Humor occurs when an incongruity can be made to follow and sense can be made of the parts of the joke. This is why we often ask "Do you understand?" or "Do you 'get' the joke?"

Another example may make the argument clearer.

One prostitute said to another, "Can you lend me ten dollars until I get back on my back?"

The ending is unexpected, because the perceiver probably expects her to say ". . . until I get back on my feet." The ending does make sense, however, and follows because a prostitute works on her back. If she had said, "Lend me ten dollars until I get back on my hands,"

---

* It should be noted that the explanation one recipient generates to reconcile the incongruent parts may not be the same as that used by another. But even if they are the same, one individual may consider his explanation to be more satisfactory than the other's. The goal of this process is to find an explanation that produces a "good fit." Individuals will differ in what they consider to be a "good fit." It is the recipient's feeling of satisfaction with his explanation which will determine his degree of appreciation. Therefore, the following joke explanations should be considered as merely illustrative rather than as the only possible explanations.

the ending would be unexpected but unfunny, because there is no rule which reconciles it with the main part of the joke.

Two questions which pose problems for the model may have occurred to the reader. The two criteria for humor—incongruity and its resolution—may seem to be possessed by other kinds of stimuli which do not evoke humor, for example, mathematical dilemmas and puzzles. The problem is resolved when we realize that incongruity and unpredictability are different. The conclusions of mathematical dilemmas and puzzles are frequently unpredictable but are not incongruous; joke endings, on the other hand, are incongruous. This is so because a joke's ending does not follow logically from its preceding text. Therefore, the ending is surprising for the recipient. A puzzle is not incongruous because it does follow logically from its premises. It does not create a rude surprise. Take, for example, the question, "What is cold in winter and warm in summer?" Its answer, "A roof shingle," is not humorous because there is no surprise brought about by it. The answer is not surprising in the way a joke's ending is, because the former follows along the lines of the initial premises. Although a roof shingle may have been unexpected, it is one of a class of quite predictable answers—car tops, trash cans, i.e., any object that the sun will warm.

The view taken here is that incongruous situations (provided that they are resolved) are funny, implying that there are no incongruous situations that are not funny. This is, admittedly, a strong assertion which may require qualifications. One of these may be that it is necessary to know that a stimulus is a joke, something intended to be funny. This then makes laughter admissible and appropriate. In this context, McGhee [see Chapter 3] maintains that it is necessary for children to know that events in a joke are fantasy and for them to assimilate these events as fantasy in order to generate a humor response. Similarly, adults may need to know that they are hearing a joke; other incongruous situations may not be suitable stimuli for humor.

It may also be asked why, if the incongruity is capable of being resolved, is there any incongruity in the first place? The answer is that a joke or cartoon is constructed to lead the recipient astray and produce surprise. Furthermore, information-processing strategies and capabilities are such that initial information is usually processed with a single interpretation. Therefore, the recipient cannot maintain a set of multiple interpretations, one of which may happen to be correct.

These arguments are in accord with common-sense observation, since a poor joketeller seems to be one who tends to lead the recipient to the correct solution before he has arrived at the end of the joke. Similarly, a poor joketeller incorrectly relates the premises of the joke by his intonation and timing so that the nonobvious interpretation becomes obvious to the recipient and the joke falls flat.

A. PROCESSES INVOLVED IN HUMOR APPRECIATION

This section describes the processes and steps of the information-processing analysis of humor (see Figure 1).

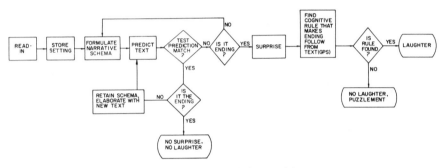

Figure 1. Humor-appreciation model.

Stage 1

Processing begins with a read-in of the introduction of the joke or of the cartoon picture. Information is extracted from this initial input, and such components as setting and context are stored. This information is used to formulate a narrative schema which is used to predict forthcoming text. This prediction-making process is used in reading, listening, and other perceptual tasks. Kolers (1968) has emphasized that "assumptions and predictions characterize most human perceiving [p. 15]." Most relevant to joke processing is Wanat and Levin's (1970) demonstration of the importance of schema production for the decoding of sentences. They have found that, given a grammatical context, the reader makes certain assumptions about the lexical items and the syntactical form of what follows. When the initial schema is confirmed, decoding is facilitated. They maintain that

> reading is an active process of accommodating the words of the text to a schema that the reader himself generates. On the basis of what he has just read, he formulates hypotheses about what his eye will next encounter.

When the words he picks can fit the schema he has generated, his hypothesis is confirmed, and he can proceed further [p. 5].

These researchers conceive these schemata to be syntactic–semantic in nature, but parallel to these are high-level thematic or narrative schemata, formulated by the reader, that structure the general story line of the text. Some evidence for the existence of these thematic schemata comes from an experiment, by Suls and Weisberg (1970), in which ambiguous sentences were presented to Ss preceded by disambiguating contexts. As predicted, the interpretation and deep structure (as defined by transformational grammar), given an ambiguous sentence, was related to the verbal context which preceded it. Apparently, from the context the reader formulates a narrative schema which facilitates and structures the decoding of the ambiguous sentence. Similarly, the reader or listener uses the preceding text of a joke to structure what will appear next by formulating a narrative schema.

The schema is formulated on the basis of the initial input. For example, the first sentence of the Ethel joke suggests a schema concerned with the ordering of food and interaction with a waiter or waitress.

Next, predictions about forthcoming text are formulated from the schema. These predictions are then compared with the most recent text input. If the predictions match the input, then one looks to see if this is the end of the joke. If it is the end, then there is no surprise or incongruity; the predicted ending is consistent with the actual ending and the process terminates with no humor resulting. This situation should occur if the person has heard the joke before or if he has somehow managed to predict its ending.

If it is not the ending of the joke, the schema is retained (since its predictions have been accurate), although it is elaborated with the new text being read in, and the individual again cycles back to predicting later text.

If predictions do not match, then one looks to see if this is the end of the joke. If it is not the end, the program cycles back to reformulate a new schema which will be more consistent with text at this point.* This new schema will be used to make predictions about later text. If predictions do not match and this incongruous text

---

* It is expected that what deviations occur will be minor and the narrative schema can easily be reformulated. This seems to be consistent with all jokes—the beginning and middle parts of a joke are generally congruent, and the middle usually follows from the beginning; it is only at the ending that one's expectations are abruptly disconfirmed.

comprises the ending, the result is surprise (in the case of a cartoon, the caption disconfirms some aspect of the picture). This is because expectations have been disconfirmed without the possibility that later text will be read in to reconcile the incongruity. In short, the individual experiences an abrupt disconfirmation of his prediction. This corresponds to Stage 1.

Stage 2

At this point one engages in problem solving to find how the punch line follows from the main body of the joke. It should be noted that Stage 1 has often been seen as the sole basis of humor by many earlier writers on the subject (Locke; Beattie; Hazlitt; Schopenhauer; Lipps) [see also Chapter 1]. However, there is no psychological dynamic offered by them which accounts for why such a surprise or disconfirmation is pleasurable. In order to understand this, a second stage needs to be postulated.

The problem at Stage 2 can be stated as follows: How does the punch line (B) follow from the preceding parts of the joke (or the cartoon picture) (A)? When the problem is framed in this manner, it is clear that the main part of the joke comprises the premises of the problem and the punch line the end product. The task of problem solving is to find out how the punch line follows or is congruent with the preceding text.

The problem-solving process is conceived to work along the lines of the GPS developed by Newell *et al.* (1958). The GPS was designed to represent and explain the process and goal-directed nature of human problem solving. The problems it can solve are those for which there are no fixed sequences of operations to assure solution. Instead, the GPS resorts to heuristics—a variety of strategies and devices which offer reasonable promise of reaching a solution. The basic heuristic is means–end analysis.

First, the premises of the problem and its goal are stated in comparable terms so that the GPS seeks to transform the premises into the goal. In means–ends analysis the problem is broken down into interlocking smaller problems. If the major goal is to transform A into B, the program first compares the two with a general routine to identify differences and then establishes a subgoal of reducing the set of differences. The GPS then seeks some transformation or operation to reduce the differences. Three methods, conceived as subgoals, are used to achieve the reduction: Transform A into B; reduce difference D between A and B; or apply operator (an allowable transformation) Q to A. These goals may occur recursively in a loop. The GPS is equipped with a table which gives the permissible transformations that are relevant to reducing particular differences.

This conception appears to be roughly applicable to the problem solving in joke resolution. As in the GPS, the recipient attempts to transform the joke's A into B by comparing the two to identify differences and then establishing a subgoal to reduce these differences. The processor has available the three methods outlined above. The operators are cognitive rules which, when applied to A, will produce a new expression less different from B than the original A. These rules are semantic, logical, or experiential. When the rule (or operator) is found, it is applied. Then the new object and B are compared; if they do not match, the process continues until the proper rules are applied to obtain correspondence. When the process reaches correspondence, the individual has found how the punch line of the joke (B) follows from the main part, or stem (A).

In the ideal case, the problem solving will be successful and will retrieve the relevant rule that reconciles the joke parts. The punch line is then perceived to make sense, and the person "gets" the joke. When the apparent incongruity has been made congruous, the program has succeeded and will terminate; the humor has been understood.

If the individual does not have the necessary rule to transform A into B, or is unable to retrieve the rule at that particular time, then the joke parts will remain incongruous and the subject will be puzzled. The joke will not be understood.

According to the present model, emotional, motivational, and situational factors influence humor appreciation in the same ways they affect other types of information processing. This is of considerable importance in humor because the most influential approach to date, the psychoanalytic, maintains that humor is principally a function of motivational factors (Freud, 1905).* The Freudian notion suggests that the arousal of a repressed motive such as sex leads to the enjoyment of humor stimuli which in some fashion depict that motive. By this reasoning, a sexually aroused individual will appreciate sexual humor more than a nonaroused person because the joke will serve to release the increase in sexual energy.

In contrast, an information-processing analysis considers the basis of humor to be the experience of an abrupt disconfirming incongruity which is reconciled by problem solving. Motivational,

* Norton ed., 1960 (see References).

emotional, or situational factors enter into the humor appreciation process by directing attention to joke content relevant to the motive state. This occurs because drive and other factors contribute to the formation of relevant perceptual–cognitive sets. These sets affect joke processing at two distinct phases. In the first phase a relevant set alters the processor's attention to the incoming information that is related to the set. This means that motivational, emotional, and situational factors will create a corresponding set, which, in turn, will direct greater attention to the related joke content. This increased attention as well as the attention paid to the incongruity should bring about an increase in comprehension. Salience will increase attention paid to the joke and facilitate the processing of the text. Therefore, a sexually aroused subject should appreciate sexual humor more than a nonaroused subject because the former has paid greater attention and processed the joke's text more readily. This also implies that ease of information processing is positively related to humor comprehension.

The second phase, in which motivational (emotional or situational) factors enter into humor appreciation, is in the problem-solving stage. The set formed by these factors should make certain cognitive rules salient and therefore accessible as operators to be used in problem solving. If a subject is sexually aroused, sexual rules will be salient and thereby accessible for the problem-solving routine. There is, then, a greater likelihood that the appropriate rule to reconcile the discrepant parts of the joke will be found. It should be noted, however, that for very simple jokes, high salience may make the problem solving too easy, to such an extent that the joke will seem trivial and, therefore, unfunny.

It should be mentioned that, while motive arousal should increase the likelihood that an appropriate rule will be found to reconcile the incongruity, its sensitization also increases the likelihood that no incongruity will be perceived in the first place. A recipient's set should make it likely that he will retrieve the relevant rule during problem solving, but it seems unlikely that the set would give the precise rule that would plausibly lead to the punch line before it was heard.

The salience hypothesis has received considerable experimental support in studies by Goldstein, Suls, and Anthony [see Chapter 8].

B. AN ILLUSTRATION

Let us follow the sequence of steps that appear to be necessary in humor by examining the following joke.

> O'Riley was on trial for armed robbery. The jury came out
> and announced, "Not guilty."
> "Wonderful," said O'Riley, "does that mean I can keep
> the money?"

This joke illustrates the properties of humor that have been hypothesized—the ending of the joke is unexpected and incongruous (Stage 1) but can be so interpreted as to make sense (Stage 2).

In the Stage-1 process, the joke text is read in. Some appropriate narrative schema concerning a jury or the course of a trial is selected. Some forthcoming information concerning a jury or a trial is expected. The later read-in verifies this, and some verdict is predicted. The verdict is then read in. O'Riley's response to the verdict, "Wonderful," is expected. He is a free man. It is then predicted that he will say, "Does that mean I can go now?" Instead, he asks, "Does that mean I can keep the money?" This is unexpected since it admits his guilt, and we have already heard that the court considers him innocent. In Stage 2, problem solving begins to resolve the incongruity. A search is made for a rule or rules that might reduce the difference between the preceding text and the punch line. What would accomplish this? The appropriate setting concerns trials, justice, sentencing. The difference between the premises of the stem and the ending is that O'Riley has been found innocent of robbery, but he wants to know whether he can keep the money which he has just been found innocent of stealing. The processor must find rules or some explanation that makes sense out of this. Clearly the rule that apprehended criminals are punished is not applicable; this does not reduce the difference. The underlying difference does indicate, however, that there has been a mistake. The processor might find the rule that juries do not always come to a correct verdict, but this experiential fact is not sufficient. O'Riley did not say, "I'm guilty; I stole the money." This is certainly implied by his statement, but there is more. He asked if he could keep the money. The rule that seems to come closer to resolving this incongruity is that which recognizes the difference between actual and legal truth. This rule, in conjunction with the fact that courts make mistakes, comes closer to a solution but is not entirely satisfactory. Thus far, the processor can determine that O'Riley could be found innocent but actually be guilty. However, the processor has missed the point of his question which refers to the consequences of the verdict. Further search may yield a rule concerning legal consequences. Applying such a rule in conjunction with the previous ones, it is realized that O'Riley can indeed keep the money. If problem solving were to take this course, then the joke's problem would be resolved. O'Riley's question points out that courts make mistakes, that legal truth and actual truth do not always correspond, and that legal truth determines public consequences. In short, O'Riley can keep the money since, by law, he did not steal it. For successful solution of the problem, some routine like this is necessary. When the incongruity has been explained, the process should terminate and laughter ensue.

But do people go through this elaborate processing when they hear a joke and laugh? Intuitively, we "get" a joke instantly. In answer, we suggest that the processing works at a rapid rate, just as sentence processing seems to occur as rapidly as the sentence is read. Nevertheless, sentence comprehension seems to involve very complex mechanisms and processes. There is no reason to think that joke comprehension is a simpler undertaking.

C. MOTIVATION IN THE MODEL

The problem posed by the joke's incongruity presents a motivational element. It is suggested that degree of incongruity is directly related to the amount of surprise experienced, and the amount of surprise that the punch line creates should produce a corresponding need to solve the problem. In a sense, the situation is analogous to one in which an individual encounters an unbalanced cognitive structure (Heider, 1958). Evidence indicates that an attempt to restore balance is instigated (e.g., Burnstein, 1967). The prediction here is that the more surprising the punch line, the more one should want to overcome the surprise. When the problem is solved, the recipient should experience greater appreciation.

It might be objected that a highly unexpected punch line would cause the recipient to leave the field, and the joke unresolved. This does not seem likely for several reasons. First, even the most unexpected punch line should not be threatening, since the joke is perceived as fantasy. Second, leaving the field would negate the effort that was made in attending to the joke initially. Third, typically, one does not leave the field before making some attempt to solve the problem.

Another objection might be that the greatest need for solution would occur at low levels of incongruity because the joke would be easily solved. However, research on cognitive consistency indicates that low levels of inconsistency are not as motivating as higher levels (Festinger, 1957).

Finally, Shurcliff (1968) has presented some data supportive of the present hypothesis. His *S*s rated a number of humor stimuli for funniness and surprisingness and Shurcliff reports a monotonic relationship between these variables, with increases in surprisingness corresponding to increases in funniness.

D. Factors that Influence the Funniness of Humor

The two-stage model suggests four factors that may contribute to the appreciation of humor.* They are

1. incongruity of the joke ending;
2. complexity of Stage-2 problem solving;
3. time taken to solve the incongruity problem;
4. salience of the joke's content (discussed earlier).

Incongruity of the joke's ending refers to how much the punch line violates the recipient's expectations. It has been explained in the preceding section that the highest level of comprehended incongruity should produce more humor than only moderate or slight incongruity.

Complexity refers to the degree of cognitive demand the joke problem requires for solution. One joke should be considered more complex than another if it involves more elaborate problem solving. It is predicted that humor should reach some maximum level with jokes that involve a moderate level of difficulty for the recipient's cognitive capability. A joke that is too easy involves a trivial solution; there would be no felt success upon resolving it. A joke that is too hard cannot be figured out at all. This notion is similar to the cognitive congruency principle proposed by Zigler, Levine, and Gould (1967). Where appreciation peaks within the moderate level is not entirely clear. However, data collected by Goldstein (1970a) suggest that humor increases with ease of information processing, which means that appreciation should peak just before the joke becomes trivial to its recipient. (It should be noted that Zigler *et al.* suggest that humor peaks just before it becomes impossible.) Obviously, more research is needed to determine the effects of complexity on humor appreciation.

The present account considers that unexpectedness and complexity are conceptually distinct—the former entering at Stage 1,

---

* Individual differences are clearly of importance in humor appreciation, but they will not be discussed in any detail here.

the latter at Stage 2. Frequently, however, the two terms have been used interchangeably in the humor literature. There may be some basis for this; for example, one may argue that highly unexpected punch lines automatically require more problem solving for reconciliation than do lower levels of unexpectedness. Still it may be profitable to treat these factors separately. Consider two recipients who both adopt the same initial interpretation of a joke. They may both find the punch line to be equally incongruous, but their problem-solving ability may differ, or one may follow more blind alleys than the other before arriving at a solution. In this instance, incongruity will not necessarily correspond to the degree of complexity that the two recipients experience in problem solving.

At any rate, it is not possible to settle this issue here. Future experiments should be designed to yield data that will permit us to determine the correspondence between incongruity and complexity.

We suggest that, apart from the number of operations needed, the amount of time it takes to solve the joke problem may be implicated in the degree of appreciation. Complexity can be distinguished from solution time, since a joke may require a certain number of problem-solving operations, and two individuals may use these, but one may work faster than the other. Furthermore, the feeling of success may be associated with the time spent on the problem irrespective of the number of operations required for the solution. Reasoning from common sense, we might suppose that the faster we solve the problem the more likely we are to be satisfied with ourselves. Evidence collected by Bergum and Lehr (1967), who used nonhumor stimuli, shows an inverse relationship between the affective value of stimuli and the time taken to respond, with reaction time being faster for positively evaluated stimuli. Goldstein (1970a) measured joke processing time and appreciation and found that appreciation decreased as processing time increased [see also Chapters 2 and 11].

In future research it will be necessary to investigate the effects of these factors in combination. An important question involves the weighting to be given to each factor. Another consideration is that some factors interact with others. Increasing complexity to a moderate level may make a joke congruent with a given recipient's level of cognitive functioning but may also increase the time needed for solution. It is necessary to know the weights of these factors to determine whether there will be an increase, decrease, or no change in appreciation and also to determine whether these factors interact with each other additively or multiplicatively. Only experimental evidence will supply answers to these questions.

E. REPEATED EXPOSURE TO HUMOR

A weakness of any humor theory based on incongruity is that it does not account for the fact that some humor can be appreciated more than once. According to incongruity theory, on a second hearing the punch line should not seem incongruous, present no problem, and, therefore, provide no amusement.

The question of why some humor may be funny more than once has several possible explanations which do not contradict the validity of incongruity theories.

One explanation is based on the retention of affective material. Kanungo and Dutta (1966) have found that the intensity of perceived affect of material determines its retention, with better retention associated with greater affect. Proceeding from this, we might expect that those jokes that are very funny would be remembered well upon repetition. For these jokes one would remember the incongruity and its resolution, so it would not be funny a second time. But jokes that were only moderately funny on the first hearing may be forgotten, so their punch lines would again be incongruous on a second exposure. These jokes, therefore, should be amusing again.

Another possibility is that a joke can be funny for more than one reason. Some jokes seem to have several levels of interpretation; therefore enjoyment might be had from working through the joke in several different ways.

One rather obvious possibility is that humor is enjoyable on repetition because the joke has been associated with the positive emotional response that the recipient experienced after comprehending the joke on its first exposure.

Finally, we should raise the possibility that the jokes may actually become more enjoyable upon repeated exposure. Zajonc (1968) has found that repeated exposure of novel stimuli, such as ideograms, faces, and nonsense syllables, may receive enhanced affect from repetition, presumably because familiarity lessens the tension aroused by novel stimuli. Perhaps the repeated exposure of a given joke may lessen the tension aroused by its novelty and thereby increase liking for it (cf. Goldstein, 1970b).

III. Comparison with Other Cognitive Theories

Aside from the pervasive Freudian theory of humor, several cognitive theories of humor have been proposed by psychologists. It will be valuable to show how these differ from the present account. (We should note that Freud emphasized that humor is a means of expressing preconscious conflict wishes, but that he also discussed the structural properties of humor, particularly in the first part of his book on wit. Unfortunately, his disciples have played down these latter aspects of his work. See Freud, 1960.)

Maier (1932) suggested that, in a joke, a change in the anticipated meaning of particular elements brought about by the punch line leads to a sudden restructuring and change of interpretation of the whole. Bateson (1969) and Koestler (1964) also proposed Gestalt-like theories. Bateson suggested that humor occurs when the punch line brings what was background material for a joke suddenly and unexpectedly to the center of attention, as in the reversal of figure and ground. Koestler (1964) suggested that humor involves what he called "bisociation," in which there is an abrupt transfer of the train of thought from one matrix to another governed by a different logic or rule.

It is difficult to classify these theories as belonging solely to one stage; all three writers recognize the importance of incongruity (corresponding to Stage 1), but they also refer to a restructuring. However, it is not clear from their writings how this restructuring is accomplished. They tend to view the restructuring as immediate and do not explain what sort of understanding of the incongruity creates a new Gestalt. They do not mention the problem-solving terms that integrate the discrepant parts.

Maier (1932) realized that other stimuli also possess the features of humor but are not humorous; so he posited certain factors that make humor unique. He claimed that the elements of the joke are to be perceived objectively; that is, the recipient must not identify with the figures involved, and the emotions of the recipient must not come into play. This suggests that the more "objective" the recipient, the more humorous the joke should be. On the other hand, the salience hypothesis proposed earlier suggests that if the joke content is relevant to the individual, he will find it funnier than a noninvolved individual. Several studies support such a notion [see Chapters 8 and 10].

Maier also claimed that a joke has a logic unique to itself, which he called the ridiculous. The present model proposes that the structure of a joke does follow logically, although its logic is not initially obvious.

Kagan (1967) has recently offered some suggestions which may be relevant here. In a discussion of the development of the smiling response, he advances the idea that the creation of a schema for an event is one major source of pleasure. An infant smiles when he is able to match a stimulus (e.g., a face) to a schema or representation of that stimulus pattern. The infant will smile when he is initially unable to incorporate an object into his existing schema system but does so after exerting a more active assimilatory effort.

Although Kagan's comments are directed to the infant smile, his model is similar to the present approach in that his is a two-stage model. The first stage comprises the initial surprise, and the second stage comprises the processing which seeks to assimilate the stimulus. However, the models differ in one important respect; Kagan seems to be suggesting that it is the assimilation of a stimulus into an already established schema which is the source of pleasure. It is not altogether clear whether this is analogous to the joke situation where the object seems to be to shift from the initial expectations and theme to new ones which are, if not provided by the joke, at least implicit in it. One does not reconcile the punch line to the main stem in accordance with one's initial schema; rather one constructs a new schema entirely.

McGhee (1971) has suggested a developmental theory of cognitive humor for jokes and cartoons. He maintains that, in young children, all that is necessary for identification of humor is a recognition of the incongruity plus some kind of cue which leads the child to think that the events could not really occur as depicted. According to McGhee's view, young children do not proceed through the second stage proposed here. (McGhee elaborates on this view in Chapter 3.) While this may be true for children, it does seem necessary to postulate a second stage for adults.

Berlyne (1969; see also Chapter 2) has presented an account of humor which is in some ways similar to the model presented here. He maintains that humor possesses collative variables that raise arousal (novelty, surprise, incongruity, complexity) and other factors that lower arousal (understanding or reintegration). This suggests a two-stage model. Berlyne (1969) claims that the rising and falling arousal may be associated with reward value, so that humor is enjoyable, and "the arousal-relieving components of the humorous situation serve to keep the rise in arousal within the rewarding range and prevent it from entering the region of aversiveness [p. 806] ." The present model differs from Berlyne's principally because of its information-processing orientation and also the specificity with which it treats the microprocesses involved in humor. Berlyne also tends to treat incongruity and complexity interchangeably [see Chapter 2], while here we think that there is sufficient reason to distinguish between them. Furthermore, Berlyne contends that the arousal-relieving elements of some kinds of humor may depend on the gratification of extrinsic motives such as sex or aggression, while the present model considers that these drives effect the salience of the joke and how it is processed.

In this section we have briefly discussed several other cognitive theories of humor. Some differ in that they seem to overlook the necessary restructuring or resolution of the joke's parts. Other theories have a developmental focus on children's humor or smiling, which may be governed by processes different than those governing adult humor appreciation. Berlyne's account shares common elements but differs in ways we have tried to indicate. In general, most theories have been vague in specifying the sequence of steps and factors involved in humor. Two conspicuous exceptions are proposals by Jones (1970) and Schultz (1970), who present two-stage models which are similar to the present model, although they differ in their focus and details. Similarly, an early investigation by Willmann (1940) was concerned with a two-stage humor model.

IV. Suggestions for Research

By postulating a series of steps that lead to the appreciation of humor, the model suggests some kinds of research that are needed to understand this elusive subject. From the previous discussion we see the need to assess the effects and find the differential weights for salience, complexity, incongruity, and solution time, as well as to test the derivations from the model for these factors. If, however, an investigator is interested in the effects of a single factor, the model indicates that the other factors should be controlled in some fashion. This control has frequently been overlooked in past research on humor, and its lack has subjected much of the research to alternative interpretations.

The effects of complexity on appreciation could be investigated by selecting jokes that vary on a continuum of complexity. The effects of complexity might also be assessed by a technique suggested by Brock and Goldstein (1969). The *S*s might be given tasks that are either cognitively easy or difficult and then given jokes of varying complexity to rate for funniness. One might predict that *S*s who had been cognitively taxed would prefer the simpler jokes.

Effects of incongruity might be investigated by developing an incongruity scale for stimuli along the lines of the sexiness scale developed by Godkewitsch [see Chapter 7] or by measuring GSR or cardiac response [see Chapter 6]. One could then correlate the surprise reaction with perceived funniness. There is a need for additional work which will require *S*s to explain what is funny about jokes. Their explanations of the incongruity and its resolution should relate to the degree of perceived humor.

It may also be possible to have *S*s solve difficult jokes out loud; their protocols can then be compared to the sequence of steps in the model, as presented in Figure 1.

Other research is needed to determine the structural properties of jokes that are funny on repeated exposures. One might also use Zajonc's procedure (1968) to determine whether the repeated exposure effect is applicable to humor stimuli. To test the retention explanation of repetition effects, it will be necessary to find the relationship between retention of jokes and their perceived humor.

V. Conclusion

In this paper a two-stage model for humor appreciation has been presented in information-processing terms. The model ties many old proposals together and offers a viable alternative to the Freudian theory, which has received so much attention from students of humor.

Obviously, the model is not in final form, and revisions will probably be necessary. Nevertheless, it serves to delineate several microprocesses that appear to be implicated in humor appreciation. In addition, this analysis indicates how humor involves other psychological processes about which, at this point, we are somewhat better informed, i.e., information processing and problem solving. In short, studying humor from this perspective may lead us to a better understanding of the complex behavior we know as humor.

Acknowledgment

This chapter was written while the author held an NDEA fellowship. The author is indebted to Roger Brown, Jeffrey Goldstein, Daniel Gutkin, Paul McGhee, Thomas Ostrom,

Ralph Rosnow, and Robert Weisberg for their comments and suggestions on earlier drafts of this chapter.

References

Bateson, G. The position of humor in human communication. In J. Levine (Ed.), *Motivation in humor.* New York: Atherton, 1969.

Bergum, B., & Lehr, D. Affect level, capillary pulse pressure and response latency. *Journal of Applied Psychology,* 1967, 51, 316–319.

Berlyne, D. E. Laughter, humor and play. In G. Lindzey & E. Aronson (Eds.), *Handbook of social psychology.* (2nd ed.) Vol. 3. Reading, Massachusetts: Addison-Wesley, 1969.

Brock, T. C., & Goldstein, J. H. *Determinants of humor appreciation.* Progress report presented to National Institute of Mental Health, 1969.

Burnstein, E. Sources of cognitive bias in the representation of simple social structures: Balance, minimal change, positivity, reciprocity, and the respondent's own attitude. *Journal of Personality and Social Psychology,* 1967, 7, 36–48.

Festinger, L. *A theory of cognitive dissonance.* New York: Harper, 1957.

Freud, S. *Jokes and their relation to the unconscious.* New York: Norton, 1960. (Originally: *Der Witz und seine Beziehung zum Unbewussten.* Leipzig and Vienna: Deuticke, 1905.)

Goldstein, J. H. Humor appreciation and time to respond. *Psychological Reports,* 1970, 27, 445–446. (a)

Goldstein, J. H. Repetition, motive arousal, and humor appreciation. *Journal of Experimental Research in Personality,* 1970, 4, 90–94. (b)

Heider, F. *The psychology of interpersonal relations.* New York: Wiley, 1958.

Jones, J. Cognitive factors in the appreciation of humor: A theoretical and experimental analysis. Unpublished doctoral dissertation, Yale Univ., 1970.

Kagan, J. On the need for relativism. *American Psychologist,* 1967, 22, 131–147.

Kanungo, R., & Dutta, S. Retention of affective material: Frame of reference or intensity? *Journal of Personality and Social Psychology,* 1966, 4, 193–206.

Koestler, A. *The act of creation.* London: Hutchinson, 1964.

Kolers, P. Some psychological aspects of pattern recognition. In P. Kolers & M. Eden (Eds.), *Recognizing patterns: Studies in living and automatic systems.* Cambridge, Massachusetts: MIT Press, 1968.

Maier, N. R. F. A Gestalt theory of humor. *British Journal of Psychology,* 1932, 23, 69–74.

McGhee, P. E. The development of the humor response: A review of the literature. *Psychological Bulletin,* 1971, in press.

Newell, A., Shaw, R., & Simon, H. Elements of a theory of human problem solving. *Psychological Review,* 1958, 65, 151–166.

Newell, A., & Simon, H. The logic theory machine. *IRE Transactions on Information Theory,* 1956, IT-2, 61–69.

Schultz, T. Cognitive factors in children's appreciation of cartoons: Incongruity and its resolution. Unpublished doctoral dissertation, Yale Univ., 1970.

Shurcliff, A. Judged humor, arousal, and the relief theory. *Journal of Personality and Social Psychology,* 1968, 8, 360–364.

Suls, J., & Weisberg, R. Supplementary Report: Processing syntactically ambiguous sentences. *Journal of Experimental Psychology,* 1970, 86, 112–114.

Wanat, S., & Levin, H. Linguistic constraints in reader strategies. Paper presented before Eastern Psychological Association, Atlantic City, 1970.

Willmann, J. M. An analysis of humor and laughter. *American Journal of Psychology*, 1940, 53, 70–85.

Zajonc, R. Attitudinal effect of mere exposure. *Journal of Personality and Social Psychology*, 1968, 9 (2, Pt. 2), 1–27.

Zigler, E., Levine, J., & Gould, L. Cognitive challenge as a factor in children's humor appreciation. *Journal of Personality and Social Psychology*, 1967, 6, 332–336.

Chapter 5

A Model of the Social Functions of Humor

William H. Martineau

Department of Sociology and Anthropology
Ohio Wesleyan University, Delaware, Ohio

I. Introduction

Humor is a pervasive phenomenon in the social fabric of most, if not all, societies. Yet, one can concur with Levine's (1968) observation that despite its obviousness humor "has evoked little serious attention from behavioral scientists as an area worthy of research and theory [p. 1]."* One also can agree with Levine's comment that "reasons for this lack of scientific interest in humor ... are unrelated to its significance in human affairs and its possible contribution to general behavior theory [p. 1]." In this chapter we shall present a model of the social functions of humor which we

---

* There are some signs that behavioral scientists are becoming increasingly aware that humor is a legitimate topic for serious investigation. This volume and the collection of materials it represents is one indication of such interest. Further evidence are the symposia, *Social aspects of humor, Humor research and theory: Towards interdisciplinary integration,* and *Cultural relativity of humor,* which were held at the 1969 annual meeting of the Western Psychological Association, the 1971 meeting of the Midwest Psychological Association, and the 1971 meeting of the American Psychological Association, respectively.

believe provides a meaningful basis from which hypotheses might be generated for empirical research. The model describes three intra- and intergroup situations for which the social functions of humor are delineated as combinations of four key dimensions of the situations are varied. These functions are presented in the form of theorems which are discussed in relation to the sociological literature. To begin, we shall take a brief look at the status of the sociological study of humor and then proceed to review the materials from which a model was synthesized.

II. A Progress Report

A. A Sociology of Humor?

The maturation of sociology has brought with it a flowering of special sociologies that now dot the discipline and characterize the presumed "need" for and growth of specialization among sociologists (e.g., the sociologies of education, religion, law, science, art, sports, occupations, and medicine). These sociologies may be viewed as attempts to bring knowledge of the elements and processes of social life to bear on a particular social system (e.g., schools, families) or on a distinctive type of behavior or aspect of social order (e.g., ethnic relations, mental illness).

Does a sociology of humor exist? If the existence of a substantial body of scientific literature is the criterion, the answer must be negative. At this time there are approximately a score of journal articles scattered over some thirty years, a few directly pertinent dissertations, and several books and monographs which refer to humor at some point but do not examine it in any comprehensive manner.

However, there are more important grounds upon which the question should be considered. We believe that if there is, or should be, a sociology of humor (a question of more serious consequence than pedantic debate), it should be regarded as an attempt to understand more precisely a widely diffused type of social process and specific medium of communication.* In addition it should be

---

* The conceptualization of humor as a means of communication is not new. Many social scientists appear to have arrived at this view independently. In one of the earliest articles, Hayworth (1928) placed great stress on laughter as a means of communication—a means which he suggests may have antedated language. In this most basic sense, laughter is a vocal signal to others. Hayworth indicated that an advantage of viewing laughter as communication is that a theory of communication serves to unite different theories of laughter. It might be well to extend and utilize his suggestion in order to unify general theories of humor as well.

directed toward incorporating such knowledge into more general explanations of social interaction patterns and the dynamics of group structure and group process.

To identify the study of the social functions of humor in this fashion highlights the major contribution it has to offer—that is, to serve as an aid to the comprehensive understanding of group structure and group process. Humor is part of every social system and can be analyzed as one social process affecting the system; humor occurs in nearly every type of human interaction and can be analyzed as to how it influences each interaction pattern and the social structure emerging from it. To realize and explore the full potential of this area of study, we advocate that humor be viewed from the sociological perspective as a "lubricant" and an "abrasive" in social interaction—especially in such common everyday interaction that constitutes the basis of the social order and makes the routine flow of social life possible. By this we mean, to use an analogy, that on the one hand, the interjection of the humorous serves as oil pumped from an oil can. Humor is intended to initiate social interaction and to keep the machinery of interaction operating freely and smoothly. Indeed, sometimes it may not be sufficient. But perhaps most often this is its intention and objective function. On the other hand, but not mutually exclusive from the former, humor may serve as an abrasive. Rather than oiling the workings of social interaction, it constitutes a measure of sand. The consequence of such abrasive humor is interpersonal friction and a juncture in the communication process which may modify the character of the interaction.

B. REVIEW OF LITERATURE

It is appropriate at this point to review the work on humor that has been produced by sociologists to date.* By considering this literature in chronological fashion, one may more easily grasp the course of progress and remaining needs in the study of humor.

* Studies to be reviewed will be restricted to those conducted by sociologists, anthropologists, and others using a sociological framework. No doubt there are many sources, ranging over an immensely diverse area of sociological and quasi-sociological literature, which make passing (and sometimes more extensive) reference to humor and its social functions. In addition, psychologists have been active in the study of humor and the influence of their work upon sociologists cannot be denied. Although some of their research is linked to sociological analyses of humor, this is not included in the present review. The nature of this volume suggests that such work will be adequately represented by other contributors. One comprehensive review which integrates much of the literature from different perspectives is that by Pitchford (1960).

The first major article to deal with humor in a sociological framework was Obrdlik's (1942) *Gallows Humor—A Sociological Phenomenon.* This work stemmed from Obrdlik's firsthand experiences in Czechoslovakia during Nazi Germany's occupation of that country. He cast humor in the role of influencing the social characteristics of the Czechs and Nazis as groups and the pattern of relationship between them. In describing it as gallows humor, Obrdlik emphasized its peculiar nature in having emerged among the Czechs from a particularly precarious and tragic situation. This led him to conclude that humor associated with such structural features (in this case, the dominant–minority relationship) is always intentional and has both positive and negative effects. For the oppressed, it operates to bolster morale and hope; the humor becomes a compensatory device, making the fear and tragedy of the moment seem perhaps only temporary. Humor therefore serves as a means of controlling the behavior of those sharing the burden. Obrdlik defined the negative effect of gallows humor as the influence it had upon the disintegration of the occupying forces against whom the humor was directed. The following excerpt illustrates the gallows type of humor:

> Do you know why the day-light-savings time has been exceptionally prolonged this year? Because Hitler promised that before the summer is over, he and his army will be in England [p. 713].

Obrdlik observed that the circulation of such humor was a symbol of resistance, granting reprieve to the Czechs and making the Nazis furious.

This particular analysis is noteworthy, not because such structural settings between the oppressors and the oppressed are unparalleled or that humor in such situations has gone unobserved, but because Obrdlik's effort seems to have been the first in the United States to recognize humor as a sociological phenomenon originating in social interaction and having explicit social functions. It took the uniqueness and flavor of his material (a dramatic example published in a major journal) to mark the initiation of serious sociological investigation of humor.

In crediting Obrdlik with the first major contribution to the sociological study of humor in the United States, we have not overlooked Radcliffe-Brown's (1940, 1949) research on joking relationships. His interest in humor, dating back as early as 1908,* no doubt had an appreciable influence on the initiation of scientific investigation of humor. Viewing humor as a problem in comparative sociology, Radcliffe-Brown (1940) defined the joking relationship as "a relation between two persons in which one is by custom permitted, and some instances required, to tease or make fun of the other, who in turn is required to take no offence. . . . The joking relationship is a peculiar combination of friendliness and antagonism [p. 90]." Although he acknowledged variations in the form of this relationship in different societies, he suggested that the basic social relationship is extremely widespread, appearing in Africa, Asia, Oceania, and North America. Thus it becomes relevant in a general comparative study of social structure. As we shall see, the concept of the joking relationship emerges in several ways in more recent studies.

In the course of his massive statement on the racial problem in the United States, Myrdal (1944, pp. 38–39) fostered the analysis of humor in the context of race relations. Myrdal suggested a number of social functions of intergroup humor: an escape route or symbolic excuse for inconsistent behavior, compensation to the sufferer, absolution in the form of an understanding laugh, and primarily indirect approval for that which cannot be explicitly acknowledged. Understandably, all such functions are developed within the conceptual framework of the "American dilemma."† Myrdal's analysis was not the first work to be done on humor in the racial context. During this historical era, several other references to humor also appeared in the general literature by and about Negroes, in

---

* In his 1949 article on the joking relationship, Radcliffe-Brown indicated that formulation of the concept began in 1908 when he was searching for an explanation of customs of avoidance between kin members in the Andaman Islands. The joking relationship came as a spin-off from his interpretation of avoidance relations as relationships of friendship: For example, although a husband avoids all contact with his wife's mother, the husband claims that she is a great friend since she has provided him with his wife. Although Radcliffe-Brown has been accepted as the most prominent representative of research on the joking relationship, there were, at that time, other anthropologists, as well, whom he cites as having observed the same phenomenon. The reader may consult Radcliffe-Brown (1940, 1949—or as reprinted in 1965) for such references.

† As the anchoring theme of his book, aimed at determining the status of the Negro in the United States, Myrdal (1944) explained the "Negro problem" as "a problem in the heart of the American." He defined the "American Dilemma" as "the ever-raging conflict between, on the one hand, the valuations preserved on the general plane which we shall call the 'American Creed' . . . and, on the other hand, the valuations on specific planes of individual and group living. . . . [p. xlvii]."

particular, in works by Dollard (1937, p. 309), Davis, Gardner, and Gardner (1941, p. 459), and Drake and Cayton (1945, p. 723). However, Myrdal's work appears to have been more prominent in generating interest in humor research.

Burma (1946) was the first to deal more systematically with the social functions of humor in race relations. He proposed that humor is well suited as a conflict device because of its adaptability to varying subject matters and its potential for subtly conveying malice. Racial humor is primarily created to attain gratification at the expense of the other racial group; its purpose is "to cause one's adversary to appear ludicrous in his own eyes . . . [or] in your eyes." Most all racial humor, Burma concludes, "definitely can be related to racial competition and conflict and the social and cultural patterns which have arisen from them."

During the early 1950s, three articles contributed to a more intensive investigation of humor. Barron (1950) advocated "an empirical and systematic classification of descriptive data" to serve as a basis for construction of a theory that might resolve the controversies among philosophers, psychologists, and sociologists of humor. Continuing the theme of intergroup humor, he sought to compile jokes on three American ethnic groups, the Jews, Negroes, and Irish. Curiously, Barron's work represents a primary focus on the humorous stimuli rather than humor's mediating influence in the interaction process, which was the concern of his sociologist predecessors. It thus constitutes an innovative departure, raising the issue of the role of the stimulus in the humor process.

Klapp (1950) was successful in linking a portion of humor directly with the social structure. He did so by showing that the fool has a specific socially defined position and role in society. To the group "the fool represents values which are rejected by the group: causes that are lost, incompetence, failure, and fiasco." His position is lowly, yet valued, and he serves as a scapegoat, butt of humor, and cathartic symbol of aggression. He has the social license to depart from the group norms of propriety, which are ordinarily subject to sanction. Through the ridicule of his behavior, he acts as a control mechanism (i.e., a negative example) enforcing the very propriety which he violates. Klapp's reference to fool making as a social process, however, appears to have even broader and more significant implications. He suggests that there is a continuous, collective process of ascribing the role of fool to people as a means of enforcing conformity, pressuring for status adjustment, or simply eliminating the deviant. Klapp's contribution integrates humor with a general understanding of participation in the process of social organization.

Also appearing at the onset of the 1950s was Richard Stephenson's (1951) article investigating conflict and control functions of humor.* Proceeding on the principle that these functions of humor served at least as convenient classifications for sociological analyses, Stephenson advocated greater study of the control functions of humor and the broadening of study beyond the context of ethnic group relations. Using joke anthologies as a source of data (as Barron had done), Stephenson explored humor in those situations involving social stratification. Such anthology-collected jokes focused on status and differentials in income and occupation. However, he interprets these primarily as serving a control function. They minimize such economic differences, ridicule the extremes of the stratification system (the aristocracy and the unassimilated immigrant), and maximize the unifying values expressed in the traditional American creed (equality, ambition, opportunity, etc.). Stephenson noted that his conclusions pertain to anthology jokes—those entering the public domain in popularly read printed form. He further acknowledged that although these emphasize social control, social conflict functions of humor about stratification are likely to prevail in other sources of humor.

The timing and contributions of these last three studies seem to mark the establishment of sociological inquiry into humor. We shall see that activity peaked during the later 1950s and early 1960s. Turning to this period, we find reports by Blau (1955) and Bradney (1957) on the social functions of humor in bureaucracies. In an extensive analysis of a state employment agency, Blau (1955, pp. 109–112) found that joking among interviewers in a competitive

---

* The conflict and control functions of humor are mentioned frequently in the literature on the social functions of humor. As a representative explanation, we cite Stephenson's (1951) analysis of these functions:

> The conflict function of humor is expressed largely by means of irony, satire, sarcasm, caricature, parody, burlesque, and the like. The particular adaptability of humor as a conflict weapon lies in the fact that humor may conceal malice and allow expression of aggression without the consequences of other overt behavior. . . . The control function of humor may be expressed in a wide variety of humor types. As a means of social control, humor may function to express approval or disapproval of social form and action, express common group sentiments, develop and perpetuate stereotypes, relieve awkward or tense situations, and express collective, *sub-rosa* approbation of action not explicitly approved. Humor as expressed in the controlled laugh or smile may serve as a means of communication, signaling the intent and nature of the communicating parties [from R. M. Stephenson. Conflict and control functions of humor. *American Journal of Sociology*, 1951, 56, 569–574].

situation was "instrumental in creating [social cohesion] by uniting a group in the pleasant experience of laughing together." The telling of jokes functioned to release tensions and reduce the disruptive effect of conflicts stemming from competitive operations in the agency. From Blau's description, one can interpret the emergence of such humor by referring to Klapp's formulation of fool making as a social process. In this instance, interviewers collectively used the hapless client as a butt of humor, as a fool type. Blau claimed that in the process, they reinforced cohesion among themselves but also stereotyped the client and created group norms about the processing of such clients (ways usually increasing client dissatisfaction and the potential for interviewer–client conflict).

Bradney's (1957) research on sales assistants in a London department store offered a somewhat different interpretation. Although structural conditions were similar to those of the employment agency, in that competition was a major feature of the routinized social relationship, fool making was not employed as the adjusting mechanism. Although humor again functioned to control conflict arising from competition, Bradney viewed its source as the socially legitimized joking relationship. It was less formalized, however, than that first described in preliterate societies by Radcliffe-Brown. Nevertheless, in the same manner joking functioned to release antagonism and minimize the strain stemming from prescribed formal relationships among the employees of the organization.

Enough studies had appeared by this time to allow Middleton and Moland (1959) to assess the literature and conclude that three major approaches had been taken in sociological studies of humor. There were those studies which focused on situations of intergroup conflict, the intragroup control functions of humor, and joking relationships. Their own research investigated joking in Negro and white subcultures. Using samples of college students at two southern universities, they tested a number of hypotheses on frequency of joke telling, differences between sex and racial groups, and frequency of telling sexual and anti-ethnic jokes in either racial group. Aside from particular findings, it is interesting that Middleton and Moland concluded that previous studies, emphasizing jokes of ridicule and therefore the conflict and control functions of humor, had neglected much of the widely circulated, popular humor. They suggested that the result has been a failure to recognize fully the important function of humor in "the creation and reinforcement of a sense of solidarity and intimacy within groups." Middleton and Moland advocated that emphasis be directed toward the study of joking as a process of seeking social approval which also, at the same time, tends to strengthen the social bonds of the group.

In a subsequent article based on the same research, Middleton (1959) pursued the hypothesis that definitions and functions of humor vary with the cultural context. His analysis explored subcultural variations in humor by comparing "the appeal of racial jokes, both anti-Negro and anti-white, to matched groups of Negroes and whites."* The findings tentatively suggested that Negroes generally found Negro jokes as funny as whites did but reacted more favorably than whites to anti-white jokes. However, three variables (acceptance of racial stereotypes, authoritarianism or ethnocentrism, and social class position) were introduced to determine their influence on these generalizations about reactions to racial jokes. Two findings emerged. Among whites, a moderately high positive association was found between authoritarianism and favorable reactions to both types of racial jokes. And among Negroes, middle class position was significantly associated with favorable reactions to both types of racial jokes.

Compared to the research done during the 1950s, the work produced in the early 1960s amounts to a flurry of activity in the brief history of the sociological study of humor. In three short years, four doctoral dissertations appeared which constituted sociological investigations of humor (Pitchford, 1960; Goldman, 1960; La Fave, 1961; Emerson, 1963). In addition, seven articles related to humor were published (Coser, 1960; Davis, 1961; Levine, 1961; Christensen, 1963; Noel, 1964; Goodchilds & Smith, 1964; Hammond, 1964). Humor also was discussed in books by Lewis (1961), Coser (1962), and Simpson and Yinger (1965).

Two of the dissertations just cited are concerned directly with the social functions of humor. Pitchford (1960) "attempts to develop a theoretical model for locating humor within the structure of social action and delineating its consequences for the adaptation of adjustment of social systems [p. 3]." The ultimate purpose of this model was to assist in explaining the social functions of humor as a universal phenomenon. Pitchford found that existing literature supported humor functioning in three ways: as a means of achieving consensus, a technique of social control, and a device for introducing competition and social conflict.

* This particular research is related to the earlier work of psychologists Wolff, Smith, and Murray (1934) who first raised the issue of why certain ethnic groups frequently employ self-disparaging humor based on the traditional stereotypes of themselves.

In 1963 Emerson studied the social functions of humor in a hospital setting. She first postulated that social conflicts arise from cultural or structural incongruities (such as "latent roles deriving from an individual's memberships outside the subculture, or contradictions of ideology and practice with the subculture") and that such conflicts lead to precarious situations in which individuals may experience disruptions such as loss of self-control or embarrassment. Findings indicated that humor may serve, on the one hand, to introduce such conflict in an informal manner, and on the other hand, to neutralize it. It appears to do so because it constitutes an acceptable form of protest, while insulating the ongoing social interaction by making light of the situation. Both Pitchford and Emerson, therefore, add strong support for two of the previously explored functions of humor, conflict and control.

In an analysis of materials dating back to the 19th century, Goldman (1960) declared "that Negro humor in form and content is a derivative of the Negroes' unique social position in American life [p. vi]." Goldman suggested that an explanation of Negro humor requires an understanding of the pattern of race relations at the time in which the humor occurred. This sociohistoric frame of reference is considered appropriate and vital. Tracing Negro humor through the history of race relations in the United States, Goldman found humor serving a variety of functions. During and after slavery, humor was a means of passing on information, a way of making an unbearable situation somewhat lighter, or at times a means of reducing one's work load. Humorous roles were often "instrumentally necessary . . . to manipulate the environment and gain advantages [p. 22]." Humor was also found to be associated with family disorganization: It functioned to heighten marital competition and conflict. Above all, however, Goldman's content analysis led him to emphasize humor as a device for expressing attitudes reflective of the tension and friction between the races; it was a surrogate form of expression permitting resentment and hostility to be publicly voiced.

The fourth thesis appearing at the onset of the 1960s focused not on the social functions of humor, but upon a social influence which evokes a humorous response. La Fave (1961) demonstrated that the concept of reference group could be an effective predictor of humor reactions. He found that among four experimental groups (Catholics, Jehovah's Witnesses, Southern Baptists, and Agnostics), "jokes tend to be judged as funny by *S*s whose reference (identification) group is esteemed, and whose outgroup is disparaged, and to be judged unfunny by *S*s whose reference group is disparaged and whose outgroup is esteemed [p. 67]."

As previously indicated, several articles and references in books reflected an increased study of humor in the early 1960s. Their contributions are somewhat diverse. There are three articles which have in common a focus on the humorous role per se and its structural consequences for the group (Davis, 1961; Goodchilds & Smith, 1964; Levine, 1961). Although each explored humor in quite different social situations, they each concluded that a humorous role enacted by a group member has expressive and instrumental functions—such as releasing tension and maintaining structure or facilitating goal attainment.

The joking relationship formulated by Radcliffe-Brown is further documented by Christensen (1963) and Hammond (1964). The former's research among the Luguru of Tanganyika directly supports the theory that joking is one social mechanism (an alternative to extreme respect or avoidance) for resolving hostility emerging from structural relationships among kin members and maintaining a stable system of social behavior. In an important extension of Radcliffe-Brown's position, Hammond (1964) contended that in institutionalized joking "the structural relationship between the participants tends to be characterized by five significantly interrelated structural attributes: separation, reciprocity, ambivalence, equality, and independence [p. 266]." Hammond related these situational features to his conception of joking among the West African Mossi as an adaptive mechanism which assumes importance for the way in which it provides concurrently for the maintenance of communication and control, and the catharsis of potentially disruptive emotions.

In an intensive study of a hospital ward, Coser (1962, pp. 84–89 especially) devoted considerable attention to the functions of humor in the adaptation of people to a new situation (the hospital) and a new role (the sick role). She found that humor in the form of jocular griping enabled patients to establish an identity and to arrive at consensus and cohesion among themselves such that a group structure emerged with boundaries vis-à-vis the hospital staff group. Coser's analysis appears important because of its applicability to other similar situations in which the individual is thrust into a new social system and new role.

Finally, the Simpson and Yinger (1965) text is noted in this review if only because the inclusion by the authors of a review of humor studies and their notation of its social functions was an indication that humor studies had become visible. The exposure in such a text was also likely to ensure additional efforts to investigate the social functions of humor.

This concludes our discussion of the brief period in which the greatest amount of sociological analysis of humor seems to have occurred. We have now but to review the literature appearing from the mid-1960s up to the present. The research interest which grew slowly, and seemed to mature in the early sixties, appears to wane. Despite the general lack of sociological study, however, there are some noteworthy contributions toward understanding humor in the social context. Historian Joseph Boskin (1966) has written with insight about the social functions of Negro humor, particularly as reflective of changing times and the history of race relations. Tracing Negro humor from early folk to the contemporary, Boskin suggests that it consists of two types: internal and external. The latter was predominately a means of accommodation to white society, a means of survival. Boskin viewed internal or ingroup humor, however, as functioning to reinforce group behavior and to overcome the obstacles of discrimination. He asserted that amid increasing racial strife (the civil-rights movement era), ingroup humor served to lessen individual and group tension and to ridicule the opposition. Boskin concluded by speculating that the newer comedians and forms of Negro humor were expressing new confidence, a reflection of growing black pride and consciousness.

Two other authors also have contributed to the analysis of humor among black Americans. Arnez and Anthony's (1968) review of contemporary Negro humor substantially supports the major thrust of Boskin's analysis. They postulated that the humorous is indeed a reflection of one's cultural experience and suggested that the character of Negro humor has mirrored the saga of the American Negro. They also acknowledged, as did Boskin, the role of ingroup humor in building social cohesion as well as in creating stereotypes. But their primary thesis is that contemporary Negro humor, illustrated by the material of comedians such as Moms Mabley, Flip Wilson, Godfrey Cambridge, and Dick Gregory, represents social satire. Arnez and Anthony viewed such humor as helping to create the "new image" of the black man conscious of his past and his identity. As social satire, this humor, the bitter as well as the more mild, is interpreted as a means of criticizing and highlighting the incongruities in American society; it is viewed as a general agent of social change.

A closer look into the functioning of humor within the black community itself is provided by Hannerz (1969). From an ethnographic study of a Washington, D.C., neighborhood, Hannerz concluded that humor, particularly the joking relationship which we reviewed earlier, is very much a part of the everyday routine and interaction process characterizing ghetto dwellers. Amid neighborhood conditions of close physical proximity, informality became the norm and relationships were formed on a person-to-person basis where direct knowledge of the individual and his background was preferred. Within this context, however, Hannerz observed that these relationships tended to be superficial and that some degree of social distance was desired. The balance between informality and social distance appeared to be maintained by the joking relationship.

Additional exploration into the role of humor at a basic level in the interaction process was performed by Miller (1967) and Emerson (1969). Commenting on the status of humor studies and types of humor, Miller emphasized the need for studying the social significance of humor. While observing sessions of a Chippewa tribal council and recording instances of humor (primarily jokes), he examined the context in which the humor occurred as well as the reaction evoked. Probing hypotheses concerning the ways in which humor contributes to the life of the group, Miller concluded that humor was seldom used to control the behavior of other council members; humor did serve as an important device for release of tension; and, most important, humor performed a communicative function. He emphasized that humor can "communicate what would be difficult to say in any other way. Through humor, human contacts, always problematical, become less fragile [p. 271]." The work of both Miller and Hannerz clearly represents continuations of the anthropological tradition in studying humor. In particular, Hannerz presents an integrated empirical approach, analyzing humor as part of the basic social fabric. We note both of these contributions as having special significance for demonstrating how the analysis of humor can be employed to assist understanding of group structure and group process.

Emerson (1969) offers a detailed analysis of the process involved in the humorous exchange itself. By focusing on jokes containing covert messages about more serious and possibly taboo topics, Emerson was able to describe the exchange in terms of a negotiation between the interacting parties. She found that humor provided a channel through which negotiations could be initiated for more serious communication. Through response and counterresponse, expectations were communicated. On the basis of such expectations, decisions could be made on suspension of the conventional guidelines surrounding the taboo topics, assignment of responsibility for such, and possible redefinitions of the original exchange. Emerson's analysis constitutes an explicit illustration of the mechanics of the humor process.

These last analyses represent the substance of humor study during the remainder of the 1960 decade and conclude this review. We reiterate that the humor studies reviewed are intended to highlight major accomplishments and shifts of interest in studying the social functions of humor in a sociological framework. To be sure, there exist numerous additional references which are concerned with the social functions of humor from other related perspectives. The remaining chapters of this volume should clearly reflect this. The studies that have been reviewed constitute the basic source of our model of the social functions of humor and are referred to again as supportive evidence for theorems of the model.

III. A Model of the Social Functions of Humor*

The basic premise underlying the model is that humor is a social mechanism with definite social functions. More specifically, humor is viewed as a distinctive type of pervasive social process and medium of communication by which acting units in the social system convey information during the ongoing process of interaction. Humor is conceived generically to be any communicative instance which is perceived as humorous by any of the interacting parties. The humorous communicative instance becomes a vehicle or social mechanism employed for interaction. Humor may assume different forms and has different functions in various structural settings. We have already seen that the general orientation of the few sociologists working on this topic has been to conceptualize some of these functions and also present some variables that have an impact on the function of humor—and which, in fact, can change the function of humor.

A number of functions of humor have been stressed in the literature. In most cases consensus, conflict, and control have been the focus of analysis. The more important variables delineated are the actor, the audience or recipient, the butt of the humor, the judgment of the humor, the cultural context, and the social position of the involved parties. The model attempts to combine some of these variables, specify combinations of them, and delineate the functions which humor performs under these combinations. In other words, rather than stressing the functions of humor directly, the

---

* A preliminary formulation of this model appeared earlier (Martineau, 1967).

procedure has been reversed. The model identifies some conditions under which the functions of humor can be further specified. In particular, the model is constructed on a basic framework of intragroup and intergroup structural settings: (1) humor analyzed totally within the group; (2) humor analyzed in an intergroup situation, but with focus on the internal structure of one group; (3) humor analyzed in an intergroup situation with the focus on the interaction and relationship between the two groups.

Within these three structural settings, four major variables are considered in varying combinations. The first is the *actor*; that is, the individual or group that initiates the humor. Second, the *audience* is the party that experiences or is exposed to the humor. The third variable is the *subject* or butt of the humor: about whom is the humor? at whom is it aimed? The "ingroup" and the "outgroup" are used as the contrasting subjects. *Judgment* of the humor is the final variable and constitutes the evaluative element. The question posed is how the humor actually is perceived or judged by the audience, apart from the content of the humor or the intentions of the actor. "Esteemed" and "disparaged" are employed as labels for the polar extremes of evaluation. The following diagram illustrates the humor process in the three structural situations considered. Shown are the first two variables, the actor (A) and audience (Au), and three basic features: Each circle represents a social group; H represents the source of humor; and arrows indicate the direction of humor flow. The shaded area indicates the focus of sociological analysis in each situation.

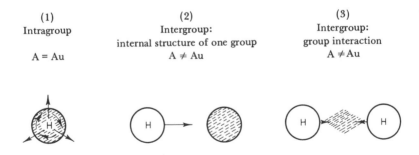

(1)	(2)	(3)
Intragroup	Intergroup: internal structure of one group	Intergroup: group interaction
A = Au	A ≠ Au	A ≠ Au

The complete model, including the remaining subject and judgment variables, is illustrated by Table 1.

From the model the following theorems are derived to identify some of the social functions of humor. These theorems are discussed

TABLE I

Social Function of Humor

	Subject			
	Ingroup		Outgroup	
	Judgment		Judgment	
Structural situations	Esteemed	Disparaged	Esteemed	Disparaged
(1) Intragroup $A = Au$	Function:	Function:	Function:	Function:
(2) Intergroup: internal $A \neq Au$	Function:	Function:	Function:	Function:
(3) Intergroup: interaction $A \neq Au$	Function:	Function:	Function:	Function:

in relation to the literature we have reviewed. In the absence of supportive studies, a brief rationale is offered for exploratory consideration.

THEOREMS

1. Intragroup Situation

Basic Premise. Humor initiated in an intragroup situation functions within the ingroup depending upon how it is judged by the group members.

(a) When the humor is judged as esteeming the ingroup, it functions to solidify the group.

Humor esteeming the characteristics of a group or group members constitutes positive reinforcement of existing behavioral patterns and strengthens the social bond. We are inclined to note also a vast amount of humor which, although not always perceived clearly as "esteeming," performs a similar function for the ingroup. This is the seemingly purposeless, inoffensive humor that Pitchford (1960) describes as the "universal short cuts to consensus." The "little jokes" and humorous banter so often observed in everyday interactions and when first acquaintances are made are ways of revealing friendship, approval, and a sharing of sentiment, and relieving a somewhat awkward situation (Coser, 1962; Miller, 1967). More specifically, the function of humor is to initiate and facilitate communication and development of social relationships: Through humor, consensus is achieved and social distance is reduced. As an aspect of the socioemotional role in informal groups, humor serves as a symbol of social approval promoting group solidarity (Davis, 1961).

(b) When the humor is judged as disparaging the ingroup, it may function in the four ways discussed as follows.

(1) To control ingroup behavior.

The common type of humor which this theorem concerns is what anthropologist Radcliffe-Brown (1965) has called the "joking relationship." While more formalized in some preliterate societies, it is recognized as a common phenomenon in nearly every society. Custom permits, or even requires, one person to tease or make fun of the other without the other taking offense. For example, Bradney (1957) found humor functioning in this manner among employees in a British department store, Coser (1962) and Fox (1959) found it among hospital patients, Hammond (1964) and Miller (1967) found it in tribal settings, and Hannerz (1969) found it among blacks in a ghetto neighborhood. A simple illustration is the violation of the norm of punctuality: If one is caught being late, the joking relationship is usually envoked immediately and jokes are made about one's tardiness. The function of humor in most such instances is to arrive at or return to a state of consensus and conformity among members. The humor arises because of a recognition that interaction either *must* continue or is at least desirable. Humor is used to express grievances or can be directed at someone in the group who either has not learned or has violated the norms of the group. Humor constitutes a symbol of disapproval—a subtle way of sanctioning the deviant and at the same time providing him with an opportunity to accept the humorous definition of the situation, acknowledge the incongruity of his behavior, correct his behavior, and rejoin the group without "losing face" (Klapp, 1950; Hammond, 1964; Miller, 1967). Humor, therefore, acts as a safety valve for expressing grievance or controlled hostility against deviance. The result is that the normative system is reinforced and social cohesion prevails.

(2) To solidify the ingroup.

This consequence is a by-product of the process just discussed. But there are ways other than the joking relationship in which self-disparaging humor functions directly to solidify the group. There is the common phenomenon of members admitting their own faults, weaknesses, or undesirable characteristics and viewing them in a humorous vein (Miller, 1967). This is usually seen as the sole prerogative of ingroup members. We have the early research of Wolff *et al.* (1934) documenting self-disparaging jokes among Jews, and that of Middleton (1959) doing the same among Negroes, as well as numerous popular references to this behavior. Such self-disparaging humor often is perceived as funny and functions to solidify. La Fave (1961) suggested that the reference group construct could be utilized to explain this phenomenon [see also Chapter 10].

(3) To introduce or foster conflict already present in the group.
(4) To foster demoralization and social disintegration of the group.

These last two functions of self-disparaging humor are not necessarily related to one another. Conflict is not always dysfunctional for the system; it does not necessarily lead to disintegration. However, in both theorems humor can be viewed as a mechanism of social change. That is, in the form of a more severe sanctioning mechanism, humor can be predicted to disrupt communication and the interaction within the group such that the basis of interpersonal associations is changed. Ridicule, as one type of disparaging humor, is often described as such a conflict weapon. One empirical question is to discover the proportion of severely abrasive humor which can be tolerated before necessary communication becomes impaired and the basis of social integration destroyed.

(c) When the humor is judged as esteeming an outgroup, it functions to solidify the group.

It is an unlikely occurrence that humor exchanged within a group will be perceived as esteeming an outgroup. When it does occur, a tentative prediction offered is that the group as a whole has adopted the outgroup as a reference group [see Chapter 10]. The humor constitutes an acknowledgment and a reminder that there is a set of interests or values in which both groups share. Mutual recognition of this through humor adds to the social bond among members. A lack of consensus in the humor judgment, however, would be labeled as disloyalty to either the membership or identification group. Rather than solidarity, dissension and conflict would ensue as consequences.

(d) When the humor is judged as disparaging an outgroup, it may function as follows.

(1) To increase morale and solidify the ingroup.
(2) To introduce or foster a hostile disposition toward that outgroup.

These two functions seem to occur simultaneously. Obrdlik's (1942) research on gallows humor illustrates these functions of humor. During World War II, his observations were that the Czechs under Nazi occupation were able to cope with the situation and maintain morale through the use of humor, which at the same time sustained hostility toward the Nazis. The sharing of jokes poking fun at the Germans sustained group cohesion and helped coalesce resistance. Additional evidence supporting this theorem comes from analyses of humor among blacks over the years (Davis *et al.,* 1941; Drake & Cayton, 1945; Goldman, 1960; Boskin, 1966), Stephenson's (1951) study of status jokes aimed at the very rich and immigrant poor in American society, Arnez and Anthony's (1968) analysis of contemporary black comedians and their material (Dick Gregory, for example), and Blau's (1955) research in a state employment agency where interviewers joked about job applicants. In each of these studies, the humor of the situation victimizes an outgroup as the butt of the humor and serves to grant reprieve to the ingroup.

2. Intergroup Situation: Internal

Basic Premise. In an intergroup situation, humor that is initiated by an outgroup functions within the ingroup depending upon how it is judged by the ingroup members. In this situation, the group under analysis (the ingroup) does not initiate the humor; it is the audience alone.

(a) When the humor is judged as esteeming the ingroup, it functions to increase morale and solidify the ingroup.

Praise from an outgroup source may be unexpected and held to be suspect. Yet, group members may accept the humor as an invitation to amicable relations. Under these conditions, we can predict that esteem would affect the internal structure of the ingroup by boosting morale and promoting increased interaction among group members.

(b) When the humor is judged as disparaging the ingroup, it may function in the three ways discussed as follows.
(1) To increase morale and solidify the ingroup.

This consequence may be predicted on the basis of a familiar principle. To rally in defense against attack, even subtle attack, is a common human response. Criticism is considered a prerogative of group members; criticism from outsiders, except in special instances, is not received warmly. The perception of an invasion of domain represented by the disparaging humor affects the internal structure of the audience group. Evidence supporting these consequences of humor takes the form of observations of the treatment of ethnic and minority groups in humor—that is, humor from the dominant group which stereotypes the minority and pokes fun at characteristics of this stereotype (Boskin, 1966; Arnez & Anthony, 1968; Moore, 1970). The impact on most American minority groups has been an eventual strengthening of internal structure and development of hostile dispositions toward sources of such humor. Most minorities, particularly the Italians, Jews, Blacks, and more recently, Mexican Americans, homosexuals, and women, have exhibited this phenomenon.

(2) To control the behavior of the ingroup.

As one example, Stephenson (1951) has pointed out that the function of disparaging humor often is to bring the group in question into conformity, i.e., into line with the higher order of prevailing behavioral patterns in the society. In the case of the aforementioned minorities, discussed as the subjects of much disparaging humor, this means conforming to the so-called "American mold" and relinquishing many of their cultural ties and characteristics.

(3) To foster demoralization and disintegration of the ingroup.

Continued bombardment of abrasive humor has a destructive effect upon its recipient. The gallows humor analyzed by Obrdlik (1942) exemplifies this social function. Obrdlik saw gallows humor as having a double effect. While it bolstered morale of the Czechs who initiated it, it also influenced the disintegration of those toward whom it was directed—the Nazi oppressors.

There is a difficulty in predicating from this structural situation which social function will obtain, an increase in group solidarity, conformity of behavior, or disintegration. As the case of the minorities demonstrates, the long-term consequence may be that all three eventually occur. Of interest at the moment, however, is the immediate social function, which could be influenced by a number of variables not controlled in the model. The model does indicate that humor judgment is one important variable involved. Studies (Smith & Vinacke, 1951; Middleton, 1959; Noel, 1964; La Fave, 1961, see also Chapter 10) indicate that humor judgments may vary considerably with the influence of the audience's reference groups or identification classes. In the present instance, if the audience judging itself disparaged in the humor identifies with the actor or another outside grouping, we would predict a control function of humor; if the audience does not identify as such, defensive reactions and solidarity or demoralization and disintegration would seem to occur, depending upon the extent of disparagement and the group's resources for coping with it.

(c) When the humor is judged as esteeming the outgroup, it may function in the two ways discussed as follows.
(1) To introduce or foster a hostile disposition toward the outgroup initiating the humor.

Although the ingroup may not be presented with this situation frequently, the theorem applies to a structural possibility. Perceiving a group bestowing praise on itself gives the observer reason to be suspicious, to be on the alert, and to develop an initial hostile disposition or reactivate an existing one. This social function is likely if the two groups are in a situation of competition or confrontation, with the outgroup occupying a dominant position.

(2) To solidify the ingroup.

This social function depends upon an identification of the audience with the outgroup initiating the humor as a reference group or upon a specific interpretation of the humor as an appeal to a system of values or interests which both groups share.

(d) When the humor is judged as disparaging the outgroup, it may function in the two ways discussed as follows.
(1) To increase morale and solidify the ingroup.

A provisional rationale for this theorem is that the audience group's judgment indicates a share in the disapproval being symbolized by the humor; it may view the disparaging humor as action being taken against behavior which it also decries. The perception of such self-criticism may influence attitudes toward that outgroup and lead to a more favorable redefinition of the intergroup setting. This could invite modifications in the internal affairs of the ingroup.

(2) To introduce and foster a hostile disposition toward that outgroup.

This consequence would stem from a preexisting state of hostility or competition between the groups; the perception of self-disparaging humor is likely to reinforce prejudicial perceptions of the outgroup.

3. Intergroup Situation: Interaction

Basic Premise. Humor initiated in an intergroup situation functions in the interaction between groups depending upon how it is judged by both groups during the humorous exchange.

> (a) When the humor is judged as esteeming one of the groups, it may function in the two ways discussed as follows.
> (1) To foster consensus and social integration.

The consequences of humor for the intergroup relationship are comparable to those in the intragroup situation. Two alternatives are presented in this situation: The humor being exchanged esteems either the audience group or the initiating group. The former, and the more likely, is seen as predictive of consensus and integration. Humor esteeming the interacting partner has a tendency to minimize differences and maximize similarities between the groups. It indicates a sharing in certain social meanings and serves as an overture for friendly interaction. The mutual exchange of such humor symbolizes the opening (or the maintenance) of communication channels through which the groups convey information likely to bring them closer together or at least to a mutually agreeable stabilized relationship.

> (2) To foster disintegration of the relationship.

If either or both groups introduce humor judged as self-praising by the other (the second alternative), the consequences should differ from the above explanation unless a high degree of integration and stability already has been reached in the relationship. To illustrate by exaggeration, groups perceiving one another conveying egotistical humor may find their relationship strained to the point of confrontation and discover that they have little in common with one another to sustain a relationship.

> (b) When the humor is judged as disparaging one of the groups, it may function in the two ways discussed as follows.
> (1) To foster disintegration of the relationship.

Two alternative predictions are again considered. If both groups mutually participate in initiating humor which is judged by the other as disparaging the initiator's audience, humor acts as an abrasive to disrupt interaction, threaten the relationship, and possibly introduce intergroup conflict. Avoidance of these consequences would occur if the relationship itself were highly valued and sensitivities insulated from the abrasion or if license were a shared norm on such occasions. Instances of the latter occur when the relationship is critically necessary for some reason or when one group occupies a higher status entitling it to disparage the other humorously or "permit" the same overtly, by the lower status party (for example, Drake & Cayton, 1945, p. 273; Boskin, 1966).

(2) To redefine the relationship.

The subject or butt of the disparaging humor may be the ingroup itself. Judgments of humor as self-disparaging in an intergroup setting may have mixed consequences. If there is a mutual interpretation that each group is being critical of itself and not of the other, the humor is likely to minimize differences and accent a larger grouping or value system which both share and have used as the basis for self-criticism. The general function of humor would be one of reassessing and redefining the relationship. As Emerson (1969) has emphasized, humor can be utilized as a subtle means of negotiating in interpersonal relations.

The case of humor in the intergroup situation, particularly, points out that an important consideration in predicting the social functions of humor are the structural characteristics of the situation. As an example, we refer to the status of the participating groups (that is, their positions in the social order relative to one another prior to the initiation of humor). Their positions and past history of interaction form the relationship in which the humor takes place. Previously developed norms of the relationship now determine the amount of license in humor exchange and who may exercise it. The humor judgment and response of the audience depend on these shared expectations. Hammond's (1964) study (see p. 111, this chapter) exemplifies the type of research needed on such structural features surrounding the exchange of humor. He has suggested how the weight of differing features may influence the quantity of humor, its content, symmetry (or asymmetry), judgment, etc., and, therefore, the social functions of humor.

IV. Conclusion

In this chapter we have presented a model of the social functions of humor derivative from three structural situations. Each of these group situations has been described in terms of four variables which, when combined in sets, are used to delineate theorems representing the social functions. As a basic medium of communication, humor assumes many forms and its social functions become complex under the influence of other social processes and existing social structures. The model begins to handle these influences systematically to provide a basis for generating research hypotheses, as well as for additional theoretical formulations of humor functions. In the case of some theorems of the model, previous research was sufficient to predict the social functions of humor for given social conditions. But the status of the sociological study of humor leaves much to be done. The social functions of humor, as well as the general nature of variables affecting them, have been recognized and documented. There is need now for a broadened study of humor types with an emphasis on the delineation and measurement of variables affecting alternative functions of humor. Such research will enable refinement of our explanatory models and increase their predictive powers.

Acknowledgment

The author wishes to thank Dr. James Davidson of Purdue University and Dr. Mary Jo Seyler of Ohio Wesleyan University for their helpful comments on this chapter.

References

Arnez, N. L., & Anthony, C. B. Contemporary Negro humor as social satire. *Phylon,* 1968, 29, 339–346.

Barron, M. L. A content analysis of intergroup humor. *American Sociological Review,* 1950, 15, 88–94.

Blau, P. *The dynamics of bureaucracy.* Chicago, Illinois: Univ. of Chicago Press, 1955.

Boskin, J. Good-by, Mr. Bones. *The New York Times Magazine.* May 1, 1966, 31–92.

Bradney, P. The joking relationship in industry. *Human Relations,* 1957, 10, 179–187.

Burma, J. H. Humor as a technique in race conflict. *American Sociological Review,* 1946, 11, 710–715.

Christensen, J. B. Utani: Joking, sexual license, and social obligation among the Luguru. *American Anthropologist,* 1963, 65, 1314–1327.

Coser, R. L. Laughter among colleagues. *Psychiatry,* 1960, 23, 81–99.

Coser, R. L. *Life in the ward.* East Lansing, Michigan: Michigan State Univ. Press, 1962.

Davis, A., Gardner, B. B., & Gardner, M. P. *Deep south.* Chicago, Illinois: Univ. of Chicago Press, 1941.

Davis, J. A. Compositional effects, role systems, and the survival of small discussion groups. *Public Opinion Quarterly,* 1961, 25, 575–584.

Dollard, J. *Caste and class in a southern town.* New Haven, Connecticut: Yale Univ. Press, 1937.

Drake, S. C., & Cayton, H. *Black metropolis.* New York: Harcourt, 1945.

Emerson, J. P. Social functions of humor in a hospital setting. Unpublished doctoral dissertation. Univ. of California, Berkeley, 1963.

Emerson, J. Negotiating the serious import of humor. *Sociometry,* 1969, 32, 169–181.

Fox, R. C. *Experiment perilous, physicians and patients facing the unknown.* Glencoe, Illinois: Free Press, 1959.

Goldman, M. The sociology of Negro humor. Unpublished doctoral dissertation. New School for Social Research, 1960.

Goodchilds, J. D., & Smith, E. E. The wit and his group. *Human Relations,* 1964, 17, 23–31.

Hammond, P. B. Mossi joking. *Ethnology,* 1964, 3, 259–267.

Hannerz, U. *Soulside.* New York: Columbia Univ. Press, 1969.

Hayworth, D. The social origins and functions of laughter. *Psychological Review,* 1928, 35, 367–384.

Klapp, O. The fool as a social type. *American Journal of Sociology,* 1950, 55, 157–162.

La Fave, L. Humor judgments as a function of reference groups: An experimental study. Unpublished doctoral dissertation, Univ. of Oklahoma, 1961.

Levine, J. Regression in primitive clowning. *Psychoanalytic Quarterly,* 1961, 30, 72–83.

Levine, J. Humor. In D. L. Sills (Ed.), *International encyclopedia of the social sciences,* Vol. 7. New York: Macmillan, 1968.

Lewis, O. *The children of Sanchez.* New York: Vintage, 1961.

Martineau, W. H. A model for a theory of the function of humor. *Research Reports in the Social Sciences,* 1967, 1, 51–64.

Middleton, R. Negro and white reactions to racial humor. *Sociometry,* 1959, 22, 175–182.

Middleton, R., & Moland, J. Humor in Negro and white subcultures: A study of jokes among university students. *American Sociological Review,* 1959, 24, 61–69.

Miller, F. C. Humor in a Chippewa tribal council. *Ethnology,* 1967, 6, 263–271.

Moore, J. *Mexican Americans.* Englewood Cliffs, New Jersey: Prentice-Hall, 1970.

Myrdal, G. *An American dilemma.* New York: Harper, 1944.

Noel, D. L. Group identification among Negroes: An empirical analysis. *Journal of Social Issues,* 1964, 20, 71–74.

Obrdlik, A. J. Gallows humor—A sociological phenomenon. *American Journal of Sociology,* 1942, 47, 709–716.

Pitchford, H. G. The social functions of humor. Unpublished doctoral dissertation. Emory Univ., 1960.

Radcliffe-Brown, A. R. On joking relationships. *Africa,* 1940, 13, 195–210.

Radcliffe-Brown, A. R. A further note on joking relationships. *Africa,* 1949, 19, 133–140.

Radcliffe-Brown, A. R. *Structure and function in primitive society.* New York: Free Press, 1965.

Simpson, G., & Yinger, J. M. *Racial and cultural minorities.* New York: Harper, 1965.

Smith, N. V., & Vinacke, W. E. Reactions to humorous stimuli of different generations of Japanese, Chinese, and Caucasians in Hawaii. *Journal of Social Psychology,* 1951, 34, 69–96.

Stephenson, R. M. Conflict and control functions of humor. *American Journal of Sociology,* 1951, 56, 569–574.

Wolff, H. A., Smith, C. E., & Murray, H. A. The psychology of humor. I. A study of responses to race-disparagement jokes. *Journal of Abnormal and Social Psychology,* 1934, 28, 341–365.

Part III

EMPIRICAL ISSUES

Chapter 6

Physiological Correlates of Humor

Ronald Langevin

Clarke Institute of Psychiatry, Toronto, Ontario, Canada

and

H. I. Day

Department of Psychology
York University, Toronto, Ontario, Canada

I. Introduction

The presence of humor is frequently identified by visible signs of expenditure of energy such as smiling or laughter, together with the report of pleasurable affect. However, overt responses are not always present, for individuals may report a situation as comic or a joke as humorous without concommitant laughter or other common signs of amusement. It is also well known that people will laugh when tickled, in sympathy with others, under stress, or in otherwise seemingly inappropriate situations. Druckman and Chao (1957) found that in ten different cases of epilepsy, laughter or smiling was present immediately before or during epileptic convulsions. Many of the subjects in their study were children, but one who was able to discuss his feelings indicated that he experienced no humor or pleasure in this laughter. While these various observations suggest that laughter may serve as a general energy discharge, they also suggest that the discharge of energy is a correlate and not a sufficient condition of humor.

II. The Essence of Humor

Why do we so often laugh in humorous situations? Spencer (1916) stated that nervous excitation, in general, tends to beget muscular motion and that the discharge of such energy has habitual pathways. In the case of laughter, the natural pathways are in the face, in particular, in the eyes and mouth. This begs the question, for how do these habitual pathways become established?

One explanation is in terms of "set" or "attention". It is possible that comic situations are socially defined, e.g., "I am about to tell you a joke" or "so and so is a comedian [and therefore funny]," and we show signs of amusement in such situations. There is some support for this hypothesis. Martin (1905) found that preexposure to serious or sad pictures reduced the reported amusement for subsequently presented humor, while preexposure to silly or funny pictures enhanced it.

This hypothesis is also congruent with the approach of Schachter and Singer (1962), who proposed a two-factor theory of emotions in which heightened arousal is coupled with a set for a particular emotion. Schachter and Wheeler (1962) showed that a necessary condition in the appreciation of humor was an increase in arousal. They found that subjects who were injected with epinephrine found a movie more amusing than control subjects who were injected with saline and who, in turn, found the film more amusing than a third group injected with chlorpromazine. Thus increased arousal was associated with greater amusement, while the tranquilizing chlorpromazine was associated with reduced amusement. Following the increase in arousal level, the set for humor in the movie made it amusing.

It may be that while energy discharge in terms of laughter is not necessary in humor, increased arousal is always present. Thus, when an individual encounters a humorous stimulus, there may not always be an obvious discharge of energy, such as laughter, but some type of physiological change seems always to be present. Spencer (1916) reported, without any definitive empirical evidence, that when one is amused, the pulse quickens, there is muscular excitement, and breathing also becomes deeper and faster. He suggested that these movements are different from other gross movements in that they have no object.

In an empirical study, Martin (1905) found that respiration quickened and the pulse increased when subjects reported cartoons to be amusing. However, she used six sophisticated subjects and presented her results on a total of 20 observations, without any statistical analysis. Similarly, Wolff, Smith, and Murray (1934) measured laughter and GSR but failed to report physiological data. A more contemporary writer, Fry (1969a, 1969b; Fry & Stoft, in press) has repeatedly obtained similar results with heart rate (HR) and respiration but again failed to report statistical evidence. Thus, while anecdotal and suggestive evidence of physiological correlates of humor appreciation can be found in the literature, there does not seem to be a single definitive study to show the correlation of humor appreciation with physiological measures.*

A. INCONGRUITY AS A FACTOR IN HUMOR

If we accept the argument that physiological responses are a necessary but insufficient condition for humor, we must seek to explore the conditions under which humor will be aroused. As noted in Chapter 1, numerous such conditions have been advanced. One of the most commonly discussed conditions is that of incongruity. However, recent investigators, Nerhardt (1970), for example, have argued that the experience of humor is a function, not of simple incongruity, but rather of the degree of divergence of the situation from an expected state. Nerhardt found that variation in expectation of weights in a "psychophysical" experiment related significantly to the amount of laughter. Clark (1970) concluded that simple incongruity in a situation with expectation of humor is a necessary but insufficient condition to account for amusement. Spencer (1916)

---

* In 1933, Perl reviewed the literature up to that time and Berlyne (1969) reviewed it for the subsequent three decades. A 1967 bibliography of empirical studies in humor compiled by Treadwell offered a scant five pages of studies from 1897–1966, none of which examined GSR.

realized this in his earlier essays when he suggested that incongruity should be a "descending incongruity" in order to generate amusement.

III. Arousal: Humor and Curiosity

In 1960, Berlyne proposed a theory that integrated incongruity into a conflict and arousal model [see also Chapter 2]. He suggested that curiosity is a state of heightened arousal induced by the presence of high levels of collative variability in the stimulation. Included in collative variability are novelty, complexity, surprise, incongruity, and other conditions under which an expectation of the characteristics of a stimulus is violated. Berlyne posited that the presence of these variables induces conflict among competing response tendencies together with elevated arousal. Such a condition is aversive, and the organism explores to seek additional information that would allow the reduction of curiosity.

If we were to accept Spencer's (1916) notion that incongruity is the source of humor, we would then be required to compare the two concepts of humor and curiosity.

In fact the parallel between the two is quite strong. One of the characteristic ways of describing a curiosity-inducing stimulus is to call it "interesting" (Berlyne, 1963; Day, 1968). Certainly humorous stimuli are also perceived as interesting.

In a number of recent studies, we used a set of 15 pairs of slides, each pair consisting of a familiar situation and a similar but incongruous situation; for example, a traffic signal with cars stopped and moving was coupled with a traffic signal in the air with airplanes stopped and moving. Another example showed an ordinary door coupled with a door with handles and hinges on both edges. In one study children at all grade levels from kindergarten to grade 8 were asked to indicate the "more interesting" alternative in each pair. Thus the intention of the study was to judge developmental change in attitude toward incongruity and so examine the concept of curiosity. The explosive reactions to the stimuli in the form of laughter, shouting, and other indications of humor appreciation, especially among the primary-level children, were convincing evidence that the children were judging the material on a "humorous" as well as "interesting" basis. In fact, though no data were collected in this regard, it was also clearly evident that what was reacted to as funny was also judged interesting.

A second parallel between curiosity and humor may be seen in the effects of familiarity. Continued exposure to a novel stimulus makes it less interesting until finally exploration ceases (Berlyne, 1960). Similarly, Martin (1905) found that repeated presentations of a cartoon reduced a subject's laughter and enjoyment.

Third, in curiosity there is an expenditure of energy directed toward approach behavior and exploration of the source of stimulation, often taking the forms of touching, looking, questioning, etc. This is coupled with attention and positive affect. In the presence of a comic stimulus, there is a similar expenditure of energy in approach behavior coupled with attention and positive affect. The expenditure of energy may take the form of smiling, laughing, slapping of the thigh, etc.

Fourth, anecdotal reports suggest that both humor and curiosity may generate similar physiological reactions and arousal changes. Although little evidence has been reported for humor reactions, it has been indicated that these changes should be measurable in GSR's and changes in HR, blood pressure, etc.

Finally, the same collative variables do not arouse all individuals equally to be curious and explore. Individual experiences differ so that a particular stimulus may fail to surprise some or seem incongruous in some cases possibly because expectations are different. Also, the degree of incongruity may be too high (or low) for optimal interest in a particular situation; thus one may not consider it interesting or perceive it as incongruous. Similarly, a person may fail to find a joke funny because he does not "get the point." Sometimes the sophistication of an individual's sense of humor may be too high (low) for a particular joke or cartoon. For example, many of the stories children find amusing are not considered comic by adults. As Clark (1970) points out, humor involves *perceived* incongruity, just as Berlyne argues that perceived incongruity is necessary for curiosity.

Shellberg (1969), using Berlyne's theoretical position as a starting point, postulated that degree of humor is an inverted U-shaped function over the amount of arousal induced by collative variables. She claimed that for the relaxed person a cartoon is a momentary rise in arousal; for the moderately aroused person the arousal increase in the humor stimulus adds to the already present arousal from other sources, and thus he experiences a greater drop in arousal, greater pleasure, and much more humor. A highly aroused person is already experiencing uncomfortable stimulation, and adding arousal from a comic stimulus accents arousal rather than reduces it; thus he will either ignore the humor stimulus or find it unpleasant. Shellberg conducted an experiment in which she attempted to manipulate arousal conditions to illustrate this theory. She compared students under five levels of arousal: relaxed; low, moderate, high, and extreme. The relaxed subjects were relaxing on campus between classes or during lunch hour. The low aroused subjects were in a typical classroom situation, while moderately aroused subjects met before midterm or the start of final examinations. Highly aroused subjects rated the cartoons prior to taking a final examination, while extremely aroused subjects rated the cartoons immediately before writing the examination. As predicted, she found an inverted U-shaped relationship between level of arousal and judged humor of the cartoons.

One question remains: Why do some incongrous stimuli induce curiosity while others induce humor? Presumably, both types of stimuli generate some arousal increment, and positive affect; yet the resultant behavior is somewhat different. The answer may be in the availability of a solution. In stimuli that induce humor, the total information, including the punch line, must be available quickly; otherwise the joke is not funny. Goldstein (1970), for example, found that jokes rated as more humorous had shorter latencies of response. On the other hand, when the situation does not allow an immediate answer or resolution of the incongruity, curiosity is aroused and exploration results. A riddle or joke that drags on too long is not considered funny.

Thus it appears that both curiosity and humor may have a large number of common characteristics: Both are induced by incongruity; both are arousing; both result in response conflict; both become less attractive with repetition; and both induce arousal-reducing behavior. The differences between these states may lie in the set in which the stimulus is presented (as "interesting" or "funny"), the length of time the arousal is allowed to remain at an elevated level, and the suddenness with which arousal is reduced.

One gap in this exposition is the failure to pin down physiological correlates to humor through studies that would parallel those showing the relationship between curiosity and measures of physiological change. While some writers present anecdotal evidence of physiological changes with humor appreciation, there is a dearth of statistical evidence to tie these together. Thus the main goal of our study was to test the theoretical positions of Berlyne (1969) and Shellberg (1969) and obtain evidence for our own thinking in this area.

In line with these theoretical formulations, the following hypotheses were derived.

1. Within limits, physiological responses would vary directly with the rated humor of a set of cartoons. Cartoons rated as neutral on a scale of humor would evoke little physiological response. With increasing ratings of humor, physiological activity would increase. However, cartoons rated as unpleasant would evoke the largest amount of physiological reaction. Responses would be measured by changes in GSR amplitude and BSR, and increases in HR.

2. If arousal were prolonged unduly, even in a supposedly comic situation, the stimulus would be rated as unpleasant rather than funny.

3. Recovery time for GSR amplitude would be an increasing function of rated humor. Unpleasant cartoons, however, would be related to an even longer recovery time.

4. The number of GSR's would be linearly related to judged funniness.

5. As humor ratings increased, latencies of physiological response would decrease.

This last hypothesis follows findings by Goldstein (1970), who showed that latencies of overt humor responses were shorter for the more humorous cartoons. Scofield (cited by Perl, 1933) also reported that the longer the period of preparation, the less hearty was the laughter.

There are many methodological problems in studying both humor and physiological measures. First, there is the problem of the generality of humor appreciation. In a factor-analytic study of humor, Eysenck (1942) found that a single factor of humor appreciation accounted for 19.4% of the total variance. This appears to be too small a proportion of the variance to argue that there is a general factor of humor appreciation. Therefore, in selecting stimuli for a humor study, it is necessary to obtain a range of materials from different individuals in order to ensure that some cartoons will be funny, whereas others may not. Second, since humor appreciation is highly subjective and physiological reactions extremely variable from one individual to another, it is more reasonable to use a within-subject design (Wickens & Harding, 1965). Thus the present study was designed so that the same subjects rated cartoons for humorousness and were measured for GSR and HR.

IV. An Experimental Study

A. METHOD

Subjects

Sixteen student child-care workers (eight men and eight women) at a local psychiatric hospital served as *S*s. Data from one female *S* were excluded because she misunderstood the instructions.

Materials and Apparatus

Twelve cartoons (with captions) were selected from 1000 clipped from current magazines. Four judges—three women and a man—rated all the cartoons for "humorousness," and the 12 for which highest concordance among judges was found were selected for the study. Two of these cartoons served as practice slides and the other ten were designated as experimental stimuli.

A Carousel projector was used to present the slide materials, and the times of presentation of stimuli were recorded on a Beckman model RF dynograph event pen. Physiological measures were recorded on PGR coupler model 9892A and Cardiotach coupler model 9857. Beckman electrodes with electrode paste were placed on the palm and back of the left hand for GSR measures, and others were placed just below the elbow on the inside of each arm for HR measures. An ear-clip electrode was also used to ground the *S* to the shielded room in which the experiment took place.

Procedure

Subjects were told that the purpose of the study was to examine physiological correlates of humor, and they were assured that the electrodes were harmless and they would experience no sensation from them.

After a 10-min hydration period for GSR and HR electrodes, the following instructions were given:

> You will see 10 cartoons on the screen before you. Rate each slide on the following scale when it disappears from the screen. If you find the cartoon very humorous, call out a "+3"; somewhat humorous, call out a "+2"; slightly humorous, "+1"; and not at all humorous, that is, neutral, call out a "0." If you find the cartoon very unpleasant, call out "−3"; somewhat unpleasant, "−2"; slightly unpleasant, "−1."

The *S*s were provided with a card showing the scale and were told to rest as quietly as possible. Two practice slides were used to ensure that the Ss understood the instructions and to overcome "warm-up effects" of the cartoons (Martin, 1905). Then the Ss were shown 10 cartoons while GSR and HR were recorded. Each cartoon was presented for 15 sec with a 15-sec interval between cartoons. The order of presentation of cartoons was randomized across subjects.

The following measures were taken for each cartoon presentation.

1. GSR conductance change $\times 10^6$.
2. Number of GSRs.
3. Latency to first GSR (the time between onset of the stimulus cartoon and the start of the first GSR).
4. Latency to largest GSR (the time between onset of the stimulus cartoon and the start of the largest GSR).
5. Basal skin resistance (BSR) at the start of each trial.
6. Change in BSR from stimulus onset to offset, which is a component of the GSR distinct from amplitude (Duffy, 1962) and offers an additional useful measure.
7. Mean recovery time GSR (the total time from onset of the GSR till its return to its previous level or to the original rate of change occurring prior to the GSR). This measure was used by Mednick (1962) and discriminated schizophrenic and normal reactions to stress.
8. Mean change in HR—average from minimum and maximum peaks of response for each stimulus (Lazarus & Opton, 1966).
9. Maximum HR response for each stimulus.
10. Minimum HR response for each stimulus.

B. RESULTS

Each measure was changed to standard scores within Ss to reduce measurement artifacts (cf. Lacey, 1956). This also provided ipsative measures which appear to have greater generality and reliability than group comparisons (Sidman, 1960). Thus a score would be

$$R_{is} = \frac{X_{is} - \bar{X}_s}{\sigma_s}$$

where

R_{is} = Z score for a given response i, for a given subject s;
X_{is} = raw score for a given response i, for the subject s;
$\bar{X}_s$ = mean raw response for s;
σ_s = standard deviation of the raw scores for s.

Subjects did not use all seven rating categories equally and the ratings were collapsed into four groups: aversive (−), neutral (0), slightly humorous (+), and very humorous (+ +). The modal rating was 6 on the 7-point scale.

An analysis of variance was performed for each of the ten physiological measures. Table I shows the values for each analysis of variance as well as the mean scores for −, 0, +, and + + ratings.

Of the GSR measures, "BSR start" was not significant suggesting that Ss were approaching each stimulus with approximately equal basal rates. Differences in change in BSR were also not significant, but GSR amplitude and recovery time were significant. A

TABLE I

The Relationship between Humor Ratings and GSR and HR Measures

	Measure	Analysis of variance F values (df = 3, 132)	−	0	+	++
	GSR					
1.	Amplitude in conductance units x 10^6	3.51*	−.144	+.116	+.223	+.306
2.	Number of responses	<1	+.082	+.104	+.092	−.044
3.	Latency to first response	2.02†	−.194	+.048	−.210	+.206
4.	Latency to largest response	1.24†	+.106	+.040	−.253	+.163
5.	BSR start	<1	+.224	−.058	−.039	+.016
6.	Change in BSR	<1	+.398	+.028	−.124	+.034
7.	Mean recovery time	5.30**	−2.200	+.052	−.342	+.328
	HR					
8.	Mean change	2.67*	+.015	+.104	−.310	+.215
9.	Maximum response	3.63*	−.406	−.075	−.209	+.322
10.	Minimum response	1.17†	−.294	+.204	+.081	−.117

* *p* < .05.   ** *p* < .01.   † Not significant.

Newman–Keuls test on the means of −, 0, +, and + + (Winer, 1962, p. 78) showed that the four means were not clearly distinct but rather overlapped with the other means. Amplitude of GSR increased from unpleasant cartoons to most humorous ones. Similarly, recovery time increased across those conditions, but this may be accounted for by the close association between amplitude and recovery time. Thus it appears that changes in amplitude of GSR were significantly related to humor ratings.

Latency to the first GSR failed to show significant differences; therefore latency to the largest response was examined. Again results failed to reach significance. The number of GSR's was also not significantly different across conditions.

Heart rate data offered support for the hypotheses. Mean change in HR was significant, and again a tendency was found for HR to increase from − to + + replicating Martin's (1905) finding. Lacey, Kagen, Lacey, and Moss (1963) suggested that HR deceleration occurs when one attends to external inputs (environmental intake), whereas internal tasks (rejection of the environment), such as mental arithmetic, produce cardiac acceleration. Similarly, pleasant stimuli produce cardiac deceleration, while those that are unpleasant produce acceleration. Thus minima and maxima were examined separately as measures of deceleration and acceleration, respectively.

Analysis of variance showed significant differences for maximum response but not for minimum response. Since mean HR consists of minima and maxima combined, these results suggest that HR deceleration did not contribute significantly to the scores. Rather HR acceleration, i.e., arousal increase, was the important factor. Like GSR amplitude, means of HR changes overlapped when examined by a Newman–Keuls test. Since the largest mean HR was 84.66 b.p.m. and the largest mean change was 10.07 b.p.m., it seems that moderate increases in arousal are positively associated with humor ratings. As in the Johnson and Campos (1967) study, the Lacey *et al.* (1963) hypotheses of HR acceleration and deceleration functions were not confirmed.

V. Discussion

The main finding in this study is that physiological changes included within the construct of arousal are positively and significantly related to subjective evaluations of humor. Galvanic skin response amplitude was positively correlated with humor appreciation, lending some support for Berlyne's (1969) and Shellberg's (1969) positions that moderate changes in arousal are reinforcing even if not followed quickly by arousal reduction. However, physiological change was not a U-shaped function of humor–unpleasantness ratings. In fact, "unpleasant" cartoons produced the smallest responses rather than the largest. However, since the cartoons had been chosen solely for their comic value, it may be that no strongly aversive stimuli had been included. A better test of the recovery hypothesis might be to compare humorous, strongly aversive, and neutral stimuli.

The results offer empirical support for the anecdotal statements of Spencer (1916) and for the work of Martin (1905) and Fry (1969a, 1969b). The results showed an increase in arousal even without an obvious external discharge of energy such as smiling and laughing. This result parallels the findings that collative variables influence arousal in curiosity situations (see Berlyne, Borsa, Homacher, & Koenig, 1966).

No support was found for Goldstein's (1970) position that latency of response is related to degree of humor. However, Goldstein used group ratings of complexity and humor, whereas the cartoons in this study were rated solely for humor, and results were analyzed using an individual's own evaluations. Moreover, Goldstein recorded skeletal muscle responses (reaction time), whereas we concentrated on physiological responses which may build up gradually beginning with anticipation of the joke.

In order to compare Goldstein's study with the present results, we had three judges rate our cartoons for complexity and three judges rate them for incongruity. On 7-point scales, the mean complexity rating was 2.5, while the mean incongruity rating was 5.2. This suggests that the cartoons in the present study were generally very simple but high in incongruity. Therefore Goldstein's cartoons and ours may have been incomparable because they emphasized different characteristics of cartoons.

While GSR and HR both indicate that arousal increase is positively correlated with humor ratings, it could be argued that arousal change is an epiphenomenon and merely a concomitant of the humorous situation, an argument that would parallel that of the controversy in the area of curiosity. The test of these alternative explanations could only be accomplished by testing individual subjects under conditions of low and high arousal, the manipulation of which would be under control of the experimenter and would be extrinsic to the nature of the subject's task. This has been attempted in curiosity studies where the responses were exploratory behavior and learning (cf. Berlyne *et al.*, 1966; Day, 1967; Day & Llewellyn Thomas, 1967; Kleinsmith & Kaplan, 1964), and a body of evidence has been accumulated that lends credence to the view that change in arousal is not merely concomitant, but essential, to the appreciation of humor. Similarly, Schachter and Wheeler (1962) have shown that arousal changes induced by drugs are closely related to humor appreciation. While this does not answer the question of whether the arousal is an epiphenomenon or a causal agent, it does support the contention that it is a necessary condition of humor. It remains yet to be demonstrated that humor can reinforce learning and shares properties of reinforcement with other stimuli such as collative variables, brain stimulation, etc. Thus, while the present study offers some support for an arousal interpretation of humor, many questions have been raised which remain unanswered.

Acknowledgment

The authors wish to thank Cathy Spegg, for programming services, and Gail Posluns, for assistance in data tabulation.

References

Berlyne, D. E. *Conflict, arousal and curiosity.* New York: McGraw-Hill, 1960.

Berlyne, D. E. Complexity and incongruity variables as determinants of exploratory choice and evaluative ratings. *Canadian Journal of Psychology*, 1963, 17, 274–290.

Berlyne, D. E. Laughter, humor and play. In G. Lindzey & E. Aronson (Eds.), *Handbook of social psychology.* (2nd ed.) Vol. 3. Reading, Massachusetts: Addison-Wesley, 1969.

Berlyne, D. E., Borsa, D. N., Homacher, J. S., & Koenig, I. D. V. Paired-associate learning and the time of arousal. *Journal of Experimental Psychology*, 1966, 72, 1–6.

Clark, M. Humour and incongruity. *Philosophy: Journal of the Royal Institute of Philosophy*, 1970, 45, 20–32.

Day, H. I. The effects of increased arousal on attention in high and low anxious subjects. *Ontario Journal of Educational Research*, 1967, 9, 185–191.

Day, H. I. Preference: Interest or pleasure. Paper presented at the meeting of Canadian Psychological Association. Calgary, 1968.

Day, H. I., & Llewellyn Thomas, E. Effects of amphetamine on selective attention. *Perceptual and Motor Skills*, 1967, 24, 1119–1125.

Druckman, R., & Chao, D. Laughter in epilepsy. *Neurology*, 1957, 7, 26–36.

Duffy, E. *Activation and behavior.* New York: Wiley, 1962.

Eysenck, H. J. The appreciation of humour: An experimental and theoretical study. *British Journal of Psychology*, 1942, 32, 295–309.

Fry, W. F., Jr. Humor in a physiologic vein. *News of physiological instrumentation*, Beckman Laboratory, July 1969. (a)

Fry, W. F., Jr. Instinctual and physiologic bases of the humor experience. Paper presented at symposium proceedings at the meeting of the Western Psychological Association, Vancouver, Sept. 1969.   (b)

Fry, W. F., Jr., & Stoft, P. Mirth and oxygen saturation levels of peripheral blood. *Psychotherapy and Psychosomatics*, 1971, 19(1), 76–84.

Goldstein, J. H. Humor appreciation and time to respond. *Psychological Reports*, 1970, 27, 445–446.

Johnson, H., & Campos, J. The effect of cognitive tasks and verbalization instructions on heart rate and skin conductance. *Psychophysiology*, 1967, 4, 143–150.

Kleinsmith, L. J., & Kaplan, S. Interaction of arousal and recall in nonsense syllable paired-associate learning. *Journal of Experimental Psychology*, 1964, 67, 124–126.

Lacey, J. The evaluation of autonomic responses: Toward a general solution. *Annals of the New York Academy of Sciences*, 1956, 67(5), 123–164.

Lacey, J., Kagan, J., Lacey, B., and Moss, H. The visceral level: Situational determinants and behavioral correlates of autonomic response patterns. In P. Knapp (Ed.), *Expression of the emotions in man*. New York: International Universities Press, 1963.

Lazarus, R., & Opton, E. The study of psychological stress: A summary of theoretical formulations and experimental findings. In C. Spielberger (Ed.), *Anxiety and behavior*. New York: Academic Press, 1966.

Martin, L. J. Psychology of aesthetics: Experimental prospecting in the field of the comic. *American Journal of Psychology*, 1905, 16, 35–116.

Mednick, S. A. Schizophrenia: A learned thought disorder. In G. Nielson (Ed.), *Proceedings of the 14th International Congress of Applied Psychology*, 1962, 4, 167–178.

Nerhardt, G. Humor and inclination to laugh: Emotional reactions to stimuli of different divergence from a range of expectancy. *Scandinavian Journal of Psychology*, 1970, 11, 185–195.

Perl, R. E. A review of experiments on humor. *Psychological Bulletin*, 1933, 30, 752–763.

Schachter, S., & Singer, J. Cognitive, social and physiological determinants of emotional state. *Psychological Review*, 1962, 69, 379–399.

Schachter, S., & Wheeler, L. Epinephrine, chlorpromazine and amusement. *Journal of Abnormal and Social Psychology*, 1962, 65, 121–128.

Scofield, H. A. The psychology of laughter. Unpublished master's essay, Columbia Univ., 1921, 1–66.

Shellberg, L. Arousal and humor preference: A theoretical formulation and empirical test. Paper presented at the meeting of the Western Psychological Association, Vancouver, Sept. 1969.

Sidman, M. *Tactics in scientific research*. New York: Basic Book, 1960.

Spencer, H. On the physiology of laughter. In *Essays on education*. London: Everyman's Library, 1916.

Treadwell, Y. Bibliography of empirical studies of wit and humor. *Psychological Reports*, 1967, 20, 1079–1083.

Wickens, D., & Harding, G. Effects of UCS strength on GSR conditioning: A within-subject design. *Journal of Experimental Psychology*, 1965, 70(2), 151–153.

Winer, B. J. *Statistical principles in experimental design*. New York: McGraw Hill, 1962.

Wolff, H. A., Smith, C. E., & Murray, H. A. The psychology of humor. I. A study of responses to race-disparagement jokes. *Journal of Abnormal and Social Psychology*, 1934, 28, 341–365.

Chapter 7

The Relationship between Arousal Potential and Funniness of Jokes

Michael Godkewitsch

Department of Psychology
University of Toronto, Toronto, Ontario, Canada

I. Arousal and Appreciation of Humor

A. LITERATURE

A small number of investigators have tried to relate the concept of arousal to the phenomenon of humor. These investigators have sought to establish some relationship between subjects' momentary arousal level and the extent to which they appreciate different kinds of humorous stimuli. The arousal level of a subject was sometimes understood to be dependent upon a set of relatively permanent traitlike properties of the subject, but most often it was operationalized in the form of an ephemeral arousal state induced by some experimental treatment extraneous to the subject or the humorous stimuli. In the latter case, the subject's momentary arousal state was assumed to motivate him in some predictable fashion, dependent upon the investigator's theoretical stand.

In most of the papers the basic hypothesis has been that if exposure to humorous stimuli leads to a positive affect in a subject, his drive state or tensions are reduced. This hypothesis appears to be common to psychoanalytically oriented, cognitive, and behavior theorists, and to authors who regard the appreciation of humor as a coping mechanism. The main findings in the body of research concerning this problem are rather inconclusive. But one may tentatively differentiate between conditions purporting to induce a moderate level of arousal in the subject and those aiming to arouse him highly. It appears then, from the literature, that a high level of arousal generally results in no greater appreciation of jokes compared with a habitual level of arousal (Byrne, 1961; O'Connell, 1960; Shellberg, 1969a, b; Young & Frye, 1966). A moderate level of arousal, induced by a hostile or aggressive treatment (Dworkin & Efran, 1967; Sears, Hovland, & Miller, 1940; Singer, 1968; Singer, Gollob, & Levine, 1967; Strickland, 1959; Tollefson, 1961), an inadequacy treatment (Williams & Cole, 1964), anxiety-inducing manipulations (Shellberg, 1969a, b; Shurcliff, 1968; but not Hom, 1966; Hammes & Wiggins, 1962), or the presentation of sexual stimuli (Davis & Farina, 1970; Lamb, 1968; Strickland, 1959) mostly result in a greater amount of appreciation for subsequent humorous stimuli (but not Goldstein, 1970). According to Shellberg (1969a) the basic data can be explained by the "inverted U-shaped curve" hypothesis: The relation between the arousal state of the subject and his appreciation of humor is curvilinear, rather than monotonic, and includes a downturn in the curve. In other words, an individual whose activation state is at a moderate level is best able to enjoy humorous stimuli, whereas individuals at either a low or very high level of activation are at a disadvantage in this respect [see Chapter 2].

The ubiquitous inverted U-shaped relation between some measure of drive state and some behavioral parameter probably represents a basic neurophysiological or, if one wishes, psychophysiological system. Through this complex regulatory system the effectiveness, integration, and adaptiveness of behavior is constantly monitored and guaranteed over an extremely wide range of possible stimulus situations. The actual value of some behavioral index is determined by the resultant of a multitude of factors constituting the organism's drive state, which is here called its arousal state. Each of these factors, whether associated with the organism itself (like primary and secondary drives) or inherent in the stimulus situation (like collative properties of stimuli), contributes some arousal to the resultant level. We assume that arousal potential is the operative factor of such stimulus situations and the means through which we can study how the various sources of arousal within and without an organism compound to achieve its momentary level.

The classical Yerkes–Dodson law is one formulation of the system mentioned. Relating drive and motivation to performance, it holds that optimum performance is achieved at an intermediate level of drive. It expresses basically the same relation that Malmo (1959) and Hebb (1955) later were to call the relation between drive and performance.

One important determinant of arousal level is emotion, which according to Spence (1956), acts as a drive. Another permissible basic assumption is that the feedback stimulation from behavior manifested on a level at, or close to, its optimal effectiveness and integration is experienced as very pleasant. (There may be exceptions, but then the disturbing factor lies outside the immediate actions of the organism.) Thus, one may argue, positive hedonic tone, according to Eysenck (1967) "the desire to prolong the stimulation, or even to increase it," is defined in terms of a particular total momentary amount of arousal. This would lead us to expect a curvilinear relation between hedonic tone, or pleasure, and arousal level similar to the Yerkes–Dodson law. To the extent that this arousal level is validly operationalized and measurable in terms of arousal potential of a set of experimental stimuli, it is conceivable that such a relation should obtain between pleasure, arising from the enjoyment of humor, and the jokes' arousal potential.

Of course the hypothesized relation of arousal potential and humor appreciation should not indiscriminately be equated with the Yerkes–Dodson law. Although the parallels have been sketched, the dependent variables are quite different. Performance of motor acts—on which the original law was based—and humor appreciation are not the same, nor are arousal potential and task difficulty, or drive, identical. Also, at very high arousal levels deterioration of performance in the overt, motor sense is seen as an interference phenomenon, while in humor experiments the downturn in the curve is interpreted as an inhibitory process. Eysenck's (1967) version of the relation posits "degrees of sensory stimulation" as the determinant of hedonic tone. Sensory stimulation undoubtedly codetermines the arousal potential of the stimulus situation and can therefore be compared with the drive dimension of the Yerkes–Dodson law in its modern version.

All the evidence for the hypothesized relationship can be brought back to the described mechanism dealing with the influence of drive or arousal on performance or hedonic tone. Some of the evidence is presented by Singer (1968) and Shellberg (1969a). Other support comes from cognitive theory: Zigler, Levine, and Gould (1967) find such a relation to obtain between appreciation and complexity of jokes. Complexity, as a collative variable, directly influences arousal (Berlyne, 1967). Levine and Abelson (1959) and Levine and Redlich (1960) reasoned, from a psychoanalytic point of view, that in jokes which arouse anxiety, the themes may be appreciated but suppress a hedonic response when the content of the joke is very threatening for the subject. Finally, Ullman and Lim (1962) note that evaluation of stimuli as humorous is likely a function of drive and habit strength. Nerhardt (1970) shows that the discrepancy of new stimuli from an established intensity level (inducing arousal) has a direct influence on the probability of these stimuli being found funny or mirth provoking.

B. CRITICISM

The relationship between arousal and humor appreciation is still far from clear. What determines a person's response to an allegedly funny stimulus is, however, reasonably well described and agreed upon: The two main factors are characteristics of the person and properties of the stimulus—excluding, for the moment, social aspects of the environment. In this study characteristics of the subject will be operationalized in terms of his permanent arousal level, and the properties of the joke stimuli in terms of arousal potential.

Before establishing a relation between the arousal potential and funniness of jokes, we must clarify what we mean by arousal. According to Berlyne (1967) arousal can well be regarded as a dimension describing the overall activity level of an organism. It must "be defined through its relations with both antecedent (input) and consequent (output) variables [p. 12]." It should be understood that the arousal dimension has a number of determining factors, as already argued.

Arousal conditions or treatments have been input variables in most of the aforementioned studies. These studies resulted in establishing some relationship between arousal conditions as independent variables and appreciation of humorous stimuli, presented under the various arousal conditions, as dependent variables. Such an experimental procedure is not objectionable if an independent check on the effectiveness of the experimental variable shows that it has affected the subject's arousal level as intended. Contradictory results from different humor studies can be partly explained by the lack of such control. Tollefson (1961) has shown how vital proper control (urged by, among others, Dworkin & Efran, 1967, and Shellberg, 1969a) can be. He exposed his subjects to one of four arousal conditions. One group saw a burlesque film, meant to induce sexual arousal; another heard a threatening lecture, meant to induce anxiety; a third group was subjected to both treatments; a fourth to neither. A subsequent measure of subjects' motivation showed no significant differences in the level of sexual or anxiety motivation, thus accounting for a lack of difference in earlier measured humor appreciation of the groups.

Even if the impact of the arousal treatment can be measured, the relation between the arousal potential of the humor stimuli and their funniness is not clarified. To that purpose one obviously has to measure the arousal potential of the joke as a dependent variable before using it as an independent variable. As yet this procedure has hardly been tried. Langevin and Day [Chapter 6] offer one good approach to the problem of measuring arousal potential. Tollefson (1961) tried to manipulate the arousal potential of jokes by altering their contents in the direction of a more arousing situation. A neutral joke, for instance, could become more arousing for a religious subject by substituting a clergyman for a neutral person as the butt of the joke. Tollefson found no difference between funniness ratings of the neutral and changed jokes by subjects who were and were not involved in religion.

The relationship between subjects' humor preference and arousal level can be clarified only if the various arousal conditions are comparable, i.e., differ only in strength and not in other respects. Unfortunately, this is difficult to achieve. Many variables contribute to the arousal level, and two treatments aiming to arouse an organism differentially are very likely to differ in more than one respect. Therefore, even if the arousal conditions in one experiment were quantitatively defined, they often were qualitatively very different. An example is Shellberg's (1969b) experiment. She employed a high arousal condition, conceptualized by testing subjects ½ hour before a term examination, and planned a postarousal condition for a subject group after another examination. That night Senator Robert F.

Kennedy was killed, and the subjects were run before the examination instead of after it. The latter subject group was now considered to be in the extreme stress condition, i.e., the treatment resulting in, supposedly, the highest level of arousal. Other conditions that Shellberg used were, for example, sitting on a bench on campus between classes, in class, etc. The confirmation of her hypothesis of an inverted U-shaped curve, relating arousal level and humor appreciation, rests on the assumption that the conditions applied can be differentiated on at least an ordinal arousal scale. Not discounting her results, we note that there is no definite evidence that this assumption can safely be made without independent proof of a quantitative difference between the levels of arousal induced by the treatments. It seems, in general, unwarranted to postulate unidimensionality of arousal on an *a priori* basis, and it is certainly unwise to impose such unidimensionality on data instead of extracting it from experimental results. Furthermore, in experiments where unidimensionality is likely, it has been implicitly assumed that the different conditions used represented equidistant points on the arousal continuum (Shellberg, 1969b; Shurcliff, 1968). Again, such an assumption remains to be supported.

The discussion about arousal and humor appreciation has been hampered by some confusion of terms. The studies described have purported to manipulate arousal. They have only shown, however, that humor varies with variables *included in* arousal potential and not with arousal itself. The latter is the result of stimulation, not its antecedent or determinant. And although arousal seems to increase with arousal potential, within certain limits, these variables are almost certainly not linearly related (Berlyne, 1963, p. 319; Hunt, 1963, p. 79). Arousal is brought about through the effect of arousal potential, and the latter must be operationalized and precisely quantified as an independent variable. If this is not done, no comparison of strengths of arousing treatments across and within experiments is logically possible. A given amount of stimulation may be called moderate by one author and highly or little arousing by another, and then only if the treatments are qualitatively similar. Mostly the contrary has been the case: Operationalizations of arousal conditions have been radically diverse. When, for instance, the relation between aggression arousal and the appreciation of aggressive jokes is the topic of study, it is doubtful whether looking at pictures of brutal and cruel war scenes (Singer, Gollob, & Levine, 1967) induces the same kind and amount of emotionality or arousal as letting the subject wait in an empty room for 20 min or treating him in an insulting manner (Strickland, 1959).

Another difficulty encountered in pertinent research has been the confined range of arousal conditions that experimenters may use. The usual ethical standards limit this range to such an extent that the role of humor in very highly arousing conditions is only partially known. Because one has to rely on incidental information (e.g., P.O.W. camp jokes) or semistructured experiments like Shellberg's (1969b) study, the debunking of hypotheses concerning the relation between arousal and humor appreciation at the extremes of the arousal scale is almost impossible. Such hypotheses are not only theoretically but also practically important. Lazarus (1966) and Keller (1966) describe how humor can function as a coping mechanism under extreme arousal conditions: It should prove fruitful to pursue experimentation in this direction.

C. PERSONALITY AND THE EFFECT OF AROUSAL POTENTIAL OF STIMULI

Humor appreciation seems to be related to the strength of particular personality traits. Williams (1946) found that children with a high appreciation of humor were extroverts rather than introverts. Verinis (1970) showed that introverts are more inhibited in their responses to humor than extroverts. Eysenck (1942, 1967), having found a similar phenomenon, explained it in terms of individual differences in excitation and inhibition. Introverts have a lower threshold for sensory stimulation than extroverts. Any given degree of stimulation would thus be experienced as effectively higher by introverts than by extroverts. The level of stimulation, or arousal potential, resulting in an optimal hedonic tone is relatively low for an introvert and relatively high for an extrovert in comparison with an ambivert or the population average. In other words, an introvert, already moderately aroused, can appreciate only stimuli that do not arouse him too much more. He will prefer a moderately arousing joke over one with a high arousal potential, whereas the extrovert will prefer the opposite. If one adheres to the inverted U-shaped relation between arousal potential and hedonic tone, one may hypothesize that the shape of this curve will be of the same general form for both personality types, but that the inflection point of the curve for introverts will fall at a point on the arousal-potential continuum indicative of a lower level of arousal than that for extroverts.

Discrimination of subjects on the basis of their habitual arousal level makes good sense if one wishes to clarify the relation of arousal potential of stimuli to their hedonic value, for this relation may well be obscured and even swamped by differences between subjects (Eysenck, 1967, pp. 26ff).

Shellberg (1969a, b) found the hypothesized curve without making such a distinction. It should be clear, however, that what she calls arousal is actually an interaction product of the arousal potential of her treatments and her subjects' habitual arousal level. It is reasonable to hypothesize a similarly shaped relation between the arousal potential of the joke stimuli and their judged funniness.

II. Measurement

Taking the preceding criticisms into account, we must find an experimental technique which offers an opportunity to relate measured arousal potential of jokes to their funniness for subjects having characteristically high and low levels of arousal. The jokes' arousal potentials must be measured independently of their funniness; the jokes must generate the same kind of arousal in order to create a unidimensional continuum; the distances between the arousal potentials of the joke stimuli must be known; and the range of arousal potentials must be as large as possible.

In principle, such a technique is found in a scaling experiment, in which joke stimuli are scaled independently for arousal potential and funniness.

The funniness scale forms no serious problem. Although funniness is undoubtedly a multidimensional affair, as shown in factor analyses by Andrews (1943), Cattell (1957), and Eysenck (1943), it appears (see Godkewitsch, 1968a) that subjects have no problem at all in rank-ordering jokes quite reliably for funniness.

Arousal potential is a different matter: It has to be operationalized in a sensible way before it can be scaled. We assume that it is the theme of the joke and its strength that determine its arousal potential. There are only a few basic joke themes, as every entertainer will maintain, and the only theme that seems relatively pure, in the sense that jokes containing this theme tend to be massed in one factor in factor analyses (Andrews, 1943; Cattell, 1957), is sex.

The property of unidimensionality of sex jokes has two important advantages for measurement: First, a scale, constructed by means of some scaling technique, will represent the true distances between the stimuli, rather than the projections of actually multidimensional stimuli on a unidimensional scale of the measured attribute (cf. Coombs, 1964, p. 346); second, not only is the arousal potential of sex jokes determined by the same factor, but also the funniness scale based on the same stimuli is likely to be just about unidimensional. Andrews (1943), using the method of equal-appearing intervals to obtain scale values for the funniness of jokes, did not consider the dimensionality of his jokes, and neither did La Gaipa (1968) when he applied the same technique to scale his jokes for aggression. Another problem with this method is that variability between subjects is considered error, while precisely such differences should form the basic data for scaling the stimuli. Finally, the method of equal-appearing intervals assumes that the observational data are of an interval or ratio level. In humor research, it seems advisable not to assume such properties (cf. Godkewitsch, 1968b).

Using sex jokes exclusively avoids the saliency effect of the theme, as suggested by Goldstein, Suls, and Anthony [Chapter 8]. They argue that the saliency of a particular theme, rather than a motivational state induced by some arousing treatment, determines preference for jokes containing that theme. In our experiment saliency of theme as contrasted with other themes cannot be a factor, since all jokes contain the same basic theme.

An additional advantage of sex jokes is that they offer an opportunity to extend the range of arousal potential relatively far through the use of jokes with a very high sexual content and the running of male subjects only. The latter is also necessitated by findings (Godkewitsch, 1968a; Williams, 1946) indicating a much lower reliability and consistency of females.

Finally, scaling eliminates the need for an independent measure of the arousal potential of the jokes, since the data used for scaling form the dependent variable of that stage of the experiment.

When stimuli of this kind are scaled on an explicit attribute, the actual technique used demands a stimulus-centered approach (Torgerson, 1958, p. 46). Paired comparison data, being preference judgments between two stimuli on one attribute, are rather reliable. This points to the law of comparative judgment (Torgerson, 1958, p. 192) as the most useful and easily applicable technique, because rank orderings may be employed to collect data for this method instead of paired comparisons. It is assumed that, in ranking stimuli, the subject compares each stimulus with every other one, and the scales thus derived are equal to those obtained from paired comparison data. This method requires much less effort from the subject, especially when many stimuli are involved, and is advisable for stimuli that are sensitive to multiple exposure, like jokes.

Thurstone's law of comparative judgment (Thurstone, 1927) is essentially characterized by a normal curve transformation of a probability (namely, the proportion of subjects judging one stimulus to have more of a particular attribute than another stimulus) into a distance (Coombs, 1964). This technique converts data of an ordinal level (rank orderings of stimuli) to an interval scale, and is therefore preferable to any technique used in experimental aesthetics for which interval data are required, since the latter are mostly less consistent and transitive across subjects, and reliable within subjects. When rank-order data are consistent and transitive, no more powerful data collection method is called for (Coombs, 1964). Torgerson (1958, pp. 173–179) describes the method used. For this experiment a least-squares solution for incomplete, rather than complete, matrices of data had to be sought, since in the case where all subjects agree on one comparison (e.g., Joke A is always judged funnier than Joke B), the resulting proportion is 1, and the unit normal deviate is infinite.

III. The Experiment

A. MATERIALS, SUBJECTS, PROCEDURE

Fourteen written jokes were selected to represent as wide a range of sexiness as possible. In a pilot study it was verified that they contained clear allusions to, implications of, talk about, or descriptions of heterosexual acts. Scatological and perverse themes were avoided, because jokes containing those themes might not fall in the sex factor as described by factor analysts. Fifty-two second-year undergraduate students were presented with a booklet containing the 14 jokes, one per page. The order was random, and different for each S. Subjects were asked to read all the jokes first, and pick the one they considered "most sexy, the one containing the highest amount of sex." They would then read them again and pick the next sexiest one, etc. A rank order of all jokes per S was thus obtained. No ties were permitted. These data were used to construct the arousal-potential scale.

Independently, 90 first-year undergraduate male students, enrolled in an introductory psychology course, were tested with the Eysenck Personality Inventory, form A (Eysenck & Eysenck, 1963), during a regular class hour. Of these Ss 14 "pure" introverts (E-score 7 or less, percentile 16 or less), 14 "pure" extroverts (E-score 14 and up, percentile 70 and up), and 18 ambiverts (E-scores 10–12, percentiles 34–52) were selected. The means of the extroversion scores of the introverts and ambiverts, and of the extroverts and ambiverts, differed significantly ($p < .005$ in both cases). Six weeks later these Ss individually read and rank-ordered the jokes for funniness. The same procedure was used as for the sexiness scale. During debriefing, it appeared that because of the time lag and the fact that a different E conducted the session, Ss had no suspicion at all that they had been selected for their personality test scores.

B. RESULTS

The method described in Section II resulted in the arousal-potential scale, the abscissa of Figure 1. The coefficient of concordance for the sexiness ratings was .64, indicating good agreement among the Ss about what is sexy. Concordances for the funniness ratings by the various subject groups were very much lower (introverts .24, ambiverts .30, extroverts .30, and another group of 21 Ss of which no personality measures were taken .36). Also, the mean funniness rankings by these four groups were highly correlated. For instance, intro- and extroverts differed significantly ($p < .05$) in their ratings of funniness on only two of the 14 jokes. According to

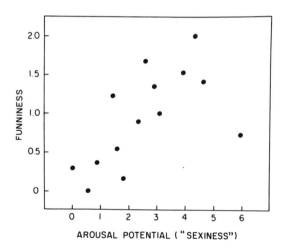

Figure 1. The relation between the scaled arousal potential ("sexiness") and the scaled funniness for 14 sex jokes.

the tables of Sakoda, Cohen, and Beall (1954), the chance of finding two p values not exceeding .05, in 14 comparisons, is higher than .05. The intro- and extrovert groups, then, did not differ significantly in their mean ratings. Therefore, the data of the 67 Ss were pooled. Overall concordance was .26 ($p < .05$); the funniness scale forms the ordinate of Figure 1. Each dot represents a joke's simultaneous position on the arousal-potential and the funniness scales. A nonparametric trend analysis shows that the bitonic tau (Ferguson, 1965) is not significant. Clearly, the hypothesized inverted U-shaped relation between funniness and our operationalization of arousal potential was not supported, nor did the two personality types differ in their funniness ratings.

C. Discussion

The apparent lack of curvilinearity in our results, illustrated by a product–moment correlation between the two scales of .62, can be attributed to various causes. One obvious explanation would be that if there is no downturn in the curve, the stimuli do not sufficiently represent the possible range of arousal potential, but rather the lower part of it. Our stimuli may have been not arousing or frightening enough to cause inhibition of enjoyment. It is, however, possible that there is an upper limit to the amount of arousal potential based on nonperverse sex in a joke, however sexy it is judged. Sex jokes may need additional arousing properties, e.g., an aggressive or perverse undertone, to be anxiety inducing. Or perhaps our subjects, exclusively male students at a large university in a big city, and presumably healthy of body and mind, were too sophisticated to be very highly aroused by even very sexual jokes.

Another explanation may be that the subjects experienced the rank-ordering of the jokes as something playful, relatively detached from reality. If this had been the case, responses of enjoyment of the sexual content of the jokes would less likely have been inhibited than if the joke situations had had more reality value (Berlyne, 1969, p. 841) [see also Chapter 3]. If such enjoyment did not have to be inhibited and could be freely expressed, a downturn in the curve would not be expected (Clark, 1955).

Sears (1947) argued that in a situation relatively free from real-life restraints, relatively free expression of impulses can be elicited. Thus, if inhibition of expression were felt to be unnecessary, as in a play or fantasy situation, one would expect a monotonic, rather than a bitonic, relation.

So far, we have assumed that despite our findings, there still is a curvilinear relation between arousal potential and appreciation. But even this may be doubted. Blum, Geiwitz, and Stewart (1967) present evidence that pleasure and mental arousal are related according to an additive model. The authors distinguish cognitive from organismic arousal, and question whether the inverted U-shaped relationship between organismic arousal and performance is applicable to purely cognitive events. If one considers sex jokes as stimuli generating cognitive as much as organismic arousal, then, reasoning along the lines of Blum *et al.,* one would not necessarily expect a curvilinear relation to obtain between the arousal potential of the joke stimuli and appreciation of the jokes. Such expectation would, of course, depend on amounts of cognitive versus organismic arousal generated by each joke. Moreover, physiological measures should corroborate such assumptions.

The puzzling lack of difference between the extroverts and introverts may be explained as follows.

Gray (1970) contends that the higher basic level of arousal in introverts results in a higher susceptibility to punishment and frustrative nonreward. He substitutes this hypothesis for Eysenck's (1967) emphasis on the higher conditionability of introverts compared with extroverts. One may argue that nonperverse sexual jokes are, for these sophisticated subjects, stimuli that arouse appetitive drives, rather than emotions associated with frustration or punishment. In that case, one would not expect a difference among extroverts, introverts, and ambiverts because they are all equally susceptible to the appetizing stimulation. Perverse jokes might generate arousal affecting the preferences of the subject groups differentially. Introverts may be more sensitive to the element of punishment in perverse sex jokes and therefore be less amused by them than extroverts would.

Future research will have to show exactly how arousal, via arousal potential, is related to funniness. This will require systematic variation of arousal potential of the stimulus situation. Thus a deeper understanding is needed of which factors are pertinent to arousal potential and how they can be quantified and manipulated. Some of these factors are suggested by our preliminary results (e.g., reality value of the joke, increased organismic arousal, sex of experimenter in relation to subject, amount of perversion depicted). Other variables (complexity, cognitive arousal) are known but need much more quantification. One way to achieve this with jokes is to manipulate the punch lines systematically, as Godkewitsch (1968b) did. Five different versions, including the original version, were constructed of a number of written jokes. The versions were (a) leave out the punch line; (b) exchange the punch line for a sentence, logically concluding the story in the joke; (c) make the punch line longer by adding unnecessary explanatory remarks; and (d) exchange the punch line for a completely irrelevant sentence. Subjects only judged one version of each joke for funniness. The manipulations decreased the funniness of the jokes in a significant and predicted way. Many other approaches can be considered (see, e.g., Nerhardt, 1970). Independent measurement of arousal potential when it is used as an independent variable is indispensable; variables like GSR recovery time and heart-rate change seem most feasible [Chapter 6].

IV. Summary

The relationship between arousal and humor appreciation has mostly been investigated by treating subjects in some more or less arousing manner and consequently having them express preference for presented jokes. In this project, an effort was made to establish the same relationship, only between the arousal potential of the presented jokes and their judged funniness. Arousal potential was operationalized as "sexiness" and determined independently of funniness. The sex jokes were scaled on both dimensions by a technique based on the law of comparative judgment. The significant monotonic relation was identical for introvert and extrovert subjects. Various explanations of the results were advanced.

Acknowledgment

The research reported in this chapter was supported by Grant APA-73 from the National Research Council of Canada awarded to D. E. Berlyne, principal investigator, who kindly commented upon an earlier draft.

References

Andrews, T. G. A factorial analysis of responses to the comic as a study of personality. *Journal of General Psychology,* 1943, 28, 209–224.
Berlyne, D. E. Motivational problems raised by exploratory and epistemic behavior. In S. Koch (Ed.), *Psychology—A study of a science.* Vol. 5. New York: McGraw-Hill, 1963.

Berlyne, D. E. Arousal and reinforcement. In D. Levine (Ed.), *Nebraska symposium on motivation.* Lincoln, Nebraska: Univ. of Nebraska Press, 1967.

Berlyne, D. E. Laughter, humor and play. In G. Lindzey and E. Aronson (Eds.), *Handbook of social psychology.* (2nd ed.) Vol. 3. Reading, Massachusetts: Addison-Wesley, 1969.

Blum, G. S., Geiwitz, P. J., & Stewart, C. G. Cognitive arousal: The evolution of a model. *Journal of Personality & Social Psychology,* 1967, 5, 138–151.

Byrne, D. Some inconsistencies in the effect of motivation arousal on humor preferences. *Journal of Abnormal & Social Psychology,* 1961, 62, 158–160.

Cattell, R. B. *Personality and motivation structure and measurement.* Yonkers-on-Hudson, New York: World Book, 1957.

Clark, R. A. The effects of sexual motivation on phantasy. In D. C. McClelland (Ed.), *Studies in motivation.* New York: Appleton, 1955.

Coombs, C. H. *A theory of data.* New York: Wiley, 1964.

Davis, J. M., & Farina, A. Humor appreciation as social communication. *Journal of Personality & Social Psychology,* 1970, 15, 175–178.

Dworkin, E. S., & Efran, J. S. The angered: Their susceptibility to varieties of humor. *Journal of Personality & Social Psychology,* 1967, 6, 233–236.

Eysenck, H. J. The appreciation of humour: An experimental and theoretical study. *British Journal of Psychology,* 1942, 32, 295–309.

Eysenck, H. J. An experimental analysis of five tests of "appreciation of humour." *Educational and Psychological Measurement,* 1943, 3, 191–214.

Eysenck, H. J. *The biological basis of personality.* Springfield, Illinois: Thomas, 1967.

Eysenck, H. J., & Eysenck, S. B. G. *Eysenck Personality Inventory.* San Diego, California: Educational and Industrial Testing Service, 1963.

Ferguson, G. A. *Nonparametric trend analysis.* Montreal: McGill Univ. Press, 1965.

Godkewitsch, M. Experimental humor: Themes in jokes and their contribution to funniness. Unpublished M.A. thesis, Univ. of Amsterdam, 1968.   (a)

Godkewitsch, M. Experimentele humor: Orientatie en een experiment. *Nederlands Tijdschrift voor de Psychologie,* 1968, 23, 409–427.   (b)

Goldstein, J. H. Repetition, motive arousal, and humor appreciation. *Journal of Experimental Research in Personality,* 1970, 4, 90–94.

Gray, J. A. The psychophysiological basis of introversion–extraversion. *Behaviour Research and Therapy,* 1970, 8, 249–266.

Hammes, J. A., & Wiggins, S. L. Manifest anxiety and appreciation of humor involving emotional content. *Perceptual & Motor Skills,* 1962, 14, 291–294.

Hebb, D. O. Drives and the C.N.S. (conceptual nervous system). *Psychological Review,* 1955, 62, 243–254.

Hom, G. L. Threat of shock and anxiety in the perception of humor. *Perceptual & Motor Skills,* 1966, 23, 535–538.

Hunt, J. M. Motivation inherent in information processing and action. In O. J. Harvey (Ed.), *Motivation and social interaction: The cognitive determinants.* New York: Ronald Press, 1963.

Keller, W. Humor, Ironie, Sarkasmus. *Heilpaedagogische Werkblaetter,* 1966, 35, 62–65.

La Gaipa, J. J. Stress, authoritarianism and the enjoyment of different kinds of hostile humor. *Journal of Psychology,* 1968, 70, 3–8.

Lamb, C. W. Personality correlates of humor enjoyment following motivational arousal. *Journal of Personality & Social Psychology,* 1968, 9, 237–241.

Lazarus, R. S. *Psychological stress and the coping process.* New York: McGraw-Hill, 1966.

Levine, J., & Abelson, R. Humor as a disturbing stimulus. *Journal of General Psychology*, 1959, 60, 191–200.

Levine, J., & Redlich, F. C. Intellectual and emotional factors in the appreciation of humor. *Journal of General Psychology*, 1960, 62, 25–35.

Malmo, R. B. Activation: A neurophysiological dimension. *Psychological Review*, 1959, 66, 367–386.

Nerhardt, G. Humor and inclination to laugh: Emotional reactions to stimuli of different divergence from a range of expectancy. *Scandinavian Journal of Psychology*, 1970, 11, 185–195.

O'Connell, W. E. The adaptive functions of wit and humor. *Journal of Abnormal & Social Psychology*, 1960, 61, 263–270.

Sakoda, J. M., Cohen, B. H., & Beall, G. Tests of significance for a series of statistical tests. *Psychological Bulletin*, 1954, 51, 172–175.

Sears, R. R. Influence of methodological factors on doll-play performance. *Child Development*, 1947, 18, 190–197.

Sears, R. R., Hovland, C. I., & Miller, N. E. Minor studies of aggression: 1. Measurement of aggressive behavior. *Journal of Psychology*, 1940, 9, 275–295.

Shellberg, L. Arousal and humor preference: A theoretical formulation and empirical test. Paper presented at the meeting of the Western Psychological Association, Vancouver, 1969. (a)

Shellberg, L. The effect of national tragedy on perceived funniness of cartoons with aggressive themes. Paper presented at the meeting of the Western Psychological Association, Vancouver, 1969. (b)

Shurcliff, A. Judged humor, arousal, and the relief theory. *Journal of Personality & Social Psychology*, 1968, 8, 360–363.

Singer, D. L. Aggression arousal, hostile humor, catharsis. *Journal of Personality & Social Psychology*, 1968, 8 (1, Pt. 2), 1–14.

Singer, D. L., Gollob, H. F., & Levine, J. Mobilization of inhibition and the enjoyment of aggressive humor. *Journal of Personality*, 1967, 35, 562–569.

Spence, K. W. *Behavior theory and conditioning.* New Haven: Yale Univ. Press, 1956.

Strickland, J. F. The effects of motivational arousal on humor preferences. *Journal of Abnormal & Social Psychology*, 1959, 59, 278–281.

Thurstone, L. L. The law of comparative judgment. *Psychological Review*, 1927, 34, 273–286.

Tollefson, D. L. *Differential responses to humor and their relation to personality and motivation measures.* (Doctoral dissertation, Univ. of Illinois) Ann Arbor, Michigan: University Microfilms, 1961, No. 61–4392.

Torgerson, W. *Theory and methods of scaling.* New York: Wiley, 1958.

Ullman, L. P., & Lim, D. T. Case history material as a source of the identification of patterns of response to emotional stimuli in a study of humor. *Journal of Consulting Psychology*, 1962, 26, 221–225.

Verinis, J. S. Inhibition of humor enjoyment: Effects of sexual content and introversion–extraversion. *Psychological Reports*, 1970, 26, 167–170.

Williams, C., & Cole, D. L. The influence of experimentally induced inadequacy feelings upon the appreciation of humor. *Journal of Social Psychology*, 1964, 64, 113–117.

Williams, J. M. An experimental and theoretical study of humour in children. *British Journal of Educational Psychology*, 1946, 16, 43–44.

Young, R. D., & Frye, M. Some are laughing: Some are not—Why? *Psychological Reports*, 1966, 18, 747–755.

Zigler, E., Levine, J., & Gould, L. Cognitive challenge as a factor in children's humor appreciation. *Journal of Personality & Social Psychology*, 1967, 6, 332–336.

Chapter 8

Enjoyment of Specific Types of Humor Content: Motivation or Salience?

Jeffrey H. Goldstein, Jerry M. Suls, and Susan Anthony

Department of Psychology
Temple University, Philadelphia, Pennsylvania

I. Introduction

A doctor, after seeing his female patient, said to her husband, "I don't like her looks."

"I haven't liked her looks for some time," replied the husband.

A number of reasons could be given as to why someone might find this joke amusing. For example, it contains an element of surprise, since the reply is largely unexpected; it requires understanding of the multiple use of the phrase "her looks"; and it may even convey the truth about the husband's feelings. It is also, quite clearly, aggressive. Although all of these explanations can be offered to account for one's appreciation of this joke, it is the last alternative which has received the most experimental attention. This may be because of the highly influential theory of humor proposed by Freud. In discussing this joke, Freud emphasizes its aggressive nature and indicates that it serves primarily as an outlet for the aggression felt by the husband toward his wife. The husband is using the joke as a means of aggressing against his wife (Freud, 1905).* That humor can serve to reduce aggressive (and sexual) drives is the most widely tested hypothesis in the field of humor research, and it is one of the central themes of Freud's theory. In the typical test of this hypothesis, drives are experimentally aroused and subjects are presented with jokes or cartoons which depict a variety of topics. It is frequently reported that subjects who are made aggressive prefer aggressive humor, while those who are sexually aroused prefer sexual humor (Dworkin & Efran, 1967; Lamb, 1968; Landy & Mettee, 1969; Singer, 1968).† Strickland (1959), for example, angered some subjects by ignoring them for 20 min, while others were sexually aroused by viewing photographs of nude models. Subjects then rated sexual, aggressive, and nontendentious (nonsense) cartoons. Angered subjects preferred aggressive humor, and sexually aroused subjects were found to prefer humor containing sexual themes.

The importance of this research extends beyond a simple understanding of the humor process. First, such research provides an opportunity to test some of Freud's notions experimentally, and second, to the extent that the Freudian humor theory is confirmed, the use of jokes and cartoons as stimuli in diagnostic and personality testing becomes feasible. The work of Levine and Redlich (Levine & Redlich, 1955; Redlich, Levine, & Sohler, 1951) and others has been aimed at the development of such humor diagnostic devices (O'Connell, 1962; Tollefson & Cattell, 1963).

Alternative theoretical approaches to humor, such as those presented elsewhere in this volume [see Chapters 1–5], stress variables quite different from motivation and humor theme in attempting to provide a basis for understanding humor phenomena. A variety of cognitive theories suggest that humor appreciation is contingent on the complexity, incongruity, or surprisingness of humor stimuli, rather than upon their specific thematic content (see Koestler, 1964; Maier, 1932). One difficulty in reconciling the psychoanalytic with other theoretical approaches lies in their emphases on different aspects of the humor situation. Tests of the Freudian theory rely on subjects' drive states and the thematic

---

* Norton ed., 1960, p. 37 (see References).

† It should be noted that the findings of such studies are not unequivocal (cf. Byrne, 1961; Davis & Farina, 1970; Goldstein, 1970b).

content of humor stimuli as independent variables, while tests of cognitive theories rely primarily on stimulus characteristics such as those already mentioned.

It is possible, however, to reinterpret experimental tests of the Freudian hypothesis in cognitive terms. In the typical test of the psychoanalytic motive arousal–humor appreciation hypothesis, subjects are presented with photographs or verbal material designed to make them aggressively or sexually aroused prior to rating humor stimuli varying in thematic content (as in Byrne, 1961; Dworkin & Efran, 1967; Goldstein, 1970b; Lamb, 1968; Singer, 1968; Strickland, 1959). In all this research it has been assumed that these inductions did, in fact, influence acute drive state. Moreover, such experiments have been entirely restricted to sexual and aggressive drives. An interpretation of these studies based on a cognitive framework suggests that what is being manipulated is not so much the subjects' motivational state, as the salience of particular types of stimuli. By showing subjects aggressive photographs, for instance, the experimenter may simply be lowering their threshold for the perception of other aggressive stimuli (Steinfeld, 1967). Thus, subjects shown aggressive photographs may rate aggressive humor as funnier than other types because they have, in some sense, an aggressive cognitive set which facilitates their processing of aggressive jokes [see Chapter 4].* In addition, manipulation checks, which have been employed in only a few of these studies, may be similarly construed; that is, they may be measuring salience as much as actual motivational states. Thus, when subjects are asked to indicate their postmanipulation moods by checking self-descriptive adjectives on a checklist, they may indicate those traits which are most salient to them, rather than (or in addition to) their motivational states.†

If this salience interpretation is correct, then it should be possible to manipulate the salience of some nonmotivational topic area and thereby increase appreciation for humor containing topic-related themes. The research to be reported in this chapter investigates the effects of salience on appreciation for specific types of humor content. Experiment I manipulates salience of both a motive (aggression) and a nonmotive (automobile) topic and examines

---

* Studies dealing with effects of observing violence on subsequent aggression may be similarly interpreted. The observation of an aggressive episode may be said to lower inhibitions against aggression, increase the strength of the observer's aggressive drive, or increase the salience of aggression to the observer (see Bandura, 1965; Berkowitz & Geen, 1966; Goldstein & Arms, 1971; Wheeler & Caggiula, 1966).

† For a fuller critical discussion on the utility of the drive construct, see Bolles (1958).

humor enjoyment for cartoons containing aggressive or automobile thema. It is predicted that when aggression is salient, subjects will prefer aggressive humor to other types of thematic content, and that when automobiles are made salient, subjects will show greatest enjoyment of cartoons with automobile content. This latter prediction is clearly incompatible with an interpretation of humor based upon the psychoanalytic model.

II. Experiment I:
Salience and Drive in Humor Appreciation

A. METHOD

1. Summary of Experimental Design

The Ss were 128 male and female students who were assigned to one of six experimental groups. Four of the groups ($N = 94$) comprises a 2 x 2 factorial design, the factors being Salience Topic (aggression or automobile) and Humor Thematic Content (aggression or automobile). In these four conditions Ss were presented with six photographs which depicted either scenes of violence or automobiles. After rating the photographs for aesthetic value, Ss were asked to rate the funniness of six cartoons which were either aggressive or which contained automobiles as a major element.

The remaining two groups of Ss ($N = 34$) served to generate manipulation check data. These groups were presented with either the aggressive or the automobile photographs, and they then completed a series of items designed to assess salience and motive arousal.

2. Materials and Procedure

Booklets were prepared which consisted of six aggressive scenes depicting physical violence or six photographs of automobiles. Following the photographs were six aggressive cartoons, six automobile cartoons, or a series of manipulation check items.

The manipulation checks consisted of the following items: (a) five subscales (hostility–aggression, anxiety, social affection, negative egotism, happiness–euphoria) from the Nowlis (1965) Mood Adjective Check List (MACL), which were found to be significant differentiators between angered and nonangered Ss in the 1968 Singer study; (b) three subscales (indirect hostility, resentment, irritability) from the Buss–Durkee Hostility Inventory (Buss & Durkee, 1957), successfully used in a previous investigation of situational influences on aggression (Goldstein & Arms, 1971); and (c) a word-association test in which subjects were asked to write the first five words they thought of in response to six stimulus words ("shop," "hood," "association," "rod," "highway," "auto"). The MACL and buss–Durkee scales were included as measures of motive arousal; the word-association test was included as a measure of salience. The word-association test was scored by two independent judges who tabulated the number of aggressive- and automobile-related word responses to the six stimulus words. The interjudge reliability was +.76.

Booklets were assigned to 128 students enrolled in undergraduate psychology courses at Temple University. Each booklet informed students that they were to serve as judges in rating various material contained in the booklets, and that these materials were to be used in a number of different studies to be conducted by the psychology department at a later date. The Ss thus believed that they were rating two different, independent sets of materials (photographs and cartoons, or photographs and manipulation check items). A postexperimental questionnaire indicated that all Ss accepted the experimental guise.

Each aggressive or automobile photograph was rated on a 7-point scale of "overall attractiveness and esthetic value," to ensure that Ss spent some time in viewing each photograph. For Ss receiving cartoons, the rating scale used was a 7-point humor enjoyment scale from (1) "not at all funny" to (7) "extremely funny."* The Ss assigned to manipulation check groups received the MACL, hostility inventory, and word-association test in counterbalanced order following their rating of the photographs.

B. RESULTS AND DISCUSSION

1. Checks on the Salience Manipulation

The word-association test was used as the most direct index of salience.† The mean number of automobile- and aggression-related

---

* The correlation between photograph and cartoon humor ratings was −.12. Thus humor ratings were not systematically influenced by the perceived attractiveness of the photographs.

† A study by Goldstein, Anthony, and Suls (1971), which investigated salience and humor, used a different salience manipulation check. After exposure to the salience-inducing stimuli, some subjects were presented with topic-relevant and topic-irrelevant words tachistoscopically. Recognition thresholds for topic-relevant words were significantly lower than for topic-irrelevant words. Thus, that salience was successfully manipulated by this procedure is further attested to by these data.

words was tallied for each S. Those viewing the automobile photographs had a mean of 8.4 automobile words while those viewing aggressive photographs had a mean of 6.7 automobile words. This difference is significant at the .05 level ($t = 1.7$, $df = 32$, one-tail). For aggressive words, those viewing aggressive photographs had significantly more aggressive responses ($\bar{X} = 2.1$) than those viewing automobile photographs ($\bar{X} = 1.0$, $t = 2.3$, $df = 32$, $p < .025$, one-tail). Thus, Ss viewing automobile photographs were more likely to give automobile-related responses to the stimulus words and less likely to give aggression-related responses than Ss who viewed aggressive photographs. To the extent that the word-association test reflects salience, the manipulation appears to have been successful in differentially arousing the two types of salience intended.

To determine whether viewing and rating photographs influences measures of aggression and hostility typically employed in such studies, analyses, comparing Ss who viewed aggressive and automobile photographs, were computed on the MACL and hostility inventory. On the MACL, Ss viewing aggressive photographs tended to describe themselves as slightly less happy than those viewing automobile photographs (happiness–euphoria, $p < .05$), but there were no significant differences between the two groups on the four remaining variables comprising the MACL. Perhaps most important, no difference between groups was obtained on the hostility-aggression subscale of the MACL. On the Buss–Durkee inventory, those Ss viewing aggressive photographs tended to have higher hostility scores ($\bar{X} = 12.2$) than those viewing automobile photographs ($\bar{X} = 9.8$), but this difference is not statistically significant ($t < 1.0$). Summarizing these findings, we seem to find that exposure to, and rating of, photographs serves to increase the salience of the topic depicted but does not substantially influence typical measures of motivational states.

2. Rating of Cartoons Varying in Thematic Content

A total of 94 Ss received cartoons following the photographs, with approximately half receiving aggressive cartoons and half automobile cartoons. The ratings for the six cartoons presented to each S were summed and analyzed in a 2 x 2 unweighted means solution analysis of variance for unequal N's (Winer, 1962). The mean humor rating for each condition and a summary of the analysis of variance are presented in Table I. The higher the score, the funnier the cartoons were perceived to be. The only statistically significant effect is the predicted Salience Topic by Cartoon Content interaction ($p < .05$).

TABLE I

Mean Humor Rating by Experimental Condition for Six Cartoons Varying in Thematic Content

Cartoon content	Salience topic	
	Aggression	Automobile
Aggression	21.4 ($N = 24$)	19.6 ($N = 28$)
Automobile	20.9 ($N = 24$)	24.0 ($N = 18$)
	Summary of analysis of variance			
Source	df	MS	F	p
A (Salience topic)	1	9.3	<1.0	n.s.
B (Cartoon content)	1	88.5	2.97	<.10
A x B	1	142.1	4.78	<.05
Error	90	29.7		

Those *S*s who rated aggressive photographs first tended to prefer aggressive humor, while those who rated photographs of automobiles first preferred humor with automobile thematic content.

Multiple comparisons among treatment means indicate that the effect of salience on humor content preference was greater for *S*s receiving automobile cartoons than for those receiving aggressive cartoons, perhaps because automobiles are quite clearly depicted in the automobile humor stimuli, while aggression is a more abstract trait which must be inferred from the aggressive humor. (This suggests that the more clearly and obviously the topic of salience is depicted in the humor stimuli, the greater will be the preference for those stimuli.)

Experiment I provides support for the notion that salience, rather than motivational arousal, can account for preferences for specific types of humor thema. It is quite evident that a specific drive cannot account for the higher rating given to automobile cartoons by *S*s who had previously rated automobile photographs than by those who had rated aggressive photographs. The findings of Experiment I support the notion that the establishment of a cognitive set which is topic-specific enables *S*s to process humor stimuli which depict that topic in a more facile, and hence, pleasurable way. Nevertheless, to establish generality for the salience interpretation and eliminate alternative explanations based on the particular manipulation of salience employed in Experiment I, a second study was conducted.

III. Experiment II:
Salience and Appreciation for Variations in Humor Thema

Experiment II was designed to employ a different and less obtrusive manipulation of salience. In addition, the second study employed a different type of humor stimuli in order to establish greater generality for the salience hypothesis. Where Experiment I employed pictorial cartoons with verbal captions, Experiment II used verbal jokes as humor stimuli.

The manipulation of salience in Experiment II consisted of having Ss read two verbal jokes based on a specific theme. Immediately following these two salience manipulation jokes, Ss were presented with additional jokes whose theme was either the same as or different than that of the salience jokes. The experiment thus consisted of a 2 x 2 factorial design.

A. METHOD

Twenty-five students, both males and females, in a Temple University evening psychology class were randomly assigned to one of the four experimental conditions. The Ss were told that they would be rating jokes which were to be used in psychological research to be conducted later in the year. They were given a booklet containing rating instructions and nine verbal jokes. The Ss were instructed to rate each joke on a 7-point rating scale, where 7 represents maximum funniness. The Ss then proceeded to rate the two salience jokes (whose theme was either medical or concerned music) followed by the seven experimental jokes. All Ss thus rated nine jokes, the first two consisting of the salience manipulation, and the remaining seven being the humor stimuli.

The hypotheses of Experiment II are that Ss who are first exposed to two medical theme jokes will rate subsequent medical jokes as significantly more funny than will Ss who are first exposed to music jokes. Conversely, Ss first exposed to music-theme jokes will rate subsequent music jokes as significantly more funny than will Ss who are first exposed to medical jokes.

B. RESULTS AND DISCUSSION

The data from Experiment II were analyzed in a 2 x 2 unweighted means solution analysis of variance for unequal N's. The analysis yielded only one F greater than 1.0, and that is the predicted interaction of Salience Topic by Joke Content ($F = 4.3$, $df = 1, 21$, $p < .06$). Cell means for this analysis are presented in Table II.

TABLE II

Mean Humor Rating by Experimental Condition of Seven Jokes Varying in Thematic Content

Joke content	Salience topic	
	Medical	Music
Medical	21.5 ($N = 6$)	18.7 ($N = 7$)
Music	14.4 ($N = 5$)	21.4 ($N = 7$)

As can be seen in Table II, all four cell means are in the predicted direction, and their absolute differences, though not highly significant, are fairly substantial. In addition, considering each of the 14 pairs of means, presented in Table III, it can be seen that 13 of the 14 means are in the predicted direction. With the exception of one inversion in means, humor stimuli are rated as most funny when they are preceded by two jokes with the same thematic content.

TABLE III

Mean Humor Rating by Experimental Condition of Each of Seven Jokes

Thematic content	Joke						
	1	2	3	4	5	6	7
Medical jokes							
Medical salience	2.50	3.33	3.83	2.83	3.50	3.00	2.50
Music salience	1.58	3.00	3.71	2.57	2.28	2.71	2.86
Music jokes							
Medical salience	1.40	1.40	1.40	2.20	3.00	2.20	2.80
Music salience	1.86	4.00	2.70	2.60	3.30	3.30	3.60

Although Experiment II uses a highly unobtrusive manipulation of salience, certain methodological difficulties are inherent in the experimental design. If the first two jokes serve to provide Ss with a medical or music cognitive set, then each succeeding joke should also serve to influence cognitive set, either by increasing or decreasing its potency, depending upon whether its topic is the same as or different from the first two jokes. In view of this, the most direct test of the salience hypothesis would be an analysis of humor responses to only the first joke following the two salience jokes, rather than an analysis on the sum of all seven humor stimuli. A 2 x 2 analysis of variance on the first joke following the two salience manipulation jokes yields only one significant effect, and that is the predicted interaction of Salience Topic by Joke Content ($F = 10.0$, $df = 1, 21, p < .01$). The means for this analysis can be seen in Table III. Thus, regardless of the effect of successive jokes on salience, the hypothesis is supported.

Nevertheless, the salience effect should diminish with the presentation of additional jokes, since following their rating of the two manipulation jokes, Ss are all repeatedly exposed to jokes with a single theme. An examination of the means in Table III lends some support to this diminishing salience effect interpretation, although the reduction is not linear.

The present study again provides support for the salience hypothesis; and in both of the replications contained in the experiment, musical jokes are funniest when preceded by music jokes, and medical jokes are most appreciated when preceded by medical jokes.

IV. Discussion and Conclusions

The effect of salience on the appreciation of humor of similar thematic content was demonstrated in two experiments which employed different manipulations of salience and different types of humor stimuli. The primary purpose of these studies was to demonstrate an alternative interpretation to motivational theories of humor, and in this respect the studies were successful. This, of course, is not to suggest that motivational factors, such as the arousal of various drive states, may not play a role in the appreciation of specific types of humor content. Rather, the purpose here is to provide *a more general analysis of humor appreciation, and one which is not restricted to aggressive or sexual humor.* It is possible that appreciation for aggressive and sexual humor themes is contingent to some degree on subjects' acute drive state, while appreciation for nontendentious humor is dependent on salience. However, a more parsimonious view would be to adopt a single explanation for both tendentious and nontendentious humor appreciation, and the salience hypothesis provides such a unitary explanation.

There are several possible interpretations of the salience effect demonstrated in the experiments reported here, no one of which can be accepted with confidence based on these data. Exposure to a specific thema, whether in the form of photographs, prose material, or even jokes, is thought to establish a cognitive set, which, in turn, facilitates the processing of related types of information. Thus heightened salience may enable subjects to process humor stimuli more easily and "get" related types of humor more readily. This interpretation implies that ease of information processing is positively related to humor appreciation and comprehension, and there are some data to support this contention. Goldstein (1970a) reported a positive correlation between speed of response, which may be one index of ease of information processing, and humor appreciation. Salience, may thus be said to facilitate the processing of humor stimuli [see Chapter 4].

An additional explanation is based on the notion of assimilation–contrast. Perhaps when stimuli which differ from those previously seen are encountered, they are rated as less enjoyable; whereas there need be no obtrusive break in thinking when successive stimuli all deal with the same general topic. Hence the latter are rated consistently positive (for related psychophysical approaches to humor see La Fave, 1969; Nerhardt, 1970; and also Chapter 7). An explanation may also be offered in terms of evaluation apprehension (see Rosenberg, 1969). The Ss may become suspicious of the experimenter's intention when there is an abrupt change in content area between the salience and humor stimuli, and this may interfere with their enjoyment of the latter. This interpretation is most applicable to Experiment II, where both salience and humor stimuli consisted of jokes; here a break in content may be most obvious and disturbing to Ss.

Finally, as already discussed, there is the possibility that salience is only a factor in the appreciation of nontendentious humor and that motivation plays a major part in appreciation of and preference for aggressive and sexual jokes. On the whole, however, the most parsimonious explanation of the data would rule out motivation as an explanatory concept, since the salience hypothesis can account for the appreciation of nonsense as well as aggressive and sexual humor.

Acknowledgment

This research was supported by a Faculty Research Award from Temple University to Jeffrey H. Goldstein. We are indebted to the following people for their assistance with various phases of this project: Kurt Ebert, Russell Eisenman, Barry Goodstadt, Susan McKenna, and Robert Menapace. Paul McGhee, Thomas Ostrom, and Ralph Rosnow kindly commented on earlier drafts of this chapter.

References

Bandura, A. Vicarious processes: A case of no-trial learning. In L. Berkowitz (Ed.), *Advances in experimental social psychology.* Vol. 2. New York: Academic Press, 1965.

Berkowitz, L., & Geen, R. G. Film violence and the cue properties of available targets. *Journal of Personality & Social Psychology,* 1966, 3, 525–530.

Bolles, R. C. The usefulness of the drive concept. In M. R. Jones (Ed.), *Nebraska symposium on motivation.* Lincoln, Nebraska: Univ. of Nebraska Press, 1958.

Buss, A. H., & Durkee, A. An inventory for assessing different kinds of hostility. *Journal of Consulting Psychology,* 1957, 21, 343–348.

Byrne, D. Some inconsistencies in the effect of motivation arousal on humor preferences. *Journal of Abnormal & Social Psychology,* 1961, 62, 158–160.

Davis, J. M., & Farina, A. Humor appreciation as social communication. *Journal of Personality & Social Psychology,* 1970, 15, 175–178.

Dworkin, E. S., & Efran, J. S. The angered: Their susceptibility to varieties of humor. *Journal of Personality & Social Psychology,* 1967, 6, 233–236.

Freud, S. *Jokes and Their Relation to the Unconscious.* New York: Norton, 1960. (Originally: *Der Witz und seine Beziehung zum Unbewussten.* Leipzig and Vienna: Deuticke, 1905.)

Goldstein, J. H. Humor appreciation and time to respond. *Psychological Reports,* 1970, 27, 445–446. (a)

Goldstein, J. H. Repetition, motive arousal, and humor appreciation. *Journal of Experimental Research in Personality,* 1970, 4, 90–94. (b)

Goldstein, J. H., Anthony, S., & Suls, J. M. Effects of salience on appreciation for specific humor thema. Unpublished manuscript, Temple Univ., 1971.

Goldstein, J. H., & Arms, R. L. Effects of observing athletic contests on hostility. *Sociometry,* 1971, 34, 83–90.

Koestler, A. *The act of creation.* New York: Macmillan, 1964.

La Fave, L. Humor as a supplemental variable to assimilation–contrast principles in psycho-social "scales." Paper presented to Western Psychological Association, Vancouver, 1969.

Lamb, C. W. Personality correlates of humor enjoyment following motivational arousal. *Journal of Personality & Social Psychology,* 1968, 9, 237–241.

Landy, D., & Mettee, D. Evaluation of an aggressor as a function of exposure to cartoon humor. *Journal of Personality & Social Psychology,* 1969, 12, 66–71.

Levine, J., & Redlich, F. C. Failure to understand humor. *Psychoanalytic Quarterly,* 1955, 24, 560–572.

Maier, N. R. F. A Gestalt theory of humour. *British Journal of Psychology,* 1932, 23, 69–74.

Nerhardt, G. Humor and inclination to laugh: Emotional reactions to stimuli of different divergence from a range of expectancy. *Scandinavian Journal of Psychology,* 1970, 11, 185–195.

Nowlis, V. Research with the mood adjective check list. In S. Tomkins and C. Izard (Eds.), *Affect, cognition and personality.* New York: Springer, 1965.

O'Connell, W. E. An item analysis of the wit and humor appreciation test. *Journal of Social Psychology*, 1962, 56, 271–276.

Redlich, F. C., Levine, J., & Sohler, T. P. A mirth response test: Preliminary report on a psychodiagnostic technique utilizing dynamics of humor. *American Journal of Orthopsychiatry*, 1951, 21, 717–734.

Rosenberg, M. J. The conditions and consequences of evaluation apprehension. In R. Rosenthal and R. L. Rosnow (Eds.), *Artifact in behavioral research*. New York: Academic Press, 1969.

Singer, D. L. Aggression arousal, hostile humor, catharsis. *Journal of Personality & Social Psychology*, 1968, 8 (1, Pt. 2).

Steinfeld, G. J. Concepts of set and availability and their relation to the reorganization of ambiguous pictorial stimuli. *Psychological Review*, 1967, 74, 505–522.

Strickland, J. F. The effects of motivational arousal on humor preferences. *Journal of Abnormal & Social Psychology*, 1959, 59, 278–281.

Tollefson, D. L., & Cattell, R. B. *Handbook for the IPAT humor test of personality*. Champaign, Illinois: Institute for Personality and Ability Testing, 1963.

Wheeler, L., & Caggiula, A. The contagion of aggression. *Journal of Experimental Social Psychology*, 1966, 2, 1–10.

Winer, B. J. *Statistical principles in experimental design*. New York: McGraw-Hill, 1962.

Chapter 9

On Being Witty: Causes, Correlates, and Consequences

Department of Psychology
University of California, Los Angeles, California

I. Introduction

Neglected areas of study abound in social psychology; humor is among them. Despite Henri Bergson's (1911) pointed warning—in what is often cited as a classically influential essay—that "to understand laughter, we must put it back into its natural environment, which is society, and above all must we determine the utility of its function, which is a social one [p. 7]," that which is social about the funny, the amusing, the humorous, the witty remains an underinvestigated, largely uncomprehended subject. We know next to nothing about the phenomena subsumed under the rubric that titles this chapter. Being witty—impromptu *in situ,* especially—is a form of human behavior that is clearly creative, that has immediate impact in an ongoing interactive sequence, and that (at least in this culture, at this time) is very frequent and generally highly valued. Yet no one, to date, has successfully experimented with the parameters of this behavior, and very few have subjected it to systematic observation. There is many a quotable deft turn-of-phrase, many an armchair insight, but there is little that can be called verified (or verifiable) fact. The problem can be studied, nevertheless, and the results should inform a wide range of interests.

II. A Paradigm for the Problem

Simply, even perhaps simplistically, considered, an occurrence of humor is an event or process that can be fairly precisely specified: If there is laughter, there has been humor; if someone is amused, something funny has happened. This is operationalism rampant, true. But whether such a blunt characterization includes too much (Is there humor in a tickle?) or too little ("Wipe that smile off your face!") is a secondary and an empirical question; unmistakably it does include the core of the phenomenon. The task then for a social psychologist of humor is to investigate those instances where *in a situation an individual says or does something which leads others to laugh or otherwise report amusement.*

Of the major components of this description—the wit, the witticism or joke, the responder (laugher, appreciator, audience), the encompassing situation—it is the *responder* who has received most of the attention of researchers. The responder demonstrating his "sense of humor" by rating how funny a series of jokes seem to him is the prototypical setting for a humor study. What sorts of things strike what sorts of people funny? What circumstances make it easier or harder to be amused? How does the relationship between responder and wit influence the response (and the initiating wittiness)? These are challenging questions, all concerned primarily with the responder component.

Analysis of *joke content* (types of witticism) has been the particular concern of the theoretically oriented. Where the professional comic may classify in terms of "sit-com" humor, sight gags, put-downs, and one liners, behavioral scientists favor differentiations involving hypothesized underlying dynamics, often assigning distinctive meanings to labels such as humor, wit, the funny, the comic. The social psychologist may, for his immediate purposes, ignore these distinctions. However, there is one content breakdown which cannot long be ignored, and that is a classification of humor as essentially either clowning and whimsical or sarcastic and biting—a classification which can be roughly equated with whether or not the humor has a target, a "butt" of the joke (who, incidentally, may or may not be a member of the interacting group and may be the wit himself). Such a differentiation, "hard" versus "soft," cannot well be ignored because it leads to very different social expectations; the effects of the two types of humor on the responder, the initiator, the relationship between them, the next behaviors in an interactive sequence, etc., would be predicted to be quite—perhaps diametrically—opposite.

Irrespective of the kind of humor he might choose to employ, the *witty person* is a focal point for the witty event, and the least studied. Furthermore, the wit as focus suggests an enlargement of the analytic scheme. As stated, the definition includes unintentional humor and excludes "jokes" that fall flat. At least three discriminable instances become evident: (a) the attempt to be funny which succeeds; (b) the attempt which fails—both of which would require a form of self-report from the wit (i.e., "I tried"); and (c) the unintended "joke," which represents either success without trying or, alternatively, what might be called an error case in this system, *sui generis* laughter ("nervous" or "polite" laughter). Phenomenally, within the intentional joking area, there also seems to be a distinction which reflects the degree of premeditation, i.e., the cautiously drawled *bon mot* versus the "it just popped out" sort of comment which surprises (and pleases) the wit and his audience equally.

Finally, there is the *situation* to be considered, the encompassing environment in which the humor takes place. There are numerous potentially significant dimensions of this aspect of the paradigm. They range from microquestions of immediate context (things about sequence and setting) to normative descriptions of the appropriateness or inappropriateness of humor for certain times, places, and persons—norms which are culturally, even social-class, bound. By far the most cutting dimension, however, is that of spontaneity: the extent to which aspects of the humor instance are or have been preprogrammed. Three degrees of spontaneity can be differentiated: (a) cases in which everything is determined beforehand, e.g., the professional comic entertainment whether it be filmed, live, or in the form of reading matter which the audience approaches with the "set" to be amused; (b) cases in which only certain aspects of the situation are predetermined, e.g., the friend relating to friends a joke he has heard, the professional comedian honestly ad-libbing; and (c) the humor instances which in frequency and, one suspects, in effect strongly dominate the scene, i.e., the entirely unprepared occurrence where an interacting individual suddenly spontaneously creates an in-context funny event, perhaps a word, an act, or a combination or series of both. Sadly, much, if not most, of the effort expended on the study of humor has—often by default and unfortunately often without recognition of the limitations incurred—dealt with category (a), the most restrictive, specialized, and from a social-psychological perspective, trivial of the three. In truth, people sometimes read humor; they sometimes watch humor; but most often they participate in humor. It is a phenomenon preeminently interactive, immanent, impromptu.

III. The Literature: What Do We Know?

Interactive, immanent, impromptu events are admittedly hard to examine and understand. Spontaneous humor, the extemporaneous "being witty" which is our topic, has not been examined and is not understood. But there are clues, hints, and beginnings.

Ungrounded theory, idle and/or incidental speculation—as well as serendipitous empirical findings—will not be discussed here. However, there are two such sources which the curious researcher might well consult, namely, the "folk wisdom" of the professional practitioners of the theater arts and the methodological "compromises with humor" forced upon students of small-group interaction. For the first, there is a much used and intriguing "College Outline Series" guide to play production, written by Nelms, which was first issued in 1950 and reprinted in 1966. This how-to-do-it "handbook for the backstage worker" is rich with lore about being funny and the effects of being funny. The author's definition of comedy, "Anything the actors do or say which is intended to make the audience laugh and which succeeds [p. 159]," differs from the one I have suggested only in its requirement of intent, perhaps because on stage the unexpected is potentially disastrous.

The second source, the serendipitous, is best seen in the interesting travels of two behavior items—"tells a joke" and "laughs"—across the categories of Bales's Interaction Process Analysis system (and modifications thereof, such as that by Borgatta, 1964), during the successive revisions of this painstakingly thorough classification scheme for recording and analyzing small-group behavior (Bales, 1950, 1953, 1970). As Bales and his co-workers have grappled with the continuously elusive question of what to do with joking and laughing behaviors in their laboratory observations of interacting groups, they have shifted the categorization of these behaviors back and forth from positive to negative, from extremely "expressive-integrative" toward "instrumental-adaptive," from being one thing to being several things. In the process, there have evolved some working assumptions about the person who is consistently humorous in his approach to others* and about the interpersonal consequences of humor occurrences in ongoing interaction ("...a kind of hidden work is being done," Bales, 1970, p. 127), which urgently need to be tested empirically.

A. HISTORICAL–ANTHROPOLOGICAL ACCOUNTS

> There have always existed men who have a peculiar faculty for taking life easily, for gliding out of awkward situations which would baffle more serious-minded and responsible human beings. Such characters are a source of entertainment to their fellows, their company is welcome [p. 3].

So reports Welsford (1935) in her detailed examination of the fool throughout history and around the world. She concludes that while the classic "jester-in-cap-and-bells" required a special cultural milieu (one steeped in sacrament and ritual), the fool, in the sense of a person who is characteristically witty, is universally present in the human group: His behavior, his costuming, his role has become more or less institutionalized. Welsford's study was enlarged 10 years later by the more systematically cross-cultural work of Charles (1945). The same line of inquiry has been pursued most recently by Klapp (1962), who introduces the concept of an "abstract social type," finds the fool to be one, and, as such, one of present-day American society's major role models.

It was anthropologist Radcliffe-Brown who made his discipline's major contribution to this area with the idea of "the joking relationship," a culturally patterned solution to the interpersonal problem that obtains when a culture constrains two persons with

---

* In the current (1970) conception, this person variously exemplifies any of three directionally labeled (upward–negative–backward, upward–backward, upward–positive–backward) group roles, depending on the perspective from which humor is defined.

divergent interests (in-laws are a kinship example) to interact frequently and intimately. It is held that an almost ritualized humorous-exchange approach in such situations allows for the harmless release of unavoidable antagonisms and, as the only alternative to a formal, very distant style, may be expected to be modal (Radcliffe-Brown, 1940). These notions have also been applied to contexts more limited than entire cultures (for instance, Bradney's 1957 study of department-store salesgirls) and recently (Abrahams, 1970) have been placed in a larger theoretical framework, wherein joking is considered one among many "conversational genres," e.g., gossip, singing, arguing, each with its own rules about personae, appropriate setting, content, etc.

Another anthropologically provided datum is the ritualized insult exchange, a most rigidly ruled form of humor behavior, which ranges in occurrence from the famous potlatch parties of the Kwakiutl Indians (Benedict, 1934) to the several kinds of "signifying" (including playing the Dozens) which are reportedly characteristic pastimes of modern American ghetto life (Berdie, 1947; W. B. Miller, 1958; Hannerz, 1969). How much, if any, *fun* there is to be had in these self-consciously staged verbal contests is questionable, since the humor is often at least partly prepared (standard off-the-shelf material) and entirely "hard," that is, a humor of sarcasm and ridicule, the target being one's opponent and/or his immediate family. It is interesting to note that hostile humor as an interpersonal style is not limited, in our society, to a lower class game; it has been observed to be the prevailing mode among upper class boys being socialized into the eastern prep school milieu (Winter, Alpert, & McClelland, 1963).

B. SYSTEMATIC OBSERVATIONS: SELF AND OTHER

In the realm of the scientifically more rigorous, one of the earliest techniques, that of systematic record keeping based on naturalistic observation of ordinary life events, remains very viable. In 1897 Hall and Allin initiated the practice by soliciting detailed descriptions of remembered occasions of laughing behavior from over 700 subjects; Kambouropoulou (1926) obtained week-long "humor diaries" from her Vassar-girl subjects; Young (1937) requested reports of weeping as well as laughing, specified a 24-hour period, and limited his sample to college students repeatedly queried. A more modern, more sociological study (Middleton & Moland, 1959) employed a sample stratified by race and sex and defined the kind of humor—the "joke–anecdote" rather than the mere "witty remark"—which subjects were to record for the reporting period of 1 week. Taken together, these self-report collections support the common-sense notions that, at least among the college student group, laughter is much more usual than tears, laughter indeed being a very frequent behavior (Young's estimate was 20-plus times per day); humor is most often socially encased and socially caused; and both the type and number of jokes heard varies by social setting, e.g., sex, degree of acquaintance, and ethnic-group makeup of the audience.

Observational data gathering by other than the participants in an action sequence represents a further refinement in method, a further step toward objective understanding. Goodrich, Henry, and Goodrich (1954) attended 23 weekly staff conferences in a psychiatric hospital and there recorded and content-coded 176 instances of "general crowd laughter" (the group numbered upward of 75 people). Somewhat to the dismay of the researchers, bluntly derogatory remarks about colleagues accounted for 35% of all laughs. A sarcastic sort of humor also characterized the work-group meetings—again conferences of a mental hospital staff—studied by Coser (1960). Jokes were recorded in this case in terms of author (the wit) and target (the butt). A reflection of the hospital status hierarchy was evident in the data: Junior personnel directed their humor shafts at patients or peers; senior staff aimed directly at their juniors. Less devisively toned humor, in fact humor described as healing in function ("promoting group solidarity and relieving tension"), dominated the Chippewa Indian council meetings observed by F. C. Miller (1967). Miller, who studied his group over a 4-year period, examined humor incidents for context and apparent effect; his conclusions stress the beneficent results of a good laugh now and then—i.e., the joking among council members was socially facilitative, making communication in essential problem areas easier.

C. CORRELATIONAL AND EXPERIMENTAL STUDIES

A more involved close-up view of the wit and the effects of his wittiness than that provided by any sideline observer is that which is obtainable from the wit's fellow group members. Although only incidentally concerned with humor behaviors, Cloyd (1964), working with 10-member college-student groups, cluster-analyzed role behavior descriptions which his subjects gave of each other at the end of a series of 20 meetings. Of six emergent patterns, one (Cloyd's "Pattern C") contains the following combination of attributes: jokes and makes humorous remarks, is liberal, challenges others' opinions, gets off the subject, is egotistical, is cynical, interrupts others. That there can be positive impressions of a witty group member is confirmed by O'Connell's (1969) explicitly humor-oriented investigation of "developmental groups" composed of neuropsychiatric patients in a Veterans' Adminstration hospital. Four times, during a 20-session sequence, these adult male group members nominated fellow members for 22 sociometric positions, among which were two positions for people who said witty and amusing things: (a) a person who said them to make members laugh, and (b) a person who was "sarcastic." In O'Connell's own words: "The 'funny' wit was regarded by his peers as an influential leader, quite popular and active but independent. His 'sarcastic' counterpart seemed more hostile and less influential and popular [p. 186] ." It is important to keep in mind that both in this and in Cloyd's investigation, the humorist is identified as such entirely by the postsession reports of group members, a perceptual filter of uncertain dimensions: Misperception of who actually said witty things can occur consequent to role stereotyping, halo and/or "forked-tail" effects, and the like.

Experimental studies, that is, studies which actively manipulate and control aspects of the phenomenon, have yet to be made in this area; the spontaneously witty person at work, so to speak, remains outside the net of the experimental social psychologist. However, planned wittiness, particularly wittiness prepared deliberately to produce specified changes in the listener—in older words, "the art of humorous persuasion"—has been subjected to some study. A pioneer contribution was made by Lull (1940), who delivered otherwise equivalent humorous and nonhumorous speeches for and against socialized medicine to college audiences, and measured relevant attitudes before and after the speeches. A methodologically excellent study for its time—the humorous speeches could not be demonstrated to be either more or less convincing, interesting, or persuasive than the nonhumorous—this work was a lone effort which did not stimulate any follow-up. However, lately (for example, Gruner, 1967; Singer, 1968) there has been a surge of activity and interest in this kind of experiment, but the issues are complex and results inconclusive.

IV. Adding Evidence: Empirical Explorations

Attempts to capture, more or less in quantitative ("scientific") form, aspects of spontaneous real-life functioning humor have occupied this writer off and on for about 15 years. In the remainder of this chapter I shall describe those attempts.*

A. FORTUITOUS FINDINGS

In the course of gathering information about small groups of people in various experimentally devised and/or natural settings, it is possible, indeed inevitable, that one will learn much about topics one had not intended to investigate. Humor can be, perhaps needs to be, such a bonus topic, piggybacked onto studies of more solemn, grandiose, or richly funded subject matters. Two examples follow; the data for both were obtained in 1958 as part of two larger separate studies of aspects of small-group functioning. In each case the experimental manipulations either were administered after or had no discernible effect upon the humor items.

1. Study A

Sixteen five-member groups of female college students partici- pated in a 1-hour laboratory problem-solving session which entailed 24 min of monitored verbal interaction. At the close of the period, Ss were asked four simple questions: Was there humor? What type? Who was witty? Did you try to be? In brief, all participants thought there had been humor (over one-third thought there had been a lot of it). Asked to differentiate humor type into (a) "mainly sarcastic: laughing *at* others in the group," (b) "mainly clowning: laughing *with* others in the group," or (c) "other," Ss resisted—two assigned nonparticipating observers reported considerable range in type—and opted almost entirely (90+%) for the polite, acceptably phrased "clowning" category. Being described as witty by one's fellow members was associated with also being described by them as "likable" (rank-order correlation, $\rho = +.63$) and "helpful to the group" ($\rho = +.52$), and with having been an active participant, in sheer volume terms, in the group discussion (with an observer's interaction count, $\rho = +.55$). A *yes* response on the final question was given by 49 of the 80 Ss (61%); these self-identified wits were generally supported in their claim by their groups ($\chi^2 = 11.46$, $df = 2, p < .01$).

---

* Lest the reader expect somewhere herein an explication of *methodological* issues, efforts, and accomplishments, let me disappoint him at the outset. Methodology may intrigue those of us sufficiently interested in a topic to tackle it ourselves, but it bores all others. Furthermore, in this instance it would require and deserves a chapter of its own, a chapter this author is not writing at this time.

2. *Study B*

A somewhat more pungent portrait of wittiness than that of Study A is provided by data from a second small-group laboratory experiment, this one involving a 75-min session, one-third of that time devoted to a discussion task. Subjects were unacquainted adults (median age 33, range 19–60) attending a university summer session; they met in 18 five-member groups, nine consisting solely of male members and nine of female members. Immediately after the discussion part of the session (and before the introduction of experimental manipulations), Ss described themselves on a series of dimensions, one of which was "witty–solemn"; in addition, each S characterized himself and each of his peers in terms of two prescribed lists of trait words, one negative and one positive. On the self-wit rating, Ss were about evenly distributed across the "witty," "neutral," and "solemn" points on the scale; there was no difference between men and women. There were differences, however, by sex in the correlates of the rating. For males, the self-rating "witty" was most strongly associated with a self-rating as *sharp* and *valuable,* least associated with *fair* and *happy.* For women, the positive correlates were *strong* and *clear,* the negative, *hard* and *deep.* In choosing trait words as descriptive, people who said they were witty differed only slightly in their own eyes from those who said they were not—male wits overchose *enthusiastic* ($p < .08$), females chose *impractical* ($p < .05$). But in the eyes of their fellow group members self-identified wits of both sexes were characteristically *loud* ($p < .02$); males were also *influential, less worried* than others, and *annoying* (all $p < .05$); females were seen as *enthusiastic* ($p < .01$).

B. The Wit as a Small-Group Participant *

Evidently, sociometric nominations, self-descriptions, postsession ratings by participants and nonparticipating observers are subject to several varieties of bias, from the indiscriminately positive to the unexpectedly negative. It is necessary to index the socially immanent, temporally fleeting phenomenon of spontaneous interactive humor directly. The work to be described next does just that. Whenever, during a monitored group discussion session, a group member said or did anything which resulted in an audible laughter-type response on the part of at least two other group

* I wish to acknowledge the importance to the work to be discussed of a colleague and friend, Ewart E. Smith, to whom also goes all credit for having secured the financing which supported our joint efforts.

members, the monitoring observer (*O*) was instructed to credit that member with a witticism. This index, the "Observer Wit Tally," is easily obtained (untrained *O*s, over a 10-min trial session, typically achieve interobserver reliabilities of +.85 to +.90); it provides an immediate objective measure of the number of group laughs; but more important it can be used to categorize subjects as demonstrably having been or not having been witty, in the situation and setting under investigation.

1. Management Development Groups

For the first application of the Observer Wit Tally (Smith & Goodchilds, 1959) the subject population consisted of seven mixed-sex groups of 11 or 12 members each, composed of supervisory personnel in a large eastern corporation (total N = 83, of whom 44 were male). The *S*s were participating in a highly interactive 5-day management development course. A noninteracting "training assistant" recorded the humor count across all of the discussion sessions and, in addition, noted which tallies represented remarks mainly "sarcastic in tone." Despite the distortion which was undoubtedly introduced by aspects of the situation that could not be controlled—especially, wide variation in participation rates of individual members and the presence of a rigid sex-linked internal status dimension—classifications derived from the *O* tally yielded some provocative results.* (And as evidence for validity, there was a positive association between the humor tally for a group and the postcourse rating by that group of the amount of humor that had occurred.)

Based on the behavioral index, more men than women made jokes; of those identified as wits, only males (in *O*'s judgment) made sarcastically toned jokes. On postcourse self-ratings, wits of both sexes, compared with nonwits, gave more positive personality profiles and saw themselves as having participated in their groups more actively and in more different ways, i.e., taking on task- and group-maintenance-type roles; members, furthermore, in describing each other, agreed with the wits' very favorable self-descriptions. The male wits who were sarcastic in their humor differed from other male wits in being still more active, more varied in role function, and more favorably rated by self and peers. There was a slight tendency ($p < .10$) for the sarcastic male to be more willing than other *S*s to acknowledge negative role behaviors on his own part.

---

* Significance levels of reported findings from this point on, unless otherwise indicated, represent two-tailed tests with $p < .05$ or better.

2. Ad-Hoc Laboratory Groups

The Observer Wit Tally was next employed with *ad-hoc* laboratory groups, 12 in one study, 18 in the second. The two studies—the second an enlarged, improved replication of the first—are described in detail in the work by Goodchilds and Smith (1964). In essence, both involved adult male six-person groups of strangers who assembled for a 1-hour experimental session "to assist in a government-sponsored study of team work"; they were recruited at a California Department of Employment office and were paid for their time. Two standard tasks, each involving an individual prediscussion answer, a monitored group discussion requiring consensus on a group answer, and a postdiscussion individual answer, were administered in a standard order. The Observer Wit Tally identified the wittiness dimension within each group and significantly agreed with S's self-ratings as "usually witty" and with postsession peer nominations as having been "witty in today's discussion."

The self-descriptions of people who were witty in this laboratory setting ("laboratory" here meaning identical across groups, minimal in social cues, totally given by experimental instructions, etc.) confirmed the findings from the quite different management training groups. Wits reported themselves to be talkative and intelligent and generally all-around good fellows. Apparently, though, the portrait should also allow for a touch of resistance to group influence, for on the one of the tasks which had no right or wrong answer but instead involved judgment, opinion, and preference, wits were significantly less willing than others to go along with the group on their final individual postdiscussion answers. On the second task there was no such reluctance, whether the group answer was right or wrong. However, groups which contained what we have called "deliberate" wits were more apt to be correct on the second task and reported more satisfaction with the group experience. The deliberate-nondeliberate distinction, available only in the second study, was derived from the S's response to a two-item estimate of attitude toward the use of humor, a favorable response from an S who was in fact himself witty indicating, we have assumed, that his wit was deliberate (or "intentional" in the paradigm's terminology).

The dimension of deliberateness is only one among several sources of ambiguity associated with the use of the simple Observer Wit Tally. The extent to which the measure taps the correlates of "being witty" as distinct from the more general (and inevitably included) "being highly participative" is hard to say. The procedure followed in the work described has been to examine any apparent wit finding against the relationship for participation, and retain—and here mention—only those findings solely or more strongly wit related. More severe problems with the index stem from the fact that it entirely ignores type of humor and any characteristics of response beyond the minimal defining criteria (e.g., how loud the laughter, how long the laughter, etc.). The latter we have not tried to catch. The first, i.e., type of humor, was scorable for the management development groups, each monitored over some 40 hours of interaction, but it just has not proved estimable in short-term groups; the hostile, sarcastic witty remark is such a low-frequency event in the setting that it has not been possible to index it reliably.

3. Real-Life Work Groups

A population of city firemen provided an opportunity to test our developing notions about spontaneous humor in real-life work groups, groups with a long history, an established role structure (including, presumably, who might and who might not be expected to play the clown), and intimate and varied association as a unit—in this case living as well as working together during 48-hour duty shifts. The same hour-long session (two discussion tasks with pre- and postquestionnaires for each) that had been used with *ad-hoc* laboratory groups was repeated in this field situation (Smith & Goodchilds, 1963). The research team, an *E* and an *O,* went to 20 individual firehouses (10 single-unit houses, 10 double-unit) which were randomly selected for us by department personnel and were scattered over the entire metropolitan area. The experimental procedures were administered in a station's kitchen–living area and involved all the firemen on duty at a station on the assigned day, making an average of 5 per single house, 10 per double (total $N = 153$).

Differences between these groups and the temporary laboratory groups in interactive behavior, solutions to the tasks, and absolute levels of response to the questionnaire items were not striking; what was striking was the absence of significant wit findings in this new setting. Whether indexed by the Observer Wit Tally (witty here and now) or by sociometric nominations (witty in general), two highly correlated measures in this instance, the witty fireman was indistinguishable from his fellow workers by any available criteria. Perhaps to establish oneself as a successful wit in a short-time short-term group requires specialized attributes and attitudes which can be discarded (or are never needed) in the long-run situation.

Effects of wittiness, on the other hand, unlike the differentiation wit–nonwit, persisted in the work-group setting, at least in the "single," simply structured firehouses. Among the 10 five-person crews, those containing deliberate wits reported more humor (in agreement with the *O* tally), were more satisfied with their group, had clearer role expectations for themselves and others, and were more efficient in the second (the problem-solving) task. In the complex, "double" houses there were no positive effects of deliberate wittiness; in fact, there was a significant negative one: Double houses with deliberate wits were less efficient problem solvers (errors seemed to be perpetuated rather than corrected during discussion).

A field setting poses its own problems; obviously the "double" house posed serious ones for our purposes. Sociologically interesting in its own right—a "double" contained, like a single, an engine crew of four men plus a captain and, in addition, a truck crew of four plus the truck-crew captain—the structurally complex larger group with its built-in dual leadership and member loyalties raises questions presently unanswerable; e.g., in a divided house would humor be expected to bridge or deepen the divide?

4. Military Teams

The specification of humor type by members of the group in which it occurs, including the humorist himself, seemed a promising technique for getting at an area of concern which had eluded our research grasp. Accordingly, for the final study in this series, we modified the two-task interaction session so that the latter half of the period consisted of a playback of the tape-recorded group discussion, with *S*s directed to note, on "Humor Record" forms, each witticism and its source person, categorize the content type (sarcastic or whimsical), and comment where possible on his own reaction to it. Teams of military airmen (four groups of eight) constituted the population.

Again, as with the double-unit fireman sample, the complexities of social-structure patterning in long-term established groups overtaxed our simple-minded hypotheses and even more simple-minded measures of them. Trends supported our previous findings, but only trends. These military teams presented us with a rigid leader–follower hierarchy (sergeants and airmen), firm expectations about who among them would and would not be witty (expectations which were unaffected by demonstrated wittiness in the session), and, unfortunately, an ethnic split (black–white) which seemed also to constitute a social split. The data gathered in this situation were unwieldy and, on the whole, uninformative; the materials specifically generated by the "full playback" approach were meaningless so far as we could determine.

Smith and White (1965), drawing from the same subject population, subsequently improved the technique and applied it, with some success, to exploring more deeply the leadership–influence aspects of the witty personality, simultaneously attempting to manipulate some of the relationships. A classification of their Ss as sarcastically or otherwise witty (based on a partial playback of the humor to group members for such categorization) yielded two suggestive bits: Sarcastic wits, so-defined, scored more highly on a paper–pencil "creativity" test, and groups containing such wits showed the most improvement, pre to post, on the problem-solving task. Although both findings are consistent with our earlier work, the typology classification is suspect (sarcastic wits tended to be undernominated as witty!). The main impediment to real progress with this subproblem remains the restriction in range of humor type which occurs in "brief encounter" group sessions.

C. BEING CREATIVE AND BEING WITTY

The person who is spontaneously humorous is, by the same token, spontaneously creative. And the group which can create humor can throw light on creative processes in general. But beyond these two research interests there is, for a social psychology of humor, yet a third interest, most intriguing of all: What are we to say of that puzzling trio—creating, creating humor, and creating humorously? How are they similar, dissimilar, related? And especially, does the last make the others more or less difficult?

1. Cartoon Captions

Ability to write funny cartoon captions was employed as a consequent variable in an experimental investigation (Ziller, Behringer, & Goodchilds, 1962) of the relative importance of two group-history variables (task accomplishment and various shifting-versus-stable membership patterns). Measured both in terms of number of captions produced and rated funniness of caption, the 48 three-person groups with variously shifting membership histories ("open groups") as compared with the 16 unchanging ("closed") three-person groups showed a significantly higher creativity level. Furthermore, groups with an induced failure experience on preliminary cognitive tasks, irrespective of membership history, evaluated their cartoon-creativity performance as significantly inadequate despite the fact that this performance, though poor, was not demonstrably so. This result was in contrast to that obtained from groups with an induced success experience on the preliminary cognitive tasks. Creating humor, for these male college-student Ss, was apparently easier in a free, flexible, happy environment.

2. Cartoon Captions and Poster Slogans

The same basic format—setting for a laboratory group the task of creating captions for line drawings—underlies an experiment just completed (Goodchilds & Green, 1971) which directly compares the two creativity processes, creating the humorous and creating the serious. Four unacquainted male college students worked as a group (there were 16 groups in all) and attempted to create in a standard time period as many captions as possible for each of eight cartoon-like drawings of interpersonal situations.* Half of the drawings were described to Ss as "cartoons" for which they would accordingly create "funny captions"; the other half were described as "posters dealing with aspects of American life," for which they were to create "serious slogans." In fact, the pictures were interchangeable and were given one-half the time under each label; the order of the two tasks (humorous—serious) was counterbalanced. Each group's eight discussion periods, which totaled approximately 50 min, were monitored, providing an overall Observer Wit Tally with, in this instance, a measured reliability estimate of +.86 (Pearson r for two independent Os).

As with each new tactic in the exploration of this subject, methodological concerns cloud initial outcomes. Nevertheless, several strong findings emerge. It appears, for example, that Ss are able to create humor on demand; that is, as indexed by (blindly) rated funniness of the group product, cartoon captions for a picture were funnier than poster slogans for the identical picture. But the Observer Wit Tally does not show any associated rise (or fall) in number of laughs: Creating humor and creating humorously are not the same. Nor does success at one imply success at the other; there was no apparent relationship between the overall wit tally for a group and the average rated funniness of a group's product. Possibly the simplicity of the wit tally as a measure is, in this case, a weakness rather than a strength; information the tally misses, such as intensity of laughter or quality of a joke-stimulus, might significantly improve the view.

* There were additional aspects to this experiment which are as yet unanalyzed and will not be detailed here.

In regard to the individual who is witty in the experimental situation (according to the Observer Wit Tally), there is agreement with the evidence from previous studies. In these groups also, the witty group-member describes himself in quite positive terms, is an active involved participant, and is seen as helpful and creative by his fellow members. He tends furthermore to ascribe to himself overtly exhibitionist-like traits (e.g., enjoying doing party stunts, wanting to sing in public, never feeling at a loss in a social situation) which suggest that the spontaneous wit may be "stagestruck." He is significantly more well disposed toward the use of humor in the small-group setting; and in the particular experimental setting, he—though not his nonwitty companions—thought his group's responses to the cartoons were superior to their work on the posters. And an interesting final note: At the end of each type of task, the Ss individually checked which among their group's answers they personally preferred; the answers chosen by the wits do not differ in judged funniness from those chosen by nonwits.

D. SARCASM AND WHIMSEY: EFFECTS OF HUMOR TYPE

The last piece of work that I wish to describe was chronologically my first, in truth forming the basis for a doctoral dissertation. The most elaborate and, in some ways, least satisfactory approach yet tried, it is nevertheless indicative, I think, of the direction in which research in this area must ultimately move. Simply put, the idea is that since the naturally occurring phenomenon of interest is easily bruised by the imposition of experimental controls, why not simulate?

Twenty-four fictional scripts were devised, each consisting of a short (1.5–2 min) conversational exchange among three same-sex college-student peers. In each script the amount of participation among the three actors was equal, and one of the three consistently attempted to be funny. In half the scripts the type of humor was consistently sarcastic (biting, barbed); in the remainder it was just as consistently whimsical—clowning. That the scripts were in fact perceived as intended—and to what extent—was confirmed by the judgments of 49 male and 24 female college-student raters. Sets of these materials in booklet form were then presented to selected subject populations, the assigned task being to read each script and, for each, indicate which of the three actors (a) "would probably have the most power to influence me," (b) "would I probably like best," (c) "probably has the most power to influence the group," and (d) "is probably best liked by the group." To the Ss the experiment was described as a study of social perception; humor was not mentioned as relevant or irrelevant to the research interest; sex of actors in the scripts was given as male for male subjects, female for female. (A more complete discussion of the design, including the rationale behind the choice of response dimensions is contained in Goodchilds, 1959.)

1. First Results

From the full 24 scripts, 12—six of each type—were selected to maximize rated funniness and clarity of humor classification; 100 undergraduate male college students served as Ss, making the required four status-judgment choices for each script. Results generally supported the hypotheses that the clowning wit would be seen as well liked and relatively uninfluential, the sarcastic wit as the reverse. However, there was an unexpected underchoice of the sarcastic wit on the influence dimension when the reference was to the self [Question (a)], and subjects tended indiscriminately to overchoose the clowning wit. Essentially the same choice pattern appeared for a female college-student sample ($N = 50$), although in absolute terms women were less favorably disposed toward female wits than men to male—particularly sarcastic wits, particularly on the popularity dimension, particularly when the self was the referent.

Status choices for all 24 scripts were obtained from the female sample (each S responding to half the sketches), enabling an estimate of the importance of rated funniness and "purity" of humor type to the wit's effectiveness. As predicted, purity more clearly differentiated the two dimensions: influence and popularity. Funniness increased the overall "times chosen" score for a wit and, in addition, it had special impact on the sarcastic wit (the unfunny sarcastic wit was totally rejected) and on the influence dimension (the successfully funny wit regardless of type was overchosen as influential).

2. Results of Replication and Extension

The original use of the "simulation" technique (Goodchilds, 1959) was followed a year later by a replication and extension employing adult, summer-session students at a different university. These 44 subjects (22 of each sex) made the same four status-judgment choices to a subset of eight scripts, representing the four best (funniest and most "pure") of each humor type. In addition, after completing the choice task, Ss ranked the sketches as to funniness and categorized the humor in each; finally, they answered a series of questions about their personal attitudes toward wit and the tendency to be witty.

With fewer sketches and an older subject population, the choice pattern nevertheless was exactly replicated. The Ss' reports of type and amount of humor in the sketches agreed also with the original ratings used to qualify sketches for inclusion, indicating that their use here was appropriate.

The new information detailing Ss' own personal wit attitudes (which were positive, the males more so than the females) permitted a division of the group into self-described wits and nonwits. This factor, inserted in the analysis of the status-judgment choices, was in two ways informative. First, in the absolute, self-described wits overchose the actor wits regardless of humor type and dimension of choice. And second, relatively, self-described wits confirmed the original hypotheses most precisely. Indiscriminate overchoosing of the clown, that is, seeing him as not *un*influential, appears to be a function of self-wittiness: Nonwits saw no lack of influence for a clown; "wits" distinctly downgraded the clown's power status.

This completes the empirical discussion.

V. For the Future

What evidence there is—relatively scientific, established evidence—concerning the topic "On Being Witty: Causes, Correlates, and Consequences" has now been marshalled and presented. For such a fertile field it seems a meager harvest. All of us together have not accomplished enough to make substantive summarizing any more than a scholastic exercise. Yet if humor truly is, as it has been interminably touted to be, tension releasing, thought clarifying, and otherways medicinally wondrous, it behooves us to discover what we can of how, when, and why it happens. The serious study of spontaneous humor by those not too serious to appreciate and occasionally create a good joke will, I am certain, contribute greatly to our understanding of the human experience and perhaps to our ability to ease and/or enhance aspects of it.

Or as novelist Aubrey Menen, in his free translation of the Sanskrit epic *The Ramayana* (1954), has the Hindu sage, Valmiki, express it, "There are three things which are real: God, human folly, and laughter. Since the first two pass our comprehension, we must do what we can with the third [p. 276]."

References

Abrahams, R. D. A performance-centred approach to gossip. *Man,* 1970, 5, 290–301.

Bales, R. F. *Interaction process analysis: A method for the study of small groups.* Reading, Massachusetts: Addison-Wesley, 1950.

Bales, R. F. The equilibrium problem in small groups. In T. Parsons, R. F. Bales, & E. A. Shills (Eds.), *Working papers in the theory of action.* Glencoe, Illinois: Free Press, 1953.

Bales, R. F. *Personality and interpersonal behavior.* New York: Holt, 1970.

Benedict, R. *Patterns of culture.* Boston: Houghton, 1934.

Berdie, R. F. Playing the dozens. *Journal of Abnormal & Social Psychology,* 1947, 42, 120–121.

Bergson, H. *Laughter: An essay on the meaning of the comic.* New York: MacMillan, 1911.

Borgatta, E. F. A note on the consistency of subject behavior in interaction process analysis. *Sociometry,* 1964, 27, 222–229.

Bradney, P. The joking relationship in industry. *Human Relations,* 1957, 10, 179–187.

Charles, L. H. The clown's function. *Journal of American Folklore,* 1945, 58, 25–34.

Cloyd, J. S. Patterns of behavior in informal interaction. *Sociometry,* 1964, 27, 161–173.

Coser, R. L. Laughter among colleagues. *Psychiatry,* 1960, 23, 81–95.

Goodchilds, J. D. Effects of being witty on position in the social structure of a small group. *Sociometry,* 1959, 22, 261–272.

Goodchilds, J. D., & Green, J. A. Inventiveness, wit, and small group behavior. Unpublished manuscript, Univ. of California, Los Angeles, 1971.

Goodchilds, J. D., & Smith, E. E. The wit and his group. *Human Relations,* 1964, 17, 23–31.

Goodrich, A. T., Henry, J., & Goodrich, D. W. Laughter in psychiatric staff conferences: A sociopsychiatric analysis. *American Journal of Orthopsychiatry,* 1954, 24, 175–184.

Gruner, C. R. Effect of humor on speaker ethos and audience information gain. *Journal of Communication,* 1967, 17, 228–233.

Hall, G. S., & Allin, A. The psychology of tickling, laughing, and the comic. *American Journal of Psychology,* 1897, 9, 1–41.

Hannerz, U. *Soulside: Inquiries into ghetto culture and community.* New York: Columbia Univ. Press, 1969.

Kambouropoulou, P. Individual differences in the sense of humor. *American Journal of Psychology,* 1926, 37, 268–278.

Klapp, O. E. *Heroes, villains and fools: The changing American character.* Englewood Cliffs, New Jersey: Prentice-Hall, 1962.

Lull, P. E. The effectiveness of humor in persuasive speech. *Speech Monographs,* 1940, 7, 26–40.

Menen, A. *The Ramayana.* New York: Scribner, 1954.

Middleton, R., & Moland, J. Humor in Negro and white subcultures: A study of jokes among university students. *American Sociological Review,* 1959, 24, 61–69.

Miller, F. C. Humor in a Chippewa tribal council. *Ethnology,* 1967, 6, 263–271.

Miller, W. B. Lower class culture as a generating milieu of gang delinquency. *Journal of Social issues,* 1958, 14(3), 5–19.

Nelms, H. *Play production: A handbook for the backstage worker, a guidebook for the student of drama.* New York: Barnes & Noble, 1950.

O'Connell, W. E. The social aspects of wit and humor. *Journal of Social Psychology,* 1969, 79, 183–187.

Radcliffe-Brown, A. R. On joking relationships. *Africa,* 1940, 13, 195–210.

Singer, D. L. Aggression arousal, hostile humor, catharsis. *Journal of Personality & Social Psychology,* 1968, 8 (1, Pt 2), 1–14.

Smith, E. E., & Goodchilds, J. D. Characteristics of the witty group member: The wit as leader. *American Psychologist,* 1959, 14, 375–376.

Smith, E. E., & Goodchilds, J. D. The wit in large and small established groups. *Psychological Reports,* 1963, 13, 273–274.

Smith, E. E., & White, H. L. Wit, creativity, and sarcasm. *Journal of Applied Psychology,* 1965, 49, 131–134.

Welsford, E. *The fool: His social and literary history.* London: Faber & Faber, 1935.

Winter, D. G., Alpert, R., & McClelland, D. C. The classic personal style. *Journal of Abnormal & Social Psychology,* 1963, 67, 254–265.

Young, P. T. Laughing and weeping, cheerfulness and depression: A study of moods among college students. *Journal of Social Psychology,* 1937, 8, 311–334.

Ziller, R. C., Behringer, R. D., & Goodchilds, J. D. Group creativity under conditions of success or failure and variations in group stability. *Journal of Applied Psychology,* 1962, 46, 43–49.

Chapter 10

Humor Judgments as a Function of Reference Groups and Identification Classes

Lawrence La Fave

Department of Psychology
University of Windsor, Windsor, Ontario, Canada

I. Problems and Paradoxes

This chapter is concerned with experimental studies of the influence of the S's reference groups (RG's) upon his humor judgments. Therefore it complements Martineau's work (Chapter 5), which relates RG's to humor.

Is there such a thing as a sense of humor? Of course almost everyone knows that a sense of humor exists! Most everyone also knows that some people have it; others do not. And should you probe further, asking anyone which of his acquaintances possess a sense of humor and which do not, you will likely learn that he possesses one but that his adversaries are sadly deficient. Whenever this subject is discussed in the humor literature, the authors seem to assume (either inadvertently or explicitly) that a select few possess a sense of humor while, for the most part, the masses are capable of being amused only at others' expense. Nevertheless, it seems desirable to question whether a sense of humor exists. Moreover, this seems a question potent enough to give rise to a host of strange and useful ideas whose existence, heretofore, has scarcely been dreamed of.

A typical definition suggests that if a person has the capacity for *laughing at his own expense,* then he has a *sense of humor.* Laughter seems to be a desirable scientific construct in that it is so operational. But as *humor* is synonymous with *amusement,* we now must ask: Is laughter synonymous with amusement? It seems immediately clear that amusement is a mental experience—an *O* in an *S–O–R* model—unlike laughter, which is a response (*R*). Obviously then, amusement and laughter are not identical. They would be equivalent if amusement were both a necessary and sufficient condition of laughter. But are they equivalent? On the contrary, a person apparently may laugh under any of the following conditions of nonamusement: when literally tickled, embarrassed, afraid, releasing tension, or pretending to have grasped the point of a "joke" which sailed over his head. Children have been found to laugh at "jokes" which they did not understand (Zigler, Levine, & Gould, 1967). Reynolds (1971) reminds us that human neurological disorders can precipitate laughter unaccompanied by amusement. Druckman and Chao (1957) summarize the pathological conditions that can accompany inappropriate laughter as follows: (1) generalized cerebral arteriosclerosis, (2) frontal lobotomy, and (3) some kinds of seizures. Reynolds notes that gelolepsy (a form of epilepsy) is such a seizure.

But is amusement a sufficient condition of laughter? An amused person may avoid laughing to keep from embarrassing the butt of the joke, to remain unnoticed, or to appear sophisticated. Dott (1938, cited in Reynolds, 1971) also relates that "at least one case involving damage of the ventral hypothalamus has been reported in which *laughter could not occur even though the appropriate emotion was present* [italics added]."

In other words, amusement is *neither* a necessary nor sufficient condition of laughter. Two suggestions for future research immediately become apparent: (1) It would seem useful to investigate distinctions between *types* of laughter (e.g., does "amused laughter" sound and look different from "embarrassed laughter"? La Gaipa, 1971, and his associates have been investigating such distinctions via video and audio tapes of cohesive groups.) (See also Chapter 11.) (2) We who lack extrasensory perception cannot read other minds directly and, therefore, must infer, from some operational indices (i.e., from responses), whether these others are amused. However, as we have seen, neither laughter nor its absence is necessarily a valid indicator of amusement per se. Sometimes smiling operationally defines amusement; sometimes the statement, "That's funny," (defines it); sometimes applause; etc. It appears then that humor research and theory must move in the direction of what Webb, Campbell, Schwartz, and Sechrest (1966) refer to as *multi-operationalism,* and Sherif (personal communication) describes as *validity cross checks.*

The preceding argument permits some rather strong conclusions: One is that "humor" theories by Freud (1917, 1928), Bergson (1911), Eastman (1936), and other well-known "humor" theorists are really not theories of humor at all but, at best, theories of laughter! Thus, since as was just shown, humor and laughter are *not* synonymous, we have demolished all such "humor" theories which equate laughter and humor (see Chapter 1).

For instance, let us single out Freud since, of the preceding theories, his has generated by far the most research. If to be taken literally was not Freud's intention, he apparently failed to warn his disciple Flugel. Observing that people laugh when tickled, Flugel (1954), following Freud's erroneous assumption that laughter necessarily indicates humor, feels duty bound to give a Freudian explanation as to why the ticklee is amused.

What is needed, however, is a theory of humor—not a humorous theory. And once we cease confounding laughter with amusement, our task as humor researchers and theorists becomes less impossible.

But the more important question seems not: Does anyone have a sense of humor? (for, depending upon our definition of "sense of humor," either the answer "yes" or "no" becomes correct). The more crucial question is: If humor theory and research would be advanced, what is the most fruitful way of defining "sense of humor"? Let us tentatively define "sense of humor" as a contradiction in terms, since the constructs "at one's own expense" (an unhappy mental state) and "amusement" (a happy mental state) are mutually exclusive. Then, denial that anyone possesses a sense of humor resolves one paradox. Yet, no one can deny that men *are* capable of being amused, and often at the expense of others. The conjunction of these premises seems to suggest that a superiority theory of humor is worthy of investigation. Now let us *social-*psychologize superiority theory, adding to it an important generalization. Consider that a mere spectator will wax triumphant if a group attractive to him achieves victory. Then perhaps, as a vicarious superiority humor theory would predict, a "joke" may prove especially funny when the "good guys" beat the "bad guys." Nonetheless, degree of funniness being a humor *judgment,* and the "good guys" a positive *reference group,* we have finally circled back to this chapter's title. Consequently, at the expense of rushing a little past our story, we are ready to review the experiments most relevant to this chapter's domain.

II. Review of Experimental Literature

It seems useful to begin with the experiment to be employed as the paradigm (La Fave, 1961). The general theoretical statement upon which the La Fave experiment bases its hypotheses is the following superiority humor assumption: *A "joke" is humorous to the extent that it enhances an object of affection and/or disparages an object of repulsion; unhumorous to the extent that it does the opposite.* La Fave's major hypothesis, however, is more specific than the above—substituting for "object of affection," "positive reference group" (+RG) or "positive identification class" (+IC), and for "object of repulsion," "negative reference group" (−RG) or "negative identification class" (−IC). In colloquial language: "Jokes tend to be funny when the good guys win and the bad guys lose; unfunny when the bad guys win and the good guys lose."

Does not such a prediction assume though, that jokes lack absolute stimulating value, that, as Flugel (1954, p. 726) observed, no such thing as a good joke exists? Exactly! In fact, jokes, strictly speaking, may nonexist too (if the above vicarious superiority assumption holds, for "jokes" then become culturally, i.e., RG, relative; one man's joke becomes another man's insult). To keep us alert to this possibility, *joke* is often placed in quotes throughout this chapter. In such case a "joke" (an *S* variable) is neither a necessary nor sufficient condition to the *O* variable, *humor* (just as, previously, the *R* variable, *laughter,* also was seen as neither necessary nor sufficient to humor). Perhaps then, with respect to *homo sapiens,* it may truly be said: *Humor lies neither in laughter nor in "jokes", but only in the minds of men.*

La Fave's major hypothesis states: Jokes tend to be judged funny by *S*s whose +RG is esteemed and −RG disparaged; to be judged unfunny by *S*s whose +RG is disparaged and −RG esteemed.

This breaks down into the following two subhypotheses:

1a. Jokes which esteem *S*s' +RG tend to be judged funny relative to those which esteem *S*s' −RG.

1b. Jokes which disparage *S*s' +RG tend to be judged unfunny relative to those which disparage *S*s' −RG.

La Fave's remaining hypothesis predicts the following: Jokes which prompt *S*s to identify positively with a more inclusive RG or

IC should prompt Ss from disjoint IC's to judge alike against the common enemy provided by a –IC disjoint with respect to their more inclusive +IC. Thus, if the three IC's–Catholics, Baptists, and Jehovah's Witnesses (JW's)–are all proper subsets of the +IC Christian, and if the IC agnostic is mutually exclusive with respect to all four of these IC's, then any good Catholic, Baptist, or JW should find jokes relatively funny when the Christian wins and the agnostic loses, and relatively unfunny when the opposite occurs. For ease of future reference, we shall call this Hypothesis 2.

Because the experimental method most suitable for measuring the influence of RG's on humor judgments differs radically from conventional methods, merely listing the techniques employed in the La Fave 1961 experiment may not prove maximally meaningful. Instead, let us imagine ourselves constructing such an experiment, contemplating the practical problems in testing the stated hypotheses and the techniques which need to be introduced to solve them.

Tests of the hypotheses involve four RG's (such that three can generalize to form a fifth). We would need to select, therefore, a social issue that is "hot" or ego-involving the whole year round, and which would supply sufficient available Ss. Also, in case our theory is correct, we should give it a fair chance to defend itself. Therefore, let us choose each RG such that each dislikes the other three. A social issue obviously satisfying the above conditions is, of course, religion. We therefore choose the four RG's already mentioned: Catholics, Baptists, JW's, and agnostics, with the first three combining (against a common, anti-Christian, agnostic enemy) to make up a fifth, Christian.

Of course we cannot afford to use so many "jokes" that our Ss, "fun-fatigued" (Martin, 1905), refuse to cooperate. Perhaps 20 is enough. Our hypotheses suggest using dialogue between different combinations of two RG's for different "jokes". Five such combinations might suffice (as shown in Table I). Thus our class of 20 "jokes" gets partitioned into five subsets of four "jokes" each. To test our general hypothesis, however, a minimum of two RG's would be needed, so, for the moment let us consider only two, Catholics and JW's.

Suppose that the jokes of this combination are all anti-Catholic and our results, consistent with superiority theory, show these to be funnier to JW's than to Catholics. A cynic could then retort: "Your prediction proved correct not because JW's were made to feel superior, but because JW's possess an easy-to-amuse personality trait which Catholics don't share!" We would have no answer; our experimental design failed to exclude this alternative interpretation.

TABLE I

Partitioning and Subpartitioning Permutations within Class of 20 "Jokes"

Set in partition class	Subpartitioning permutation	"Joke" number	Group esteemed	Group disparaged
1	1	4	Catholic	JW[a]
1	1	17	Catholic	JW
1	2	1	JW	Catholic
1	2	18	JW	Catholic
2	1	14	Catholic	Agnostic
2	1	19	Catholic	Agnostic
2	2	10	Agnostic	Catholic
2	2	20	Agnostic	Catholic
3	1	6	Catholic	Baptist
3	1	13	Catholic	Baptist
3	2	5	Baptist	Catholic
3	2	16	Baptist	Catholic
4	1	7	Baptist	Agnostic
4	1	12	Baptist	Agnostic
4	2	2	Agnostic	Baptist
4	2	15	Agnostic	Baptist
5	1	8	Christian	Agnostic
5	1	9	Christian	Agnostic
5	2	3	Agnostic	Christian
5	2	11	Agnostic	Christian

[a] Represents Jehovah's Witness.

Wolff, Smith, and Murray (1934), using Jews and gentiles, faced this problem. Apparently consistent with superiority theory, their anti-Jewish "jokes" proved funnier to gentiles than Jews. To rule out the alternative interpretation, these authors added some anti-Scottish "jokes," predicting these "control jokes" (unlike the former "experimental jokes") would not significantly differentiate Jewish from gentile humor judgments. Counter to their prediction, the Jewish Ss found the anti-Scottish "jokes" significantly less funny than the gentiles did. One might argue that the personality trait explanation fits the data, while a superiority theory does not. However, *serendipitously,* Wolff *et al.* achieved a *vicarious* (social-psychological) interpretation. They reasoned that, since the anti-Scottish "jokes" emphasized Scotch stinginess—a negative stereotype from which the Jews themselves suffered—so the Jews sympathized (i.e., positively identified with the Scots), finding such "jokes" relatively unfunny.

Our hypotheses of course bet on the Wolff *et al.* serendipity. Had they known of the RG construct (invented later by Hyman, 1942), they possibly would have realized the experimental–control joke distinction represented an inadequate method of testing their hypothesis. (Incidentally, Middleton, 1959, was apparently the first to apply the RG construct to humor research—though not until his *ad-hoc* interpretation as to why some of his Hobbesian superiority theory predictions were wrong. He, like Wolff *et al.* had failed to anticipate that Ss may positively identify with an RG not of their membership group. Thus Middleton did not foresee that university Ss of lower class parentage might identify positively with the middle class and that Negroes—perhaps Uncle Toms and Aunt Jemimas—would find anti-Negro jokes as funny as whites would.)

High ego involvement with a new RG is not easily induced in a few laboratory sessions; also, validity problems concerning the social psychology of the psychological experiment are created thereby. For these reasons, it seems necessary, in RG experiments, to select groups from *different* populations. Yet such is merely a *matching design.* The difficulty with a mere matching design has been stated by Siegel (1956):

> A matching design is only as good as the experimenter's ability to determine how to match the pairs, and this ability is frequently very limited. This problem is circumvented when each subject is used as his own control; no more precise matching is possible than that achieved by identity [p. 62].*

How could each S be made his own control? Each joke could consist of dialogue between representatives of rival groups in which the last speaker always squelches the other. Furthermore, the set of jokes could partition into combinations of four jokes such that each combination includes both possible permutations. Thus, for the combination of four Catholic-versus-JW jokes, let one permutation of two jokes be a Catholic win and JW loss, and the remaining two jokes be the other permutation, i.e., a JW win and Catholic loss. Using each S as his own control in this manner reduces a host of otherwise troublesome variables to random error.

Now a nondisguised humor judgment experiment could be structured as a disguised attitude test since, if the superiority hypothesis should prove true, Ss could unconsciously expose their likes and dislikes by their humor judgments. In their pioneering research, Wolff *et al.* (1934) exhibited awareness of this projective test potential. If such research is to be valid, its design needs to keep the Ss' defenses down. One way the La Fave experiment tried to do

* From *Nonparametric statistics for the behavioral sciences* by S. Siegel. Copyright 1956, McGraw-Hill. Used with permission of McGraw-Hill Book Company.

this was by referring to the research as sociological (not psychological) in the Ss' instructions. Another was to convince the Ss (by requesting them not to write their names on the questionnaire, and testing in groups of at least five) that their results were anonymous. (Names were unnecessary since all Ss in a given experimental session presumably esteemed the same RG.)

However, testing Ss in groups created the possibility that one S's laughter at a "joke" might influence other Ss' humor judgments. Shuffling each S's deck of "jokes" into a different order randomized this *social contagion* variable. Such shuffling also randomized out order effects (cf. Martin, 1905, regarding effects of "fun fatigue" and "fun accumulation").

Another problem was to weed out the *compliant conformist,* since his membership group is not his +RG. Conversely, a nonmembership group may be a +RG for him. Insufficient allowance for such possibilities helps explain why the Wolff *et al.* and Middleton experiments provided no solid support for a vicarious superiority theory of humor. Thus, as discussed earlier, Wolff *et al.* failed to anticipate that Jewish Ss might, under the conditions of their experiment, positively identify with Scots (a nonmembership + RG for these Jews), while Middleton overlooked the theoretical and technical implications of the fact that some Ss with Negro *ascribed* status might hold Negroes as a membership–non-+RG; and that lower class Ss might identify positively not with the lower class but with the middle.

Thus La Fave (1961) needed to ensure that the religious membership groups were also the +RG's. An *external validity check* seemed needed to guard against Ss belonging to their religious groups "in name only." For this purpose a "spy system" was used; members in good standing of the given religious group (usually La Fave's students) were to select carefully only *loyal* members for Ss. As a further cross-check, a brief questionnaire administered to Ss, after they had finished sorting the "jokes," asked them to check the religious groups they preferred. A Catholic S had to check Catholic; a JW, JW; etc., for S's humor judgments to be counted. Also, all Ss except those in the agnostic group needed to answer "Yes" to: "Do you prefer to consider yourself a Christian?" while agnostic Ss needed to check "No." Only two of the checks by the potential Ss failed to confirm the "spy's" predictions.

One other apparently relevant experiment historically preceded La Fave's 1961 study. Roberts and Johnson (1957), deriving their major hypothesis from the theories proposed by Freud (1917, 1928) and

Mead (1934), correctly predicted that "empathic identification" and humor would be positively related. However, the superiority predictions of Wolff *et al.* and Middleton would seem to predict a *negative* relation between empathic (or positive) identification and humor (since sympathy or empathy for the butt of a joke would render it relatively unfunny). Therefore, the Roberts and Johnson finding appears to contradict the predictions of Wolff *et al.* and Middleton. La Fave's 1961 hypotheses, if substantiated, would apparently resolve this contradiction, since he predicts that humor and positive or empathic identification are sometimes positively related and sometimes negatively. Thus La Fave's predictions assume that apparent contradictions between the predictions of Roberts and Johnson and the others could be shown to vanish by incorporating the needed improvements into a theoretical framework and experimental design.

One valuable contribution of the Wolff *et al.* and Roberts and Johnson experiments is their use of *multi-operationalism* (cf. Webb *et al.,* 1966). Laughter, smiling, humor judgments, and GSR's positively correlated sufficiently under conditions apparently analogous enough to those of La Fave (1961) to dissuade him from the use of multi-amusement measures.

The results of La Fave's 1961 experiment on the major hypothesis are that, on a *sign test,* all 20 jokes came out in the predicted direction ($p < .00004$).* (For purposes of statistical analysis, the data were treated dichotomously; i.e., "very funny" and "funny" judgments were scored as funny; judgments in the remaining three categories were scored as unfunny.)

Hypotheses 1a and 1b each predict for only 16 jokes (see Table I). Table I also shows that Hypothesis 2 predicts only for four jokes. (Recall that in Hypothesis 2, three groups, Catholics, Baptists and JW's, are all treated as included in one "supergroup," namely, Christians.) On Hypothesis 1a, 12 of 16 jokes score in the predicted direction; on Hypothesis 1b, 13 of 16; and on Hypothesis 2, 4 of 4. Correcting for interdependence resulting from use of means in the predicting relation, the probability for Hypothesis 1a becomes $p < .08$; for Hypothesis 1b, $p < .03$; and for Hypothesis 2, $p < .02$.

However, some very extenuating circumstances on Hypothesis 1a suggest considering it tentatively significant until replication shows

---

* I am indebted to Professor Robert F. Priest of the University of Missouri, St. Louis, for kindly pointing out that, in earlier reports of my research, I had failed to allow for the reduction in degrees of freedom for each mean, for each combination of jokes.

otherwise. First, Hypothesis 1a would have easily been significant if measured in another conceivable way. If vicarious superiority theory is correct, wrong predictions should deviate less from chance than right ones. When absolute percentage difference from chance is recorded, the four wrong predictions are the last four of the 16 in rank order ($p < .001$, one-tailed). Also, the failure to substantiate Hypothesis 1a was clearly based on two technical errors by La Fave. First, he failed to understand that his N (16), rendering only 12 degrees of freedom, would be too small to expect significance, with any confidence, when dealing with subhypotheses which would be expected to show, on the average, only one-half the trend of the major hypothesis. The other technical mistake concerns the careless "spy work" on Catholic Ss. Catholic pretest results showed humor judgment trends as strongly in line with predictions as any group's. Yet, in the actual experiment, of seven wrong predictions across all hypotheses [four on Hypothesis 1a and three on 1b], Catholics clearly accounted for six. These Catholics chosen for the actual experiment were coeds in a Catholic college in a midwestern city. La Fave simply failed to be sufficiently certain whether the "spy system" adequately weeded out nonloyal Catholics prior to testing, as he had carefully done for the vast majority of the Ss from the other groups.

The La Fave 1961 experiment appears to offer essentially four original contributions: (1) Rather unequivocally supporting, for the first time, Hobbesian superiority theory, it also generalizes to a *vicarious* superiority theory in which humor judgments prove a function of RG's and IC's. (2) This experiment apparently reconciles the "conflicting" findings of Wolff *et al.* and Middleton with those of Roberts and Johnson. (3) Substantiation of Hypothesis 2 (regarding switching levels of generality) employs the (hitherto unused) IC's model, which is capable of suggesting how to control and/or systematically vary a number of important variables previously ignored. (4) Developed for the humor judgment area is a new experimental methodology employing interrelated subhypotheses and, more centrally, by counterbalancing permutations, using each S as his own control. In a sense, however, the theoretical improvements suggested by RG's and IC's generate all the above-listed contributions, for it was these theoretical advancements which also indicated the necessary improvements in technical controls.

A critic, however, might doubt that the support of vicarious superiority theory by this nontraditional methodology will still be found on other social issues. Therefore, three stripped-down experimental replications of the major hypothesis were performed on three other social issues. These three replications repeat the methodology of La Fave (1961). However, since only the major hypothesis is tested in each of these replications, only two RG's are needed for each experiment (with a slight qualification on the Women's Liberation experiment, to be discussed).

The first replication was by La Fave, Haddad, and Marshall (1970). La Fave learned that the latter two authors (students of his already pursuing a vicarious superiority humor experiment in his class) had suddenly become participants in a 10-day sit-in in the Theology Department at the University of Windsor (February, 1969). The humor experiment's social issue was consequently changed to that of the sit-in or occupation, so that Ss could be tested while they were still ego-involved in the issue. It was possible to run the Ss the following month, and they comprised two IC's (pro-occupiers and anti-occupiers). All 20 jokes were again predicted in the correct direction; i.e., pro-occupiers tended to find pro-occupier jokes funnier than anti-occupier ones, while anti-occupiers tended to judge the anti-occupier jokes funnier than the pro-occupier ($p < .000002$).

The next replication (La Fave, McCarthy, & Haddad, in preparation) involved the issue of Canadian–American relations. Results found 16 of 20 jokes scoring in the predicted direction ($p < .005$).

The third replication by this group (La Fave, Billinghurst, & Haddad, in preparation) concerned Women's Liberation. To paraphrase the hypothesis rather loosely, promale males were predicted to find promale–antifemale jokes funnier than profemale–antimale jokes; while profemale females (members or sympathizers with Women's Liberation organizations) would tend to find profemale–antimale jokes funnier than promale–antifemale. Here, results found 17 of 20 jokes predicted correctly ($p < .003$).

The questionnaire administered after the humor sorting in this last experiment asked which sex ought to rule—"Males?" "Females?" or "Both equally?" It was predicted also that males who responded "both equally" would make humor judgments less male than "male" males and less female than "both equally" females. This prediction was also substantiated.

Thus the four experiments by the La Fave group seem to lend strong support to the assumption that RG's and IC's *do* influence humor judgments in predictable ways. The only remaining experiments in this area are, to my knowledge, by Priest and his associates.

Two of these (Priest, 1966; Priest & Abrahams, 1970) concerned United States presidential elections (1964 and 1968, respectively).

Priest and Abrahams summarize the Priest (1966) study as follows:

> It was shown that Ss rated jokes hostile to their preferred candidate as less funny than jokes hostile to the opposing candidate.
>
> [In the Priest and Abrahams (1970) experiment:] Hostile jokes about Wallace, Nixon, Humphrey and Senator McCarthy's "disaffected liberal" were rated by college students on the day before the 1968 election. The difference in their response to jokes about Humphrey and Nixon correlated .42 with candidate preference for psychology students . . ., .58 for political science student volunteers. . . . The difference in response to jokes about "disaffected liberals" vs. jokes about other groups correlated significantly with attitude toward the Democratic party but not with candidate preference. The results support reference group theory, replicate two other studies of election humor and suggest that the enjoyment of hostile humor depends upon who is being aggressed against [p. 779].*

We can only find one other experiment in the humor literature which explicitly mentions the construct RG—an unpublished study by Priest and Phillips (1966). However, it is not clear that their experiment (which attempts to measure ratings of hostile and sexual jokes when in the presence of same or opposite-sex partner) can answer whether RG's influence humor judgments. A basic reason their research has no unambiguous interpretation is that the authors seem to use the constructs *membership group* and *RG* interchangeably; hence, no adequate validity cross checks are employed to insure that the membership group is really also the RG.

Although the Priest (1966) and Priest and Abrahams (1970) results suggest that RG's influence humor judgments, yet their insufficient controls leave interpretation ambiguous. For instance, besides (1) consistently confounding membership and RG, they also fail (2) to control the heard-before variable, and (3) to employ each S as his own control. However, a relevant experiment by Gutman and Priest (1969) does apply the conventional experimental methodology. The authors summarize:

> Under what conditions is one person's aggression toward another judged to be funny? It was . . . predicted that a good person's hostile act would be seen as less hostile and more humorous; secondly . . . that a victim who "deserved" the hostility he received would elicit more humor than an undeserving victim. Both hypotheses were tested by manipulating the perceived goodness or badness of the two protagonists in four

---

* Reprinted with permission of author and publisher: R. F. Priest & J. Abrahams. Candidate preference and hostile humor in the 1968 elections. *Psychological Reports,* 1970, 26, 779–783.

experimentally written "squelch" jokes. College students ($N = 192$) rated the amount of hostility, the justifiability of the humorous hostility, and the humor of these jokes. Both hypotheses were confirmed [p. 60] .*

The authors' four experimentally written "squelch" jokes have: (a) good aggressor, bad victim; (b) good aggressor, good victim; (c) bad aggressor, bad victim; and (d) bad aggressor, good victim. Although the experimental methodology of the Gutman and Priest study differs from that of the La Fave studies, a close analogy exists between three of these four conditions and those of La Fave's 1961 experiment. Thus, in La Fave's major hypothesis, from the perspective of the victorious group in a particular joke, there was (a) a good aggressor and a bad victim, but from the perspective of the group which was the butt of that joke, there was (b) a bad aggressor and a good victim. Consider, however, any of the 16 jokes which had neutral groups (i.e., groups which were neither esteemed nor disparaged by that particular joke). From the perspective of such neutral groups the particular joke would (c) have a bad aggressor, bad victim. [La Fave's 1961 experiment had nothing analogous to (d) good aggressor, good victim—such was irrelevant to his hypotheses.]

Gutman and Priest used personal (not RG) names for aggressors and victims in their jokes. They defined either the aggressor or victim as good if he "behaves in a socially acceptable manner," and bad if he "behaves in a socially unacceptable manner." However, had the authors employed RG names (like Catholic) rather than personal names (like Jane), they could have defined a "good" aggressor or victim as a member of S's +RG and a "bad" aggressor or victim as a member of S's —RG. Doing so would have, first, connected the hostility-and-humor area to the RG-and-humor area and, second, avoided the unfortunate ethnocentrism of treating "socially acceptable behavior" and "socially unacceptable behavior" (though culturally relative) as absolutes. We must ask: Socially acceptable to which RG? Socially unacceptable to which RG?

My attitude toward the experimental literature on humor and hostility has, for the most part, vacillated between hostility and amusement. Incredible though it may seem, these experiments (performed usually in a psychoanalytic tradition) have typically failed to raise such obvious questions as: Hostility by whom? Hostility toward whom? Hostility toward what theme?

* J. Gutman & R. F. Priest. When is aggression funny? *Journal of Personality & Social Psychology*, 12, 1969, 60–65. Copyright 1969 by the American Psychological Association and reproduced by permission.

Fortunately, movement toward merger of these two humor research areas seems to have begun recently (Berkowitz, 1970; Gutman & Priest, 1969).* Ironically, however, these authors themselves seemed unaware of the emerging merger—for neither can I find in their articles nor in any others on hostility and humor at the time of this writing, any reference to RG's.

III. Reasons Why IC's Construct Is Preferable to RG

(1) The RG construct is often used in reference to a mere category of people which lacks group properties, thus abusing the meaning of the construct *group.* The word *class* enables IC's to be a more general construct than RG can legitimately be.

(2) *Class* is more comprehensive than group; a one-man group is a contradiction in terms, but one-man classes exist.

(3) As Kelley (1968) has observed, *reference* is ambiguous; it can mean either *identification* or *comparison.* Therefore, Turner's (1956) phrase *identification group* would be less ambiguous. However, comprehensiveness would also seem reduced. Yet this lost comprehensiveness can be restored without ambiguating by treating comparison not as a value for the variable reference, but as a mathematical relation which the subject conceptualizes between classes (e.g., when he prefers one of his IC's to another).

(4) By its plural form IC's suggests the possibility of multi-ordinality; RG does not. Some of the most fascinating data in social psychology concern the "irrational" behavior resulting from switching levels of generality.

(5) The RG either refers only to positive identification or negative identification but ignores neutral. The IC's is again more comprehensive than RG, since IC's have emotional components which vary on a continuum from positive *through neutral* to negative.

(6) The IC's model distinguishes the extension (denotation) of a predicate symbol from its intension (connotation) and treats distinct intensions with coextensive extensions in different planes—thus helping clarify discussion with respect to switching dimensions of identification (e.g., from the political dimension to the economic).

(7) The IC's are defined in subjective (psychological) intension rather than either conventional (sociological) or objective (meta-physical) intension. Thus cognitions of abnormal persons can also be handled within this model.

* A symposium at the annual convention of the American Psychological Association, Washington, D. C., September, 1971, emphasized the need for theoretical integration of these two humor research areas.

(8) Many advantages of rigor and precision accrue to the IC's construct by virtue of its mathematical nature. Various types of comparisons (i.e., mathematical relations) can be distinguished, and new, useful deductions, not available to the RG theorist, can be generated.

An *S*'s IC's may now be defined as *those cognitive sets of elements which are attitudes of S.* (Thus, any IC has both an emotive and a cognitive component.) Not only does *S*'s set of IC's represent a proper subset of his set of attitudes, but this chapter is only concerned with that proper subset of *S*'s IC's in which the elements refer to *persons.* Also, *S* must have some *symbol* (such as a noun or noun phrase) by which he represents each IC to himself.

IV. Conclusion

Review of relevant literature suggests that the superiority construct is very valuable in humor research and theory. It becomes yet more valuable when allowance is also made for *vicarious* superiority by incorporating the construct of RG. However, greater rigor and generality result from replacing the RG construct with that of the IC's. These constructs also have potency enough to move into the humor-and-hostility area.

Despite all this, superiority (unless used so loosely as to lose all meaning) is neither a necessary nor sufficient condition to amusement; sometimes we feel superior without being amused, at other times we are amused without feeling superior. The essence of humor still awaits its discoverer.

Acknowledgment

I wish to thank my many students, too numerous to mention here, who helped with the four experiments reported in this chapter. William A. Maesen and Mrs. Eleanor Lee were especially helpful with my dissertation experiment, as was my major professor, Muzafer Sherif.

References

Bergson, H. *Laughter: An essay on the meaning of the comic.* New York: Macmillan, 1911.

Berkowitz, L. Aggressive humor as a stimulus to aggressive responses. *Journal of Personality & Social Psychology,* 1970, 16, 710–717.

Dott, N. M. Surgical aspects of the hypothalamus. In W. E. Clark, R. J. Le Gros, and D. M. Dott (Eds.), *The hypothalmus. Morphological, clinical and surgical aspects.* Edinburgh: Oliver and Boyd, 1938.

Druckman, R., & Chao, D. Laughter in epilepsy. *Neurology,* 1957, 7, 26–36.

Eastman, M. *Enjoyment of laughter.* New York: Simon & Schuster, 1936.

Flugel, J. C. Humor and laughter. In G. Lindzey (Ed.), *Handbook of social psychology.* Vol. 2. *Special fields and applications.* Reading, Massachusetts: Addison-Wesley, 1954.

Freud, S. *Wit and its relation to the unconscious.* New York: Moffat, Ward, 1917. (Originally: *Der Witz und seine Beziehung zum Unbewussten.* Leipzig and Vienna: Deuticke, 1905.)

Freud, S. On humor. *International Journal of Psychoanalysis,* 1928, 9, 1–6.

Gutman, J., & Priest, R. F. When is aggression funny? *Journal of Personality & Social Psychology,* 1969, 12, 60–65.

Hyman, H. The psychology of status. *Archives of Psychology,* 1942, No. 269.

Kelley, H. H. Two functions of reference groups. In H. Hyman & E. Singer (Eds.), *Readings in reference group theory and research.* New York: Free Press, 1968.

La Fave, L. Humor judgments as a function of reference groups: An experimental study. Unpublished doctoral dissertation, Univ. of Oklahoma, 1961.

La Fave, L., Billinghurst, K., & Haddad, J. Humor judgments as a function of identification classes: Women's liberation. In preparation.

La Fave, L., Haddad, J., & Marshall, N. Humor judgments as a function of identification classes: The student sit-in issue. Paper presented before Canadian Psychological Association, Winnipeg, May 1970. (Abstract, *Canadian Psychologist,* 1970, 11, 187–188)

La Fave, L., McCarthy, K., & Haddad, J. Humor judgments as a function of identification classes: Canadian vs. American. In preparation.

La Gaipa, J. J. Social psychological aspects of humor. Paper presented before Midwestern Psychological Association, Detroit, May 1971.

Martin, L. J. Psychology of aesthetics: Experimental prospecting in the field of the comic. *American Journal of Psychology,* 1905, 16, 35–116.

Mead, G. H. *Mind, self and society.* Chicago, Illinois: Univ. of Chicago Press, 1934.

Middleton, R. Negro and white reactions to racial humor. *Sociometry,* 1959, 22, 175–183.

Priest, R. F. Election jokes: The effects of reference group membership. *Psychological Reports,* 1966, 18, 600–602.

Priest, R. F., & Abrahams, J. Candidate preference and hostile humor in the 1968 elections. *Psychological Reports,* 1970, 26, 779–783.

Priest, R. F., & Phillips, W. Dyad composition, social perception, and the appreciation of jokes. Unpublished manuscript.

Reynolds, D. V. Brain mechanisms of laughter. Paper presented before Midwestern Psychological Association, Detroit, May 1971.

Roberts, A. F., & Johnson, D. M. Some factors related to the perception of funniness and humor stimuli. *Journal of Social Psychology,* 1957, 46, 57–63.

Siegel, S. *Nonparametric statistics for the behavioral sciences.* New York: McGraw-Hill, 1956.

Turner, R. H. Role-taking, role standpoint and reference group behavior. *American Journal of Sociology,* 1956, 61, 316–328.

Webb, E. J., Campbell, D. T., Schwartz, R. D., & Sechrest, L. *Unobtrusive measures: Nonreactive research in the social sciences.* Chicago, Illinois: Rand McNally, 1966.

Wolff, H. A., Smith, C. E., & Murray, H. A. The psychology of humor. I. A study of responses to race-disparagement jokes. *Journal of Abnormal & Social Psychology,* 1934, 38, 345–365.

Zigler, E., Levine, J., & Gould, L. Cognitive challenge as a factor in children's humor appreciation. *Journal of Personality & Social Psychology,* 1967, 6, 332–336.

Chapter 11

Humor, Laughter, and Smiling: Some Preliminary Observations of Funny Behaviors

Howard R. Pollio, Rodney Mers, and William Lucchesi

Department of Psychology
The University of Tennessee, Knoxville, Tennessee

I. Introduction

In many ways the job of an empirical scientist is often a good deal less complicated than that of a philosopher or literary critic. In order to understand a particular cultural or behavioral phenomenon, the philosopher or critic can appeal only to his own experiences, intuitions, and judgments. If these are good, his analysis rings true; if not, he is likely to be monumentally wrong in painfully obvious ways once the data are in.

One aspect of human behavior that seems to have attracted a great many nonempirical approaches is that of humor. The list of philosophers, and wise men generally, who have tackled this problem includes almost all of the distinguished philosophers of this and all preceding ages. Writing in 1947, Eysenck provided six pages of tightly written prose that merely abstracted the content of some four dozen speculative theories of humor.

Now this is really quite surprising, for humor would seem to lend itself so readily to emprical observation. As Koestler put it as recently as 1964:

> Humour is the only domain of creative activity where a stimulus on a high level of complexity produces a massive and sharply defined response on the level of physiological reflexes. This paradox enables us to use the response as an indicator for the presence of that elusive quality, the comic, which we are seeking to define—as the tell-tale clicking of the geiger-counter indicates the presence of radioactivity [p. 31] .*

But what is the nature of this tell-tale geiger counter? It consists of a series of enormously complicated, yet highly patterned, movements that go by the names of laughing and smiling. Perhaps the best description of these patterns is to be found in classical sources such as those provided by Darwin (1872) and Sully (1902), sources from which the following composite description has been drawn:

The primary focus is laughing and smiling is, of course, the face—more particularly the mouth and eyes. A smile is produced when the upper lip is drawn back and the corners of the mouth lifted slightly. As the upper lip is raised, it partially uncovers the teeth and also brings about a downward curving of the furrows which extend from the wings of both nostrils to the far corners of the mouth. This, in turn, produces a puffing, or rounding out of the cheeks on the outer side of these furrows. Creases also occur momentarily under the eyes, and in older people it is possible to see permanent "laugh creases" at the side edges of their eye sockets. The eyes themselves also undergo general changes which can best be described by the phrase, "a bright and sparkling eye."

This brightening and sparkling of the eye can be attributed to many causes, the most important of which are the small amount of moisture squeezed from the tear glands during smiling and moderate laughter and the slight engorgement of the eye by various fluids brought on by an increase in circulation. Paraphrasing Darwin, we could express it as follows: Any cause which lowers circulation

---

*Reprinted with permission of the Macmillan Company from *The act of creation* by Arthur Koestler. Copyright© Arthur Koestler 1964.

deadens the eye and any cause which increases circulation causes it to sparkle.

So far all of these signals are visual, yet superimposed over this basic visual pattern is an auditory one—that of laughter. In low-level or moderate laughing, individuals tend to produce sounds that are short and broken and, as Darwin noted, "as different as possible from screams or cries of distress." The sound of a laugh is produced by a deep inspiration of air followed by short, interrupted, spasmodic contractions of the chest and especially of the diaphragm: hence, side-splitting laughter. But low-level laughter sometimes gives rise to more violent forms characterized by a change in the sound produced (a sound which now seems to come from deep in the throat), as well as by the addition of further more violent and extensive body movements. Darwin (1872) notes that

> during excessive laughter the whole body is often thrown backward and shakes, or is almost convulsed; respiration is much disturbed; the head and face become engorged with blood, with the veins distended; . . . the orbicular muscles are spasmodically contracted . . . to protect the eyes. Tears are freely shed [p. 206].

On the basis of these descriptions, it seems possible and reasonable to arrange these bodily responses in the form of a graduated series defined by a simple low-level bodily expression of cheerfulness at one end and paroxysms of violent laughter at the other. This series can perhaps be best represented by using common-sense terms in the following order:

1. No response noted.
2. Smile—varying in magnitude from a gentle smile with small cheek furrows to a broad smile producing a total pattern.
3. Laugh—ranging from a laugh with normal voice sounds to a deep-throated one involving moderately active head and shoulder movements.
4. Explosive laugh—profound body movements, changes in respiration, tears, etc.

Although finer gradations can and have been made by Koestler (1964) and others (e.g., Darwin, 1872), most empirical analyses focus primarily on these four categories. In actual fact, no one has ever reported the occurrence of a Level-4 response under laboratory conditions; and we have as yet not recorded a single instance in our own work.

But what do people laugh and smile at in their everyday world? Surprisingly, most studies dealing with this topic were done prior to

1940; and most dealt not with smiling but with laughing. Typical of these are studies by Young (1937) and Kamboroupolou (1926). Young, for example, asked 184 college students to estimate the number of times they laughed during a 24-hour period and then to describe the incidents which made them laugh. On the average (median value) women estimated they laughed 13 times per day, while male subjects estimated a median value of 19 times per day. A rough classification of the laugh-inducing situations described showed the greatest single cause of laughter to be jokes or wisecracks produced by peers (62%). Among other significant causes were humorous situations and incidents (15%) as well as the unintentional antics of other people (4%). Formally humorous materials such as contained in books, movies, plays, lectures, and radio programs constituted the remaining 18% of the total laughter reported by respondents.

Kamboroupolou (1926) had a group of introductory psychology students at Vassar College keep a "humor diary" for a week, asking them to record all of the things they laughed at each day. The distribution of laughs per day varied from a low of 2 to a high of about 18, with the general average between 4 and 5 per day. Kamboroupolou categorized laughter-evoking situations on the basis of a much more complicated category system than that of Young; and if these are roughly coordinated with Young's more common-sense categories, the results show that 25% of the laughs reported by Vassar students were caused by the physical actions and antics of other people, while 33% were caused by humorous remarks made by peers. The largest single category described by 38% of the diarists comprised "instances of laughter where the objective cause is the mental inferiority of another person: stupidity, ignorance . . . etc. . . ." In not one of the categories did these students mention formally humorous materials such as plays, books, or magazines. It seems as if Vassar girls of 1926 never went to plays nor read books or magazines for fun; or if they did, they never told anyone about it, least of all Kamboroupolou.

Although laughing and smiling can, and often do, have a great many different interpretations depending on the situations in which they occur, it should also be obvious that much of the time they are evoked by complex symbolic events specifically set out to produce them, i.e., jokes, comic stories, wisecracks, etc. It is under such circumstances that these very overt and observable responses come to serve as Koestler's tell-tale geiger counter, ticking—more or less loudly—in response to the comic aspects of these situations. In view of this rather ordinary yet pervasive fact, it seems quite reasonable to begin an analysis of humor by observing what people do in situations specifically set up to provide laugh-inducing materials under optimum conditions. The most common-sense locale would seem to be an impersonal audience setting, a setting in which there are no special constraints for either suppressing or forcing laughter and smiling, as there might be in problem-solving or teaching–learning situations (e.g., Coser, 1959, 1960; Goodchilds & Smith, 1964).

It was with this rather straightforward assumption that we began the present set of observations. Largely because laughter is considerably easier to record than smiling, our first series of studies was concerned simply with tape recordings of laughter in various audience groups attending plays and movies. At a very fundamental level, we were interested in finding out whether different audiences laughed at the same place over two separate performances of the same show or movie.

Laughing, considered simply as a dependent variable, has a lot to recommend it; not only is it possible to determine whether or not it occurs, it is also possible to describe the latency with which it occurs, the amplitude it reaches, and the duration it maintains before ending or being stopped by the next line of the performance. Laughter is surely as good a response as any tough-minded psychologist could want, particularly one who keeps Pavlov in mind. Then too, laughter is surely more appealing than salivation. In addition to these quantitative properties, we were soon to discover that audience laughter could also be described in terms of specific temporal patterns. That is, some laughs seem to explode immediately over an audience while others reach their peak after a much longer period of time. This patterned aspect of group laughter will be dealt with more extensively in later sections of this chapter.

Although field studies provided interesting data, we also found it necessary to move into the safer precincts of a more controlled quasi-laboratory situation for at least two reasons: (1) It was difficult to pick out the precise event in a play or movie giving rise to the laugh; i.e., both visual and auditory cues were often involved, as in the case of pantomime or comic song-and-dance routines. For this reason it seemed wiser to use recorded materials like that found in comic phonograph records. Such records are easy to obtain commercially and allow for precise latency measures. (2) It was difficult, if not impossible, to get videotape recordings of an audience attending a movie or play, which are necessary in order to investigate smiling, as well as to establish precise coordinations between the punch line of a joke and an audience's response to that joke.

These then are the situations in which we have made our observations. Like Topsy, they "growed" in ways that were not always easy to predict in advance; yet like Topsy they seem to have a natural coherence that more strictly controlled studies might not have at this preliminary level. The data to be presented were gathered in both completely natural audience situations as well as in more constrained quasi-natural ones. It is to a preliminary presentation of these observations that we now turn.

II. Naturalistic Observations of Audience Laughter: In the Wilds of Knoxville and Elsewhere

A. GENERAL METHODOLOGY

Since we decided initially to study humor through an analysis of laughing, we needed some way in which to describe laughter quantitatively. One way this can be done—and the way we actually did do it—is to use a sound-level recorder such as the one manufactured by Bruel and Kjaer (Model 2305A). Such a device graphically records the properties of taped audience laughter played through it by producing an oscillographic record (intensity over time) similar to the example presented in Figure 1. With such a

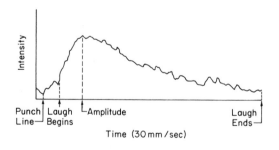

Figure 1. Sample oscillographic tracing of audience laughter—movie performance, 1970.

record at least three measures can be derived for each laugh: (1) the latency of the laugh, which is the distance on the graph occurring between the punch line and the onset of the laugh; (2) the duration of the laugh, which is the distance between the onset and the end of the laugh; and (3) the amplitude of the laugh, which is the distance between the prelaugh base line and its highest intensity peak.

Laughter was studied in three different situations. In each of these situations the microphone of a single-channel Wollensak tape recorder was placed as near the center of the audience as possible to pick up sounds from the audience as well as from the artistic production in progress. Once audience laughter had been recorded in this way, the tape was replayed through the Bruel and Kjaer level recorder in order to transpose it into more convenient graphic form.

The first of these three situations dealt with audience reactions to the musical play *Once Upon a Mattress*—an amateur production by The University of Tennessee Drama Department. A 25-min segment of Act II was selected for recording largely because, during this time, no pantomime or music occurred in the script. The actual recording took place at the Carousel Theater on the campus of The University of Tennessee. Audiences from two consecutive performances (one performance per night) were recorded. The audiences were of approximately the same size—full houses in both cases—but an actual head count was impossible.

The second of these situations involved an audience attending a local movie. As fate would have it, the movie *Bob and Carol and Ted and Alice* was playing at a local theater at the time of our early recordings. The theater manager was contacted, and he allowed a member of the Humor Research Group to record audience laughter from two consecutive showings of *Bob and Carol and Ted and Alice,* the 8:00 and 10:00 p.m. performances on a Friday night. The audiences were of approximately the same size (full houses); but, as was true for *Once Upon a Mattress,* a head count was impractical. The microphone was located in the center of the audience, picking up both the movie sound track and the audience's laughter.

The third situation involved recording canned laughter from a television comedy show *I Love Lucy.* Recordings were made by placing a microphone near the television speaker in a quiet room.

The procedure used in analyzing these data was the same for all three sets of observations. The initial step involved locating each audience laugh on the tape recordings. This was done by listening to the tapes and then marking in the punch lines as they occurred. In the case of *Once Upon a Mattress,* each sentence or phrase in the script that immediately preceded the beginning of a laugh was marked. Since scripts for *Bob and Carol and Ted and Alice* and *I Love Lucy* were unavailable, the last two or three words of each punch line were noted and recorded.

The second step in analyzing the data involved transposing auditory laughs from the tape recordings to visual representations produced by the Bruel and Kjaer recorder.* In order to do this, tape recordings were played into the level recorder such than an observer could also hear the content of each tape. Only in this way was it possible to mark the end of the punch line and the beginning and end of each laugh. This procedure resulted in a separate graph for each laugh—a graph similar in all respects to Figure 1.

Once graphic records had been obtained, it was possible to quantify each of the three measures describing a laugh. Latency and duration were recorded in millimeters, while amplitude was measured in terms of the number of calibration lines occurring from base line to highest peak on the Bruel and Kjaer record. Once these measures were recorded, correlations were computed among the various measures.

B. Results for *Once Upon a Mattress*

The first night's recordings of this show contained 31 identifiable laughs; that is, 31 places on the tape where two raters independently agreed a laugh had occurred. Twenty-two laughs occurred in the comparable section on the second night. Of these 22 laughs, 20 laughs were common to Performances I and II; i.e., 20 punch lines produced laughter in response to the same punch line on both nights.

The correlations between the three measures describing each laugh are presented in Table I for both Performances I and II. In both cases correlations for amplitude and duration are significant, with $p < .05$ for Performance I and $p < .01$ for Performance II. All other within-night correlations are nonsignificant. Cross-night correlations for the three measures are also presented in Table I. All three of these correlations are significant, with $p < .05$ for latency and $p < .01$ for amplitude and duration.

Although these correlations do show some commonality over the two nights, the actual magnitudes were surprisingly small. Most of us not in the performing arts would assume that audiences, while varying a bit from performance to performance, would probably yield the same laughter patterns over successive performances, an assumption that would have been reflected in larger cross-night correlations. In order to determine if the values obtained over two

* For those interested in technical details, the level recorder was maintained at the following settings for all groups: input potentiometer, 7; input attenuator, 0; potentiometer range, 32 dB; rectifier response, rms; drive shaft speed, 36; writing speed, 100 mm/sec; paper speed, 30 mm/sec.

TABLE I
Intercorrelations for **Once Upon a Mattress** *(1969–1970)*

Dependent measures	Performance				Cross-night correlations
	I		II		
	Amplitude	Duration	Amplitude	Duration	
Latency	−.19	+.22	−.38	−.14	Latency = .52*
Amplitude		.47*		+.67**	Amplitude = .60**
					Duration = .56**
Number of cases	31		22		20/31

*p < .05.   **p < .01.

performances of a musical comedy production were typical for amateur performances, we decided to look at past literature in the area. A reasonably exhaustive search of prior research literature turned up only two earlier studies on this point, and the time has come to consider these earlier studies.

C. A LITTLE HISTORY: LANGE AND MORRISON

The first of these prior studies dealing with audience laughter was done by Lange (1927), and the second by Morrison in 1940. Lange hand-timed (with a stopwatch) the duration of audience laughter at four different productions of Gilbert and Sullivan's *Iolanthe* as well as at several other amateur plays going by such intriguing names as *In the Garden of the Shah,* and *Tangerine.* For some unknown reason Lange did not compute cross-performance correlations, but her raw data were presented in sufficient detail so as to allow us to compute the appropriate correlations. The cross-performance correlations for the four professional productions of *Iolanthe* were all on the order of .75 or more, while all amateur productions produced correlations ranging between .45 and .74, with a median value of about .57. This value is extremely close to that found for the contemporary production of *Once Upon a Mattress,* which was, of course, also an amateur production.

In a study done in 1940 Morrison recorded audience laughter for highly skilled amateur performances as well as for movie comedies such as those starring Laurel and Hardy. Unfortunately, Morrison did not compute correlations; he did, however, provide proportions of agreement for the duration of laughter over different audiences. These proportions are considerably smaller than those Lange would have obtained had she handled her data in this way. Morrison's major result, however, was the finding of a very strong relationship between duration of audience laughter and audience size, with this correlation equal to .92. If, however, we examine laughter for audiences of about equal size, Morrison's results more closely approximate Lange's data. It can be concluded that while Morrison's findings must always be kept in mind in analyzing audience laughter, audience size had only a negligible effect on Lange's results since all of her observations were recorded over full houses.

The results of two sets of observations—those taken by Lange in 1927 and those taken by us in 1970—seem fairly consistent and conclusive: Cross-performance correlations of laughter duration are nowhere as large as might be expected on the naive assumption that two performances of the same show produce comparable durations of audience laughter. While it is true that laughs do occur at many of the same points in the script, the difference in latency and amplitude, as well as in duration, are still somewhat surprising. How can these differences be explained? Since Lange had found such good correlations for highly skilled professional performers and since we had tested primarily amateur performers, it seemed reasonable to assume that amateurs were far more variable in their stage performances and, therefore, so were the audience responses to these performances.

In order to test the possibility that audience response variability is related to actor variability, we decided to go to the movies where cross-performance variability could clearly be ruled out as a factor. The movie audiences selected for observation were recorded during a 20-min segment of *Bob and Carol and Ted and Alice* which played in Knoxville in the winter of 1970. Two different performances were recorded on a Friday night—the first at 8:00 and the next at 10:00 p.m. Friday night was chosen on the basis of the manager's opinion that Friday night audiences laugh a lot largely because they are composed of relatively young dating couples in good spirits. Such audiences are very responsive to comic movies, particularly when the humor is sexually tinged.

D. RESULTS FOR *BOB AND CAROL AND TED AND ALICE*

In accordance with the procedure used to record audience laughter for *Once Upon a Mattress,* the microphone from a Wollensak tape recorder was placed in the central part of the theater in order to record audience laughter. Following this, the recordings were translated into graphic form by playing them through the level recorder. All data to be reported were taken from these latter records. From an examination of these data, we found that the 8:00 p.m. performance produced 26 discernible laughs while the 10:00 p.m. performance produced 22. The correlations for all three components of a laugh as well as the cross-performance correlations are presented in Table II. Once again the only significant

TABLE II
Intercorrelations for Bob and Carol and Ted and Alice (1969–1970)

Dependent measures	Performance				Cross-night correlations
	I		II		
	Amplitude	Duration	Amplitude	Duration	
Latency	.35	+.32	−.13	+.22	Latency = .60**
Amplitude		+.65**		+.56**	Amplitude = .20
					Duration = .40*
Number of cases	26		22		21/26

* *p* < .05.   ** *p* < .01.

intercorrelations are between amplitude and duration for both performances. The cross-performance correlations were significant for latency (*p* < .01) and duration (*p* < .05) but not for amplitude. More important for the point at issue, the cross-performance correlation for duration produced a value of .40, a value no higher than that obtained for amateur performances.

This latter result was a bit surprising; we had assumed that amateur performances produced smaller cross-performance correlations because the "stimulus" varied more between amateur than between professional performances. Clearly this could not be true in the case of a movie comedy which provides a stimulus that is always the same. This in turn implied that differences in cross-performance correlations might be due to *cross-audience* rather than cross-performer differences and that these differences were larger for audiences viewing *Bob and Carol and Ted and Alice* than for *Iolanthe*.

But does such an assumption make sense? Although it is impossible to know for sure, it does seem reasonable that a 1926 audience attending a Gilbert and Sullivan play probably contained a majority of individuals who were devotees of Gilbert and Sullivan and that many of these individuals knew both the book and the score. If this is true, then successive Gilbert and Sullivan audiences probably represent as homogeneous an audience as can be found. On this basis, high cross-night correlations may have been due not to identity of performance but rather to identity (in certain critical respects) of audience. With the exception of a Shakespearian audience, there would seem to be no more highly "trained" audiences than those attending successive productions of Gilbert and Sullivan operettas.

E. Results for *I Love Lucy*

Another setting in which it is possible to record laughter is the television show. For some shows audience laughter is dubbed in; and, given this fact, we were interested in seeing if there were differences in the properties of canned laughter compared to more naturally occurring spontaneous laughter. In the case of certain older shows, such as *I Love Lucy,* canned laughter has a decidedly unnatural sound; and we decided to see if we could pinpoint the locus of the "unnaturalness," i.e., discover inconsistencies between the properties of natural and canned audience laughter.

The 30-min *I Love Lucy* show chosen for observation had about 20 min of script producing a total of 64 laughs—almost triple the number of laughs found in both of our prior situations. Of these 64 laughs 30 were free of overlapping dialogue or music and served as our primary data. These data were handled in exactly the same way as the data for *Once Upon a Mattress* and *Bob and Carol and Ted and Alice.*

The three intercorrelations possible between latency, amplitude, and duration all turned out to be nonsignificant (.15, .05, .28). This means that the usual correlation between duration and amplitude failed to appear in these records. In addition to correlational results, frequency distributions for latencies from the *I Love Lucy* show were also established. These distributions, along with a frequency distribution established on the basis of results provided by the preceding two sets of observations, are presented in Figure 2, where it can readily be seen that the distribution of latencies for canned laughter is quite different from distributions obtained from live audiences. When these distributions were computed over a larger number of intervals, the canned distribution had a J-shaped

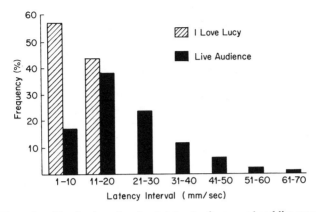

Figure 2. Distribution of prelaugh latencies for canned and live responses.

configuration, while the live distribution approximated a normal curve. Although time intervals are plotted in terms of millimeters, the modal time value for canned laughter falls in the interval between .000 and 330 msec, while the modal value for live laughter falls in the interval between 660 and 1000 msec. The values obtained for canned laughter, in terms of both absolute value and distribution, most closely approximate a distribution of simple reaction times rather than a distribution of laughs. This leads us to suspect that somewhere inside the television set there must be a little engineer told to listen for, and respond to, particular punch lines. The distribution of latencies for canned laughter looks very much like a distribution of reaction times, probably because it *is* a distribution of reaction times given in response to a set of predesignated words.

One additional aspect of these records also lends some support to this conclusion; in going over the Bruel and Kjaer records produced by canned laughter, we noticed two points: (1) The shape of the output graph was almost identical for all 30 laughs; and (2) there was always a blank (no sound) period immediately following the last word of each punch line. In no case do results obtained for *Bob and Carol and Ted and Alice* and *Once Upon a Mattress* yield similar blank periods. In all cases there was always some (nonlaugh-related) noise(s) occurring during this period. Figure 3 presents a single laugh tracing from *I Love Lucy* and one from *Bob and Carol and Ted and Alice.* The differences between the two are striking and show that not only is sound quality bad on canned laughter but that its latency and waveform deviate markedly from natural laughs in seemingly obvious and comprehensible ways.

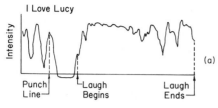

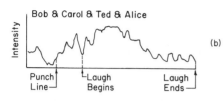

Figure 3. Comparison of oscillographic tracings for (a) canned and (b) live laughter.

F. Summary and General Conclusions

The general conclusions emerging from our observations of audience laughter can be summarized as follows: (1) Latency is essentially uncorrelated with amplitude and duration; (2) moderate correlations exist between amplitude and duration; (3) correlations computed over two different audiences show that such audiences do laugh at many of the same places across performances and that these laughs display comparable, even if not identical, cross-performance properties; and (4) naturally occurring laughter is quite different in a great many specifiable ways from canned laughter used in older television shows.

All of these results were obtained from tape recordings of an entire audience. In looking at what was going on, we often noted that many individuals smiled but failed to laugh at individual jokes. This suggested that it might be helpful to find a situation in which we could have greater control over the audience and could videotape specific individuals. It was largely for these reasons that we moved our base of operations from the theater and movie houses of Knoxville to a comfortably furnished room in the post-World-War-II barracks we usually call—among other things—the Humor Research Laboratory.

III. Laboratory Studies: Cosby and Diller, and Cambridge Too

A. General Methodology

Before we could study laughing and smiling in a quasi-laboratory setting, we had to find appropriate stimulus material. Preliminary investigations were carried out using a number of different comedy records, including some by Don Rickles, Lenny Bruce, Bill Cosby, Phyllis Diller, and Godfrey Cambridge.

The records performed by Bill Cosby and Phyllis Diller were chosen for more intensive study because pilot work showed that these records consistently produced a larger number of laughs than did any of the others. Two routines from the Cambridge album also produced a substantial number of laughs, and these were used in all subsequent experiments as warm-up material.

The stimulus materials used in the major part of the experiment included a Diller album called the "Best of Phyllis Diller" (Verve, #V-15053) minus the routine called Tightward Airlines. For Cosby we used four routines (Two Brothers, The Tank, Cool Covers, and Planes) from the Album "Revenge" (Warner Brothers #1691) and five routines (Lumps, Playground, Shop, Special Class, and Niagra Falls) from an additional album called "Wonderfulness" (Warner Brothers, #1634). Insofar as possible, we tried to damp out most of the laughing that usually occurs on records of this type. In most cases we simply left blank or indistinct sound periods on the stimulus record actually used. All in all, the Cosby material ran a total of 24 min, 4 sec, while Diller's material ran a total of 23 min, 8 sec.

The subjects used in these observations were all University of Tennessee undergraduate students observed in groups of from 13 to 15 students each. All were enrolled in introductory psychology courses and participated in our observations to fulfill a course requirement. Most were from 18 to 21 years of age, and males and females were about equally represented in all four groups.

Each of the four subject groups was seated in a circular arrangement in a comfortably furnished room. A Sony television camera was placed in the room behind a glass door so that the facial expressions of three of the subjects in each group could be recorded for the entire session. One microphone was hung from the ceiling in the middle of the room. This microphone recorded total group laughter. The microphone associated with the Sony video recorder was placed above the three students being videotaped and recorded only their laughter. Three other microphones were placed throughout the room but were inoperative. The recorded comedy routines were played through a loudspeaker located near the ceiling. Since a parabolic microphone was used, i.e., a microphone which records only sounds falling within its auditory umbrella, very little of the actual stimulus record appeared on the audio recordings obtained.

After all subjects were seated, they were instructed to listen to the records and give honest reactions. They were told that a camera would be filming facial reactions of different people at different times and that the various microphones would be recording their laughter. After these brief instructions two Godfry Cambridge routines were played to give the subjects time to relax in the experimental situation. Following this, either the Cosby or Diller records were played. Two of the four groups were played material taken from Cosby records, while two other groups were played material taken from Diller records. After these recordings were completed, each student was given a sheet of paper and asked to rate the funniness of each routine on a scale from 1 to 5, with 1 being "not funny at all" and 5 being "among the funniest things I've ever heard." They were also asked to indicate whether or not they had heard any of the routines before. No subject said he had heard it before.

After laughing and smiling had been recorded, segments of the total-group (audio-) tape containing laughter were run through the sound-level recorder and graphical representations of each laugh obtained. The videotapes containing each of the three subjects filmed per group were played back on the videomonitor, and the sound of the stimulus tape and its attendant laughter were recorded on one track of a two-track tape recorder. The second track of this tape was used to record either a high- or low-pitched tone or both. A low-intensity, low-pitched tone (100 Hz) was placed on the tape whenever the single subject being observed was judged to have smiled. A higher intensity, higher pitched tone (500 Hz) was recorded whenever the subject was judged to have laughed. In order to test interrater reliability, two raters independently judged when each subject laughed or smiled. A similar procedure was followed for all three subjects resulting in three separate tapes, one for each subject.

Through the use of two different tones to indicate laughs and smiles, the resulting tapes could be run through the Bruel and Kjaer Recorder and thereby produce a three-level graph. The lowest intensity level would be the stimulus recording alone, the middle intensity would represent the occurrence of smiling, and the highest level would occur only when the subject laughed. Patterns of laughing and smiling for each individual could now be conveniently examined from a single Bruel and Kjaer tape.

B. RESULTS FOR COSBY AND DILLER

Although Cosby and Diller were able to get our student subjects to laugh quite often, both comedians obviously approach their material in vastly different ways. First, there is the question of topic: For Cosby most themes deal with the relationship of children to their human and nonhuman environments, whereas for Diller most deal with herself, her fables, her husband, her armpits, her sex life, and so on. Cosby traffics in muted hostility, while Diller traffics in blatant self-derision and sexuality. It was largely because of these obvious and significant differences that we felt any findings common to both Diller and Cosby would represent highly regular and highly replicable characteristics of the way in which audiences respond to comic performances independent of the particular performer.

We began our analysis of these data with a rather simple and straightforward question: Is there any correlation between the mean funniness rating a group gives to a particular routine and the number of laughs evoked by that routine? In order for this question to be answered, mean funniness ratings scores were computed from the ratings of subjects in each of the four groups—two for Cosby and two for Diller—for each of the routines performed. Since each of the Cosby and Diller routines was of unequal length, a group laughter score was developed by dividing the total number of group laughs by the number of sentences in the routine. A Spearman rank-order correlation of .57 was obtained for the first Cosby group. With only 9 pairs of data points, this correlation fails to reach statistical significance. The second Cosby group produced a correlation of .78, which is significant at $p < .05$. Comparable values of .01 and .36 were obtained for Diller I and II, with neither of these values reaching an acceptable level of significance. In three of four cases then, nonsignificant correlations were found between number of laughs and mean funniness ratings.

Intercorrelations for latency, duration, and amplitude measures, as well as cross-group correlations for each measure, were calculated for all four subject groups and these results appear in Table III. For the first Cosby group the correlations between latency and amplitude and latency and duration were virtually zero. The correlation between amplitude and duration, however, was high and positive, reaching statistical significane at the .01 level. Contrary to prior field results, Cosby II produced moderate negative correlations between latency and amplitude and latency and duration. The correlation between amplitude and duration, however, was high and positive as was true for Cosby I. Cross-group correlations were moderately high and positive for latency but insignificant for amplitude and duration.

Unlike prior field studies, there was a large discrepancy in the number of places at which students in both groups laughed. Of the 76 places producing laughter in Cosby I, only 38 produced laughter

TABLE III
Intercorrelations for Bill Cosby and Phyllis Diller (1970–1971)

Dependent measures	Performance				Cross-night correlations
	Cosby I		Cosby II		
	Amplitude	Duration	Amplitude	Duration	
Latency	+.03	.00	−.42**	−.35	Latency = .42**
Amplitude		+.59**		+.61**	Amplitude = .25
					Duration = .20
Number of cases	76		38		38/76

Dependent measures	Diller I		Diller II		Cross-night correlations
	Amplitude	Duration	Amplitude	Duration	
Latency	−.43**	−.02	−.26	−.06	Latency = .41*
Amplitude		+.44**		.45*	Amplitude = .39*
					Duration = .37*
Number of cases	49		29		29/49

* $p < .05$.   ** $p < .01$.

in Cosby II. The most significant aspect of this result, however, was that all of the places at which Cosby-II subjects laughed had been places at which Cosby-I subjects laughed. In other words, Cosby-II laughs were a subset of Cosby-I laughs, with Cosby-I subjects laughing a good deal more often than Cosby-II subjects.

The intercorrelations for latency, duration, and amplitude for each Diller group and the cross-group correlations for each of these measures are also presented in Table III. For both Diller groups correlations between latency and amplitude were slightly negative, while those between latency and duration were small and insignificant. Correlations between amplitude and duration were moderately high and positive. The three cross-group correlations also were all moderately high and positive.

As was true for Cosby, members of both audience groups did not always laugh at all of the same punch lines. Twenty nine of the 49 laughs produced by Diller I were repeated (i.e., produced at the same places) by Diller II. As with Cosby, the smaller number of laughs turned out to be a proper subset of the larger number. Although students laughed more during Diller I than during Diller II, when they laughed in Diller II, they did so in places similar to Diller I.

Given these results for both Diller and Cosby, it seemed reasonable to assume that those places where subjects in both groups laughed represented "better" jokes. If this were true, we might expect to find differences in duration and amplitude for jokes producing laughter in both groups as compared to those producing laughter only in Group I. The top part of Table IV presents the mean duration,

TABLE IV

Means for Unique and Common Laughs and Associated t-Values for Cosby I and Diller I

Audience group	Laugh category and t-test results	Dependent variables		
		Amplitude	*Duration*	*Latency*
	Common laughs	10.59	47.17	11.79
Cosby I	Unique laughs	7.83	39.55	9.17
	t-Test values	3.78**	2.10*	5.82**
		Amplitude	*Duration*	*Latency*
	Common laughs	15.83	79.60	10.14
Diller I	Unique laughs	11.78	69.73	20.20
	t-Test values	5.15**	.85	3.19**

*$p < .05$.   **$p < .01$.

amplitude, and latency for those laughs in Cosby I which were common to both groups (i.e., where both groups laughed at the same joke) as well as means for those laughs which occurred only in Cosby I. The bottom part of Table IV presents comparable results for both Diller groups.

For Cosby subjects, these results indicate that common laughs had longer durations, higher amplitudes, and longer latencies than unique laughs, with all three differences being statistically significant. For Diller subjects common laughs also had longer durations and higher amplitudes than unique laughs, although only the difference for amplitude was significant ($p < .05$). Contrary to results found for Cosby, the latency for common laughs was significantly shorter than for unique laughs.

In going over the data for all four groups, we were also struck by differences in the form of the Bruel and Kjaer recordings produced. Most of these laugh curves seemed to be categorizable into one of three categories which creatively we have called early, middle, and late risers. Figures 4a, b, and c illustrate each of these three different categories. The early-riser pattern is characterized by a loud burst of sound energy occurring in the first third of the total laugh produced, followed by a slow diminution in laugh intensity over time. The middle-riser pattern is characterized by having its most intense laughter peak in the middle of the total laugh duration, followed by a faster diminution of sound intensity. The late-riser pattern reaches

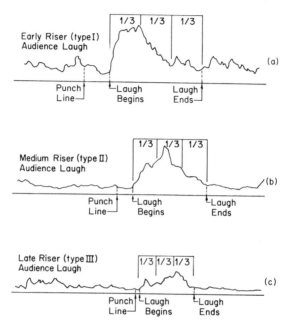

Figure 4. Oscillographic tracings for (a) early-, (b) middle-, and (c) late-riser laugh patterns.

its highest peak in the last third of the laugh, with total sound intensity diminishing quite rapidly from that point. Although all of the laughs produced in response to Cosby and Diller could be classified into one of these three categories by determining in which third of the laugh the highest peak occurred, only those jokes with general shapes similar to those of Figures 4a, b, and c were counted in the appropriate category.

About 30% of the laughs obtained did not comfortably fit into any of these general patterns. Some laugh curves, for example, produced a biomodal shape and were placed in a fourth, or "uncategorized," laugh grouping. In order to see if there were differences among the three laugh types, mean latency, duration, and amplitude values were computed for early, middle, and late risers for Cosby I and II and Differ I and II. With one exception these t-tests revealed no significant differences among the quantitative properties of laughter. Only the difference between latency for early and middle risers produced a significant t value in favor of longer latencies for early risers.

Another question about these patterns concerns their consistency over audience groups; i.e., does a late-riser pattern for one audience occur at the same place for a second audience? Table V presents the

TABLE V
Co-Occurrence of Major Laugh Types for Cosby and Diller Groups

		Cosby II			
		Early	Middle	Late	Percent total
Cosby I[a]	Early	3	3	0	26%
	Middle	2	7	0	38%
	Late	0	1	0	5%
	Total (%)	25%	40%	2%	
		Diller II			
	Early	6	3	0	31%
Diller I[a]	Middle	1	1	1	24%
	Late	0	1	0	10%
	Total (%)	51%	17%	3%	

[a] Figures do not include those laughs falling in the uncategorized grouping for either the first or second Cosby and Diller groups.

data for co-occurrence of laugh types between Cosby I and II and between Diller I and II. For Cosby there is some commonality across patterns, particularly for the middle-riser category. In comparison with Cosby, Diller produces more early and fewer middle-riser patterns with both comedians producing only a few late risers. Largely because of this difference, Diller audiences show greater consistency for early-riser patterns than for either of the other two categories.

One of the major reasons for moving to a laboratory setting was to examine the patterns of smiling and laughing produced by individual subjects. One major problem that had to be resolved before this could be done was the degree to which independent raters could reliably detect the occurrence of these behaviors. In addition, we hoped to describe specific laugh–smile patterns and then use these as a basis on which to categorize joke types. As a starting point, we simply asked two judges to go through the tapes of each subject and determine what categories seemed to describe the behaviors observed. From this preliminary screening, four different categories were developed: (1) smile only; (2) laugh–smile sequence; (3) smile: laugh–smile sequence; and (4) laugh–smile chains in which it was possible to count at least two (or more) smile: laugh–smile sequences.

With these categories in hand, the same two judges independently went through the 12 videotapes again, this time categorizing each student's response into one of these four categories. For all subjects observed, raters agreed between 75 and 85% of the time that a ratable event had occurred; i.e., in only about 20% of the cases did one judge record the occurrence of one of the four categories while the other did not. An initial examination of the specific events rated showed that both judges found it difficult to distinguish between the *laugh–smile* and the *smile: laugh–smile* categories for 10 of the 12 subjects rated. After further discussion, we decided to use the category *smile: laugh–smile* for all subjects observed; and when this was done, about 85% of the cases were assigned by both judges to the same category.

TABLE VI

Mean Number of Response Events in Each of the Major Laugh–Smile Categories

| Comedy situation | Response category | | | | | | Mean number of total subject events recorded |
| | Smile | | Smile: Laugh–Smile | | Chains | | |
	$\bar{X}$	Percent	$\bar{X}$	Percent	$\bar{X}$	Percent	
Cosby I	31.3	51%	26.6	44%	3.0	5%	61
Cosby II	26.6	68%	12	31%	.3	1%	39
Diller I	33.3	74%	8.1	19%	3.3	7%	45
Diller II	15.6	61%	9.3	36%	.6	3%	26

For purposes of further analysis we considered only those patterns which both raters independently placed in the same category. These results are presented in Table VI for all four groups. In this table the mean number of responses is presented for each category along with the mean number of subject events recorded. In addition, each mean is expressed as a proportion of the total.

Despite the fact that Cosby-II subjects produced far fewer total events, the relative proportions are reasonably comparable, with students in both groups smiling more than any other single event. In both cases *laugh–smile* chains did not occur very frequently, comprising between 1 and 5% of the total events scored. In looking at the data for both Diller groups, we can see that more events were recorded for Diller-I than for Diller-II subjects. In general, smiling seemed to occur more frequently for Diller subjects than for Cosby subjects. These between-comedian differences, however, are not large and, in agreement with Cosby results, smiling again proved to be the most frequent category. Over both groups Cosby subjects produced a greater number of total responses than Diller subjects, and this makes sense in that the mean funniness ratings of all 9 Cosby routines was 3.22 (range: 2.50–3.92), while the comparable value for all Diller routines was 2.69 (range: 1.60–3.67).

The most interesting category from a theoretical point of view is represented by the *smile: laugh–smile* category. If laughing and smiling represent different levels of response to a joke situation, it should then be possible to discover systematic relationships between the duration of a smile that precedes or follows a laugh and the laugh itself. For the six individuals filmed during Cosby I and II, only five produced a sufficient number of *smile: laugh–smile* sequences to compute meaningful correlations. For these subjects correlations between laugh duration and postlaugh smile duration ranged between .16 and .51, with a mean value of .35. Only two of these correlations even came close to statistical significance. Because we were concerned that these insignificant correlations might be due to restricted ranges, an examination of laughter duration was made and showed these values to vary between .5 and 4.0 sec, with a median value of 1.2 sec. The duration of a postlaugh smile varied from .9 to 9.8 sec with a median value of 2.1 sec. These ranges are sufficiently wide as to allow the conclusion that no meaningful correlation exists between laugh and postlaugh smile durations.

A number of other correlations were also computed, e.g., between pre- and postlaugh smile durations, between the prelaugh smile and the laugh duration itself, and between total smile time (pre- and post-) and total laugh time. In all cases these correlations were either zero or only slightly positive. Of the 12 additional correlations computed, only two reached acceptable significance levels, with both of these contributed by a single individual. Although it is possible to obtain reliable judgments of laughing and smiling durations, such durations do not correlate with each other for individual subjects.

Of the six subjects observed during both Diller records, only three—two from Diller I and one from Diller II—produced a sufficient number of response events to compute correlations between laugh and smile durations. For these subjects correlations between laugh and postlaugh smile ranged from .08 to .55 with a median value of .43 with only one subject producing significant positive correlations. A number of other correlations were also run and as was true for Cosby subjects, only one of these additional correlations was significant. Over both groups then, few significant correlations exist between laugh and smile durations for individual subjects. For demographic purposes the median prelaugh smile duration was .32 sec, the median laugh was 1.30 sec, and the median postlaugh smile was 3.41 sec. These values are only slightly different from those reported for Cosby.

C. SUMMARY FOR COSBY AND DILLER

In common with results obtained for more naturally occurring movie and theater groups, results obtained from students listening to comedy records performed by Bill Cosby and Phyllis Diller showed that, of the various components of a laugh, only amplitude and duration were consistently intercorrelated. In contrast to audiences in more natural settings, separate audiences produced a widely differing number of laughs; but in agreement with earlier results, the smaller number of laughs was almost a subset of the larger set. In addition, nonoverlapping or unique laughs were generally smaller in amplitude and of shorter duration than common laughs. No conclusion could be drawn in regard to latency.

A more detailed analysis of group laughter showed that it could be reliably categorized into one of three laugh types and that the same punch line tended to evoke the same pattern over two successive performances. More specifically, Diller and Cosby seemed to produce differing numbers of early and middle risers, with Diller producing mostly early risers and Cosby mostly middle risers.

In analyzing smiling, we found these behaviors could be reliably recorded and categorized by independent judges and that the vast majority of subjects smiled more than they laughed in response to comic materials. About 35% of the time laughs were preceded by smiles, whereas all laughs were followed by a smile. An analysis of the degree to which laugh and smile durations correlated showed essentially no relationship for almost all subjects. Laugh duration did not seem to predict the length of a pre- or postlaugh smile.

IV. Conclusion: Future Directions and Speculations

We have followed a long, if meandering, path in this chapter and there is still a long way to go. We began our analysis of humor by trying to determine what types of events made special groups known as audiences laugh. The rather obvious fact is that people do laugh and smile at "funny" situations or events, and this fact would seem to provide the wherewithal for understanding humor. The overall strategy of the present set of observations is to begin with these very observable behaviors and then attempt to trace back and categorize the antecedent conditions giving rise to them. As a preliminary goal we hope to be able to describe some properties of humorous material that give rise to laughing and smiling in reasonably nonthreatening environments. In attempting to deal with these antecedent conditions, it will be necessary to make a careful analysis of the situations in which laughing and smiling occur and to relate this analysis to prior theoretical work in the area. This latter step will be taken only if our analysis suggests that such work will be useful in conceptualizing why people laugh and smile at material designed to produce these behaviors.

One aspect of laughter, which suggests that a good deal of this prior theoretical work will be relevant, starts from the obvious fact that laughter is not a unitary response—rather, it has three separate components: latency, amplitude, and duration. If we disregard the specifics of prior theoretical analyses and respond instead to their general tenor, such analyses suggest that there are at least three different aspects involved in responding to humorous or witty material: one relating to the cognitive difficulty of the joke, one relating to its arousal (or motivational) properties, and one relating to the social conditions under which it is presented. If this is the case, it seems a reasonable starting point to determine whether each component of laughing relates to one or more of these aspects of humorous situations. So, for example, latency might relate to the cognitive difficulty of a joke; amplitude, to the emotional arousal of a joke; and duration, to a combination of factors involving both emotional arousal and the social approval or disapproval afforded a laugh once underway.

The cognitive and affective dimensions involved in wit and humor, however, are not mutually exclusive in a given joke; therefore, it is probably inaccurate to categorize jokes solely in terms of such a dichotomous category system. Rather it seems better, as Eysenck (1947) has proposed, to consider the motivational dimension (or orectic dimension as he called it) as only one significant factor in wit and humor and to recognize that cognitive dimensions can and do combine with such motivational factors in producing a comic response. If we describe jokes in terms of a two-dimensional space encompassing both cognitive and orectic dimensions, it then becomes possible to represent any given joke in terms of a specific location in this two-dimensional space.

The advantage to such an approach is that it now becomes possible, indeed necessary, to consider the joint contribution of motivational and cognitive factors in humor appreciation. Each dimension not only represents one aspect of humorous stimuli but also captures the theoretical thrust of a particular class of hypotheses about wit, humor, and the comic. So, for example, in the psychological literature psychoanalysts such as Freud (1905) and Kris (1938) emphasize the motivational aspects of wit and humor, while Gestalt writers (Maier, 1932; Harrower, 1932; Koffka, 1940) emphasize the cognitive–perceptual aspects. Once we look at the problem in this way, it becomes clear that methods must be developed to locate specific jokes within the confines of this space and then to observe the relationship between specific joke locations and appropriate dependent variables such as laughing and smiling.

Although there are a number of different ways in which to proceed with an analysis of wit and humor based on an analysis of laughing and smiling, this chapter has focused on an attempt to describe the properties of humorous materials as these are presented by two different comedians in a reasonably nonthreatening environment. Obviously this analysis is, and must remain, incomplete until some consideration is given both to the nature of the social setting in which laughing and smiling occur and to the social relationships that characterize the composition of a particular audience. We have started our work by analyzing an impersonal audience situation, i.e., where most people are strangers to each other; yet it is quite clear that observing groups selected on other bases must be done in order to extend and supplement this type of analysis. Social variables that should be considered in this regard include such things as the aim of the group (i.e., laughter in a problem-solving group should have a different form and function than in an audience group), the dominance roles in the group (laughing at a comedian's joke might turn out to be quite different from laughing at the "boss's" joke), the sexual composition of the group (all males or all females), and a great many other variables that serve to change the meaning of both the joke and the situation for an individual subject.

Certain serendipitous aspects of the present results suggest one further way in which to study the social function of laughter; and this involves the possible function of early-, middle-, and late-riser laugh patterns in group formation. In addition to being easily and reliably differentiated on the basis of oscillographic records, these patterns are also readily discriminable on the basis of their sound properties. Thus, the explosive laughter characteristic of an early riser is quite distinct from the more slowly building middle and late riser and may imply that these patterns serve as naturally occurring signals in response to jokes told about present or prospective group members. Casual observation suggests that laughter arising over a joke about some group member can serve as a method whereby the individual is either excluded from a group or welcomed into it. As Lorenz (1963) put it "laughter produces simultaneously a strong fellow-feeling among participants and joint aggressiveness against outsiders. . . . Laughter forms a bond and simultaneously draws a line [p. 253]."

But how do we know which is which? Only if different patterns serve one or the other of these functions does it seem possible for an outsider to decide whether or not to join a group, as well as to make some estimate as to his ultimate comfort in that group. Although this is only a speculation at present, the fact that discriminably different laugh patterns do exist suggest that these differences may have social functions. It is a long step from the present data but an intriguing one if correct.

For the more general purpose of understanding what makes people laugh and smile, it would also seem necessary to study the role of different comedians in evoking these behaviors. Over and above social, cognitive, or motivational factors in humor—and in many cases perhaps even more important—is the "imaginary world" created by the storyteller or comedian. If we consider for only a moment the nature of successful comedians, it is apparent that they are able to create an imaginary world for their audience, a world which functions on its own terms and under its own logic and which moderates everything the comedian says and does. It is quite one thing when Bill Cosby (or Danny Kaye before him) tells a hostile joke and quite another when Don Rickles (or Bob Hope before him) tells what would appear to be the same or a similar joke. Cosby's world is a "nice-guy world" where hostility is always meant to be taken with a shrug, while Rickles' world is an aggressive one in which every exaggerated hostility is emasculated by comparison with the overall ambience created.

Now, while it is easy to characterize the mental world created by some comedian or other in general terms, it is quite another to determine whether this same world is created for every, or for even most, individuals in a given audience. In more general terms what is needed is a comedian space within which it would be possible to locate individual comedians. Once this is accomplished, it would seem quite a simple task to determine whether comedians occupying similar locations produce similar audience responses.

While these and other extensions of the present work come readily to mind, it seems best at this relatively preliminary stage to continue further descriptions of laugh and smile patterns and to be sensitive to the demands of new data and new hypotheses as these emerge. Hopefully, such sensitivity will allow for a meaningful attack on a problem—that of humor—which only infrequently has been studied by a straightforward combination of empirical and theoretical considerations.

Acknowledgment

We would like to thank Robert E. Arthur, who is presently doing his dissertation on humor and laughing, for his many contributions—both theoretical and operational—to the present project. Part of this work was supported by Research Grant MH20442 from the United States Public Health Service.

Our thanks also go to Thomas Miller for gathering and analyzing much of the data reported in this chapter.

References

Coser, R. L. Some social functions of laughter. *Human Relations,* 1959, 12, 171–182.

Coser, R. L. Laughter among colleagues. *Psychiatry,* 1960, 23, 81–89.

Darwin, C. R. *The expression of the emotions in man and animals.* London: Murray, 1872.

Eysenck, H. J. *Dimensions of personality.* London: Routledge, 1947.

Freud, S. *Jokes and their relation to the unconscious.* New York: Norton, 1960. (Originally: *Der Witz und seine Beziehung zum Unbewussen.* Leipzig and Vienna: Deuticke, 1905.)

Goodchilds, J. D., & Smith, E. E. The wit and his group. *Human Relations,* 1964, 17, 23–31.

Harrower, M. R. Organization in higher mental processes. *Psychologische Forschung,* 1932, 17, 56–120.

Kamboroupolou, P. Individual differences in the sense of humor. *American Journal of Psychology,* 1926, 37, 268–278.

Koestler, A. *The act of creation.* London: Hutchinson, 1964.

Koffka, K. *Principles of Gestalt psychology.* London: Kegan-Paul, Trench, Trubner and Co., 1940.

Kris, E. Ego development and the comic. *International Journal of Psychoanalysis,* 1938, 19, 77–90.

Lange F. E. A statistical study of crowd laughter. Unpublished M.A. thesis, Columbia Univ. 1927.

Lorenz, K. *On aggression.* New York: Harcourt, 1963.

Maier, N. R. F. A Gestalt theory of humour. *British Journal of Psychology,* 1932, 23, 69–74.

Morrison, J. A. A note concerning investigations on the constancy of audience laughter. *Sociometry,* 1940, 3, 179–185.

Sully, J. *Essay on laughter,* New York: Longmans, Green, 1902.

Young, P. T. Laughing and weeping; cheerfulness and depression: A study of moods among college students. *Journal of Social Psychology,* 1937, 8, 311–334.

Part IV

OVERVIEW AND CONCLUSIONS

Chapter 12

Advances toward an Understanding of Humor: Implications for the Future

Paul E. McGhee

Department of Psychology
State University of New York, Albany, New York

and

Jeffrey H. Goldstein

Department of Psychology
Temple University, Philadelphia, Pennsylvania

I. Contributions of the Present Volume

Since our original goal in preparing this volume was to bring together a group of investigators studying humor outside of a psychoanalytic framework, the result has been a highly diverse theoretical and empirical attack on the humor process. The wide range of approaches opens many potential new avenues of research to those interested in studying humor. On the other hand it also makes a systematic summing up and integration of the chapters a cumbersome task. Consequently, we shall discuss individually the theoretical, methodological, and empirical advances of each chapter, relate them to other contributions and point out implications for future research.

A. KEITH-SPIEGEL

Although in the past several writers have summarized the types of theories or concepts offered as explanations of some aspect of humor, the chapter by Keith-Spiegel constitutes the first extensive analysis of key issues emphasized by early humor theorists. This analysis of long-standing issues provides a valuable perspective for assimilating the new data and theoretical views advanced in this book. While some of the issues discussed by Keith-Spiegel (such as the relation between laughter and smiling, and the problem of equating humor with either of these) continue to concern contemporary investigators of humor, including contributors to the present volume, others seem to have lost their appeal to interested researchers. In our view, this is entirely appropriate and not surprising, since many of the issues frequently discussed in the past raise questions which are not empirically answerable (e.g., whether humor is essentially good or evil in character, or whether it involves an increase or saving of mental effort). The long history of many unresolved issues attests to the need for future investigators to direct their research efforts toward empirically answerable questions.

Of course, the clarification of the concerns of prior theorists and writers also opens the door to translation of earlier issues into contemporary language. For example, it may be that the "nervous energy release" issue may be fruitfully conceptualized in terms of arousal changes operative in the humor process. Berlyne has led the way in this regard, drawing from various sources of data on determinants of arousal change to make predictions about arousal changes characteristic of humor. The major obstacle to this and other reformulations of earlier views, as emphasized by Keith-Spiegel, may lie in the inadequate definitions and inconsistent usage of many humor terms. Considering the persistent tendency humor has to evade our understanding, it would seem paramount for all investigators in this area to provide clear operational and conceptual definitions of humor-related terms, and to strive for greater consistency of usage of these terms across experimenters.

B. BERLYNE

While Berlyne does not claim to have a theory of humor, he does draw from theory and empirical findings in the areas of arousal, curiosity, and exploratory behavior in advancing an explanation for the pleasure experienced during the humor process. However he is quick to point out that the mechanisms described also operate in nonhumor situations, so that additional factors must enter in to determine the occurrence of humor.

Perhaps the greatest contribution of this chapter lies in the effort to link humor to other types of related behaviors (play, art, music, curiosity) and to specify the nature of the underlying mechanisms presumed to mediate the humor process. While acknowledging the role of such traditional mediating factors as sex and aggression (i.e., tendentious factors), Berlyne is mainly concerned with the structural properties of the stimulus situation. Drawing from a wide range of behavioral and physiological evidence, he makes a strong case for the importance of collative stimulus properties in generating the pleasure experienced in humor.

While many prior theories have emphasized the importance of the reduction of tension, release of energy, or relief of various emotional tendencies or drives through humor [see Chapter 1], they have generally failed to specify why the humor mechanisms described should be pleasurable. In hypothesizing the importance of the arousal-jag and -boost mechanisms in humor, Berlyne does provide such an explanation. Furthermore, he concludes that in light of our present knowledge of the functioning of the nervous system, there is little basis for considering as tenable the "surplus-energy" notion of Spencer or the notion of a "discharge of psychic energy" in the Freudian system. We are inclined to agree with Berlyne that there is much to be gained from reinterpreting older psychic or surplus-energy theories in terms of contemporary arousal theory.

Berlyne's cognitive emphasis in explaining humor derives from his more general view that human behavior is not determined simply by the properties of the present stimulus situation but rather depends on recollections of the past and anticipations of the future; i.e., it involves a collative process. Within his model it is clearly the cognitive processing of collative stimulus properties which leads to any arousal fluctuations observed. The degree of positive or negative affective tone associated with a stimulus depends on its arousal potential, such that moderate levels of novelty, surprisingness, incongruity, etc., are likely to generate positive affect, while low or very high levels may yield either indifference or negative affect. While smiling and laughing are considered to be closely related to both affect and cognition, the specific nature of the relationship remains unclear.

The basic tenets of Berlyne's view remain untested. While the Godkewitsch and Langevin–Day data do bear on Berlyne's model, their designs do not permit the drawing of any conclusions regarding operation of the arousal-jag and -boost mechanisms. While it seems likely that future research will demonstrate that these mechanisms do operate in humor situations (this would be consistent with related behaviors in which their operation has already been demonstrated), the fact remains that this will merely add to the ways in which curiosity, play, humor, and exploratory behavior are similar. What is needed, as Berlyne implies, is a determination of how humor is different. This goal should probably be pursued along both behavioral and cognitive lines. Specific attention should be given to changes in the continuum of arousal during the presentation of humor stimuli. Also, along the scaling lines adopted by Godkewitsch, comparable humorous and nonhumorous stimuli might be presented to Ss so that the differential manifestation (if present) of the arousal-jag and -boost mechanisms might be observed. This would permit determination of whether humor can be distinguished from nonhumorous experiences at the physiological level.

Regarding cognitive factors, Berlyne's suggestions that cues precluding seriousness may play an important role in leading a subject to interpret the stimulus situation in a joking fashion is consistent with McGhee's model. This factor might be tested by manipulating such cues and observing their influence on the degree of humor perceived in the stimulus situation at hand.

C. McGhee

Like Berlyne, McGhee emphasizes the importance of studying the role of structural properties alone in the humor process. If most humor situations contain both motivational and structural bases for humor, it would seem a sound approach methodologically to study their significance separately before in combination. Most studies use stimuli containing both bases for humor and are unable to separate the effects of the two factors. Since a cartoon must always utilize some structural vehicle to carry the humor content, the influence of motivational and structural variables must be studied by using stimuli which (1) have little affective value, (2) are equated for affective value but vary in terms of structural properties, or (3) are equated along structural lines but vary in affective value. Scaling procedures similar to those used by Godkewitsch would be required to reach these ends.

McGhee has taken a valuable step toward filling the void in our understanding of children's humor. Drawing from the Schachterian conclusion that the specific nature of an emotional experience depends on the way in which additional information present at the time of arousal is processed, he introduces the notions of fantasy assimilation and reality assimilation to describe the types of cognitive processing of stimulus discrepancies operative in humor and nonhumor experiences. The differential operation of these mechanisms in the humor process, however, remains to be tested. Also in need of empirical testing are McGhee's views regarding the role of conceptual thinking as a prerequisite for humor. While this position is consistent with the psychoanalytic theorists' emphasis on mastery, McGhee has placed his view in a different cognitive framework. Future research might investigate this dimension by presenting children who either lack or possess a given concept with humor stimuli based on that concept.

McGhee notes that the problems associated with determining the relationship between the cognitive or experiential and behavioral components (smiling, laughter, verbal reports) are especially great in dealing with children's humor. Since children cannot be relied upon to give accurate verbal reports, investigators of preschool children must rely on overt expressions of affect. If arousal measures prove to bear systematic relationships to other measures of appreciation, it might be fruitful to use physiological measures in conjunction with smiling and laughing in very young children.

McGhee also draws attention to the importance of distinguishing between comprehension and appreciation of humor stimuli. While this dimension is especially important in research on children's humor, it should also be given attention in future studies using adult subjects. It now seems clear that a wide range of stimulus, personal, and cognitive processing variables influence measures of humor appreciation. If high levels of appreciation are found to occur among subjects showing either high or low levels of comprehension, the dynamics operative for these subjects clearly must be different and are worthy of further study. Preliminary attention, however, must be given to the development of measures of comprehension. McGhee (1968, 1971) has initiated efforts along these lines, but a great deal remains to be done.

Finally, McGhee's discussion of the role of cues conducive to a humorous interpretation of stimuli suggests promising new avenues of research, since both the external and internal cues described are readily amenable to experimental manipulation.

While McGhee is in agreement with Berlyne regarding the goal of a global theory capable of accounting for all instances of humor, he feels that this goal will be reached more quickly by the preliminary development of alternative mini-theories designed to account for more limited aspects of the humor situation. While Berlyne's approach comes closer than any other to tracing common processes (i.e., arousal fluctuations) in all humor situations, McGhee's conviction that the key to the distinction between humorous and nonhumorous situations will not appear in the analysis of the arousal continuum has led him to a more purely cognitive model in which the *occurrence* of affect is assumed to depend on arousal-influencing collative properties, but its *quality* upon the way in which these properties are processed.

D. Suls

Suls has done an admirable job of incorporating humor into an information-theory framework. His model is concerned primarily with the cognitive components of humor, specifying a two-stage process: (1) perception of incongruity or expectancy violation and (2) resolution of the incongruity. Only if the perceiver goes through each of these stages, can he perceive the humor depicted by the joke. While these two stages seem necessary for humor appreciation, they are not sufficient. In this sense, the basic components of Suls's model form a theory of *comprehension* rather than a theory of *appreciation*. While he does acknowledge the influence of additional factors in determining appreciation (e.g., degree of incongruity, complexity, speed of incongruity resolution, and salience of content), these are not systematically incorporated into the model. Accomplishment of the latter would provide Suls with one of the few models to deal with both of these essential elements of the humor process.

While the data of Goldstein, Suls, and Anthony provide support for peripheral aspects of the Suls model, the basic tenets of the theory remain untested. Although the general information theorists' approach of asking subjects to think aloud while listening to jokes should provide some insight into the actual cognitive processes used by subjects in their efforts to understand jokes, a more fruitful approach might be to actually manipulate the number of steps subjects are capable of completing. While one group of subjects would be provided only with incongruity, another group could be provided with information capable of resolving the incongruity. This would permit a direct test of the role of resolution in determining appreciation. Assuming that comprehension is necessary for a genuine humor experience, we would expect the second group to show greater appreciation. This finding would then extend the analysis to such factors as ease of information processing or level of comprehension. Varying degrees of necessary information or strength of cues suggesting the nature of resolution required could be presented to subjects and subsequent levels of appreciation noted. Then the Suls model might be extended beyond a theory of comprehension to a theory of appreciation as well.

Since Suls has specified the nature and sequence of processes assumed to operate in cartoon and joke humor, it might be of value to develop a computer simulation of the process described. This would serve at least two functions: It would enable comparison of individual processing protocols with the program's steps at various stages of problem solving, and it might ultimately lead to the development of a program capable of generating humor situations.

Finally, while Suls restricts the application of his model to cartoons with captions and jokes, where expectations are created and violated within the stimulus setting, it might be of value to extend the model to additional humor situations where incongruities are simply based on the violation of expectations a subject brings with him to the stimulus situation. This would make the model more applicable to everyday humor situations, thus adding to its predictive power. The model might also be fruitfully extended to the creative aspects of humor; while Goodchilds and others have studied various factors influencing the creation of humor, the differential nature of cognitive processes operating in the initiation versus perception of humor remains unclear. The integration of the Suls model with the concept of "bisociation" advanced by Koestler (1964) might be the most valuable first step in this respect.

E. MARTINEAU

Like the research of Goodchilds and La Fave, Martineau's model for social functions of humor is more concerned with the broader social implications of humor for the study of group processes than with the dynamics of humor.

It is clearly recognized by students of humor that various dimensions of the social context may have a great influence upon both the spontaneous initiation of humor and the appreciation of humor initiated by others. After reviewing the relevant social-psychological, sociological, and anthropological research, Martineau presents a typology of social situations in which humor can occur and then proceeds to discuss the functions which humor would serve in each of those situations. Rather than discussing some finite functions of humor—as has typically been done in the past—he focuses on situations from which humor functions can be derived.

The variables contained in each social situation—actor, audience, subject, intent—are of course, present in every humor situation. However, the judgment (perceived intentionality) variable, which is such an integral part of Martineau's model, has not received the empirical attention it deserves (although La Fave's research along this line is one exception). Part of the problem lies in the lack of a satisfactory measure of judgment. Such a measure must be devised if this model is to achieve its maximum predictive value. Initial attention in this direction might be given to knowledge of the social setting or verbal and paralinguistic cues provided by the actor or source of humor.

A great many postulates of the model are consistent with previous research, although several postulates have not, as yet, been subjected to test. The research presented in this volume by Goodchilds has direct bearing on the intragroup functions of humor and might serve to provide a methodology by which additional aspects of the model can be tested. Furthermore, Goodchilds' research suggests that, not only can intragroup humor function to increase group cohesion, but it may also serve to facilitate (and presumably in some instances to impede) problem solving by the group. The potential number of functions which humor can serve in or between groups is limited only by the number of ways in which group processes and structures can be conceived. As methodology and theory advance with respect to group dynamics, the functions which humor serves in these new conceptual schemes can be quite easily added to the model.

F. LANGEVIN AND DAY

The Langevin and Day research is concerned with the behavioral aspects of humor, in particular, the relationship between physiological and verbal humor indices. However, as from the Godkewitsch chapter, it should be clear that the intensity of autonomic arousal is due in part to the nature of the stimulus and is hypothesized—both here and in the Berlyne and Godkewitsch chapters—to mediate the intensity of the humor response.

There exists in the humor literature fewer than a half-dozen studies on physiological correlates of humor, and so it becomes difficult here to relate the Langevin and Day findings to any larger body of literature. Their research, however, is pertinent to Berlyne's theoretical discussion of humor, in which moderately arousing stimuli are predicted to be maximally pleasurable. For arousal, as for so many psychological variables, a number of measures are available, although not necessarily related in a linear fashion. Langevin and Day measured GSR and heart rate (HR), including amplitude, latency, and recovery time of each. These are essentially the same measures taken by Pollio, Mers, and Lucchesi on audience laughter and support their data on a much more reductive level. While Pollio *et al.* found consistent significant positive relationships between duration and amplitude of laughter in small groups and live audiences, Langevin and Day found GSR recovery time to be significantly greater for humorous than nonhumorous cartoons.

While Langevin and Day have conceptualized funniness ratings along a scale ranging from very unpleasant, through a neutral reaction, to very humorous, their findings of a significant positive linear relationship take on a different interpretation if the aversive end of the scale is placed on the upper end of the arousal-potential continuum described by Berlyne. Langevin and Day's Table I [Chapter 6, p. 138] shows that such a transformation of the scale yields the familiar inverted-U function between humor ratings and GSR amplitude and maximum HR response. This type of finding supports Berlyne's contention of a close bond between curiosity, exploratory behavior, play, humor, etc.

It should be remembered that these data are only correlational data, so that a causal interpretation cannot be placed on the findings. It would be of value in future research to manipulate arousal potential in the fashion of the Godkewitsch experiment and replicate the Langevin and Day study. If scaled arousal-potential values are found to correspond to fluctuations in arousal, we would be a step closer to determining the influence of arousal upon humor appreciation. In one form or another (as noted by Keith-Spiegel), the arousal dimension has long been emphasized by humor theorists; thus additional physiological studies of this type should make significant progress toward resolving this controversy.

G. GODKEWITSCH

The strongest contribution of the Godkewitsch chapter is a methodological one. He criticizes studies claiming to manipulate arousal for only manipulating variables included in arousal potential. These studies do not manipulate arousal itself and also typically fail to evaluate the effectiveness of the manipulations that are made. Arguing that it might be valuable to define arousal level operationally, in terms of arousal potential, he uses a Thurstone scaling technique to develop an interval scale of arousal potential of sexual jokes. This marks a significant advance over earlier efforts to manipulate arousal or develop interval scales for humor stimuli.

A major problem confronting investigators studying behavioral correlates of arousal has been arriving at a consistent definition of the meaning of low, moderate, and high levels of arousal. Since different researchers have defined these levels differently, it has been very difficult to compare and integrate the data obtained. The development of ratio scales for various dimensions believed to influence arousal would establish comparability of data and permit evaluation of the source of arousal potential as a factor in determining the relation between arousal potential and humor.

Godkewitsch's suggestion, in attempting to account for his failure to find a curvilinear relationship between arousal potential and funniness, that stimuli with purely sexual themes may not be sufficiently arousing to reach the unpleasant level suggested by Berlyne, is an interesting one and deserving of empirical attention in the future. As suggested by Godkewitsch, it may be that aggressive or other dimensions are needed, in addition to sexual themes, to create a sufficiently high level of arousal to generate the downward turn of the inverted-U curve described by Berlyne. The significant positive linear relationship between arousal potential and funniness ratings is, however, consistent with Langevin and Day's findings of a linear trend between humor ratings and GSR amplitude and maximum HR response. While Langevin and Day's cartoons may have also failed to sample highly arousing stimuli, thus reducing the probability of finding an inverted-U curve, it can only be concluded here that a great deal of methodological sophistication has yet to be achieved before the relationship between arousal level and humor can be most satisfactorily tested.

In light of Tollefson's (1961) failure to find motivational differences between his aroused and nonaroused groups, it might be of value to hold in mind the possibility that arousal itself is not the key factor in behavioral differences found to occur as functions of arousal. Rather, along the line suggested by Goldstein *et al.,* it may be that cognitive salience is the important factor leading to heightened appreciation. Again, further research on this issue is clearly needed.

H. GOLDSTEIN, SULS, AND ANTHONY

The research of Goldstein, Suls, and Anthony deals primarily with the cognitive aspects of humor through their examination of the effects of salience on the recognition, understanding, and processing of particular joke themata. Although basing their studies on cognitive theories, such as Sul's information-processing model, implications are also apparent for the psychoanalytic theory of humor. Like the research of Godkewitsch, the Goldstein *et al.* findings suggest that appreciation of specific types of humor may be independent of motivational states. This calls into question the utility of psychoanalytic theory for predicting such a phenomenon in at least two ways: First, the salience interpretation is able to predict and explain the earlier psychoanalytic findings, as in the first Goldstein *et al.* study on aggressive humor; second, even if the psychoanalytic hypothesis is correct, the salience hypothesis is a more general and parsimonious one, and therefore of greater utility. It should be noted, however, that a specific dynamic for the salience effect is not offered by Goldstein *et al.* Although the salience prediction can be made from any number of cognitive theories (not necessarily concerned with humor), it was not systematically derived from any particular humor theory. Therefore, whether salience is related to the comprehension of humor and thence to appreciation, or whether it relates directly to appreciation is not known. This aspect of the process, as well as extensions of the salience hypothesis (e.g., to cross-cultural situations), clearly deserves further empirical attention.

Methodologically, the Goldstein *et al.* chapter makes use of systematic replications of their original research. The generality of the salience hypothesis was examined by systematically replicating Experiment I with verbal jokes rather than cartoons, with a different manipulation of salience, and with different salience topics. This use of multiple but conceptually identical stimuli and manipulations (an approach also used by Goodchilds, La Fave, and Pollio *et al.*) goes far in eliminating alternative interpretations of the data.

Results of the experiments reported by Goldstein *et al.* provide considerable support for the salience hypothesis. But additional findings were also obtained which may be worthy of future exploration. In Experiment I, for example, the salience effect was found to be stronger for automobile than for aggressive humor. The authors suggest that this could be related to the abstractness–concreteness dimension of the themata. McGhee has also suggested that behavioral, as opposed to purely perceptual incongruities, may represent a developmentally more complex level of humor. These alternatives bear further empirical scrutiny.

I. GOODCHILDS

A particularly social-psychological approach is taken by Goodchilds in her studies of spontaneous humor in small groups. In addition, her research is unique in its specific focus on the behavioral implications of humor. She goes beyond the immediate situation to an exploration of the implications of humorous behaviors for further social interaction. Implications of humor for an understanding of group dynamics and structure are clearly indicated by her data and are also linked to Martineau's theoretical model for the social functions of humor.

Theoretically and methodologically the research presented by Goodchilds may be seen as an extension of the small-group interaction process analysis of Bales. The Observer Wit Tally, which is used to obtain quantitative measures of humor acts, is similar to the kind of observer coding employed by Bales, though its focus is on a specific type of act, rather than, as in Bales's coding system, on *all* behavior acts.

In addition to the development and use of the Observer Wit Tally, the series of studies by Goodchilds and her associates includes a number of methodological improvements over earlier humor research: Multiple subject populations are sampled, including naturally occurring and artificially constructed groups consisting of students and adults of both sexes; multiple indicators are used, including the Observer Wit Tally, sociometric measures, and self- and other reports; humor creation and its implications are examined by employing spontaneous humor and having subjects devise cartoon captions and rate fictional scripts containing humor.

The data from these studies are all the more striking and valuable because of their consistency across settings, subject populations, group tasks, and dependent measures. For example, wits were found to be more active participants than nonwits among female college groups, mixed-sex management development groups, and groups of male students. This was true for both natural and laboratory groups varying in size from 4 to 12 members and groups engaged in both problem-solving and humor production tasks, regardless of whether the measure of humor was the Observer Wit Tally or ratings by group members.

Nonetheless, there are several findings from the nearly dozen studies presented by Goodchilds which need further attention: Sex differences were not always apparent nor consistent across groups, nor were wits always distinguishable from nonwits on self- and other ratings. It is also unclear why likability and influence are inversely related for sarcastic and nonsarcastic wits, although this finding is a reliable one.

J. LA FAVE

The chapter by La Fave begins with important distinctions between humor, laughter, and amusement. It is his position—and ours also—that laughter is neither a necessary nor sufficient basis for inferring a humor response and that humor per se resides within the organism; it is an internal process, of which laughter and humor judgments are only indices.

La Fave presents social-psychological modifications of superiority theories of humor, based on the notions of reference groups and identification classes. The central problem attacked by La Fave (and also alluded to by Suls, Martineau, Godkewitsch, and Goldstein *et al.*) can be reduced to the following question: Why do some people laugh at a joke while others, presented with the identical joke, do not? This problem has been examined previously in terms of personality, motivation, autonomic arousal, and salience. The theoretical analysis of this problem by La Fave centers on the recipient's identification class (IC). If the joke disparages a positive IC or esteems a negative IC, it will not be perceived as amusing; while if it esteems a positive IC or disparages a negative IC, it will be judged as humorous.

The research conducted by La Fave and his associates provides strong support for his hypotheses. Research using students highly ego-involved in a variety of social issues provided reliable replications of La Fave's original findings obtained using subjects of different religious denominations. By using repeated measures and designs, La Fave avoids several alternative theoretical and methodological interpretations of his data. Nevertheless, the limits of the IC hypothesis are not known and need to be elaborated. Furthermore, research is also needed to distinguish between several remaining alternative explanations of the data, such as the salience hypothesis offered by Goldstein *et al.* and the cognitive balance model of Heider (1958).

K. POLLIO, MERS, AND LUCCHESI

The concern of Pollio, Mers, and Lucchesi with behavioral aspects of humor and their interrelations is also tied in with attempts to determine stimulus qualities which reliably differentiate various types of humor behaviors. To these ends, an original and quite useful methodology was developed—the use of oscillographic records of laughter—which yields measures of the latency, amplitude, and duration of laughter. The use and development of this technique highlights the view that laughter (and smiling) is a continuous, rather than dichotomous, variable.

In addition to using this new measurement technique, Pollio *et al.* sampled a wide range of humor stimuli—musical plays, films, television canned laughter, and comedy recordings—in both naturalistic and laboratory settings. Their research across these various settings (with the exception of canned audience laughter, which was found to differ from spontaneous laughter in a number of ways) yields several consistent findings: Amplitude and duration of laughter are positively related to one another, but neither is related consistently to latency; audiences are fairly consistent across similar performances, particularly on the latency measure.

There are several suggestions for future research which arise from the Pollio *et al.* data. The authors themselves suggest that the three components of laughter may each be stimulus-specific, such that, for example, latency is related to the cognitive difficulty of a joke, amplitude to the arousal potential of a joke, and duration to both social and arousal variables. Future research and theory should be directed to an examination of both arousal (motivational–emotional) and cognitive dimensions, including variables present in the social situation. The finding that there are early, middle, and late risers among laughs also deserves further study in order to determine their significance and what stimulus, cognitive, and affective conditions bring them about. Finally, the suggestion by Pollio *et al.* that characteristics of humorists themselves be explored with the aim of arriving at a multidimensional space, in which any single comedian may be located, deserves empirical development.

II. An Overview

The preceding section makes it clear that while the present volume provides a number of first steps, on several different fronts, toward a greater understanding of the humor process, these remain initial steps only—and small ones at that. If the complexity of humor phenomena were ever in doubt, that doubt should now be dispelled. We have only scratched the empirical surface of this most interesting phenomenon whose nature man has pondered over the centuries. The diversity of approaches represented in this volume may be seen in Table I, which summarizes each chapter's concern with stimulus, organism, and response variables. As we have stated earlier, these diverse theoretical and empirical papers lead us toward more precise and testable conceptions of humor than has hitherto been available.

References

Heider, F. *The psychology of interpersonal relations.* New York: Wiley, 1958.

Koestler, A. *The act of creation.* London: Hutchinson, 1964. (Also: New York: Dell, 1964.)

McGhee, P. E. Cognitive development and children's comprehension of humor. Unpublished doctoral dissertation, Ohio State Univ., 1968.

McGhee, P. E. Cognitive development and children's comprehension of humor. *Child Development,* 1971, 42, 123–138.

Tollefson, D. L. Differential responses to humor and their relation to personality and motivation measures. Unpublished doctoral dissertation, Univ. of Illinois, 1961.

TABLE I

Stimulus, Organism, and Response Variables

	Stimulus variables	Organism variables		Response variables	
		Cognitive functioning	Personal traits	Humor measures	Nonhumor measures
Keith-Spiegel	Review	Review	Review	Review	Review
Berlyne	Collative properties	Arousal jag and boost		Physiological Smiling Laughing Verbal	
McGhee	Perceptual and behavioral discrepancy	Fantasy and reality assimilation	Conceptual and logical thinking	Smiling Laughing Verbal	
Suls	Cartoon and joke incongruity	Perception and resolution of incongruity		Smiling Laughing Verbal	
Martineau	Esteem or disparage in or out group		Relation to initiator of humor		Perception and cohesion of in or out group

Langevin and Day	Nondifferentiated cartoons				GSR HR Verbal
Godkewitsch	Arousal potential	Arousal level	Introversion Extroversion	Verbal	
Goldstein et al.	Cognitive themata	Salience		Verbal	
Goodchilds	Spontaneous humor, sarcasm and whimsey		Self and other ratings; sociometric measures		Perception of wit
La Fave	Esteem or disparage + or − RG or IC		Membership in RG or IC	Verbal	
Pollio et al.	Plays, films, TV, records			Smiling Laughing Verbal	

APPENDIX

Chapter 13

An Annotated Bibliography of Published Papers on Humor in the Research Literature and an Analysis of Trends: 1900–1971

Jeffrey H. Goldstein

Department of Psychology
Temple University, Philadelphia, Pennsylvania

and

Paul E. McGhee

Department of Psychology
State University of New York, Albany, New York

I. Introduction

Although the research in selected areas has been reviewed in each of the preceding chapters, no exhaustive review of all discussions and data related to humor has been attempted here.

However our own review of this literature has revealed some interesting methodological trends over the past seven decades. These trends will be briefly summarized with special attention given to empirical studies after 1950. Following this is an annotated bibliography of published work on humor in the research literature of the behavioral sciences.

II. A Survey of Methodology in Empirical Studies: 1950–1971

The literature covering the past 20 years has been selected for detailed analysis, since this period marks an increased concern with an empirical approach to the topic of humor. The 100 studies selected for this analysis constitute 66% of the total number of studies completed in this period and are a representative sample of these studies.

A. EXPERIMENTAL DESIGN

In this book, on more than one occasion, it has been suggested that researchers have become increasingly interested in various aspects of humor and that this renewed interest has been accompanied by an increase in methodological sophistication. If the transition from a correlational to experimental approach may be accepted as an index of improved methodology, these assertions are borne out by the data. As shown in Table I, not only did the total number of empirical studies of humor sharply increase in the second half of this period, but the percentage of experimental studies also increased greatly. While this increasing concern with the effect of specific experimental manipulations on humor has generated a better understanding of the influence of various personal, stimulus, and

TABLE I
Type of Experimental Design in Two Decades

Years	Type of experimental design		
	Correlational	Experimental[a]	Total
1950–1960	19	5	24
1961–1971	44	32	76
Total	63	37	100

[a] Any study which contains at least one manipulated variable is classified here as experimental.

social characteristics upon humor, many studies have failed to relate their results to theory. Correlational studies, however, have been even less frequently derived from theory. While the trend in Table I is promising, future research can make maximal contributions by developing theoretically based experimental studies.

B. Subject Samples

Psychology has often been described as the study of rats and college sophomores. While research on humor has managed to avoid concentration on the former, Table II clearly shows that our understanding of humor continues to be based mainly on the behavior of the college student, hardly a representative sample of

TABLE II

Subjects Employed in Sample Studies

Sex	Subject population						
	Children	High school	College	Normal adults	Psychiatric patients	Other or not specified	Total
Male	3	1	15	1	7	5	32
Female	0	1	5	1	2	1	10
Both	9	1	22	7	2	3	44
Not specified	0	0	5	3	4	3	15
Total	12	3	47	12	15	12	101[a]

[a] Total is more than 100 because of use of multiple subject populations in six studies. The table excludes five content analyses from the sample.

mankind. If developmental, social, and cultural factors do play an important role in the humor process, the need for a broader sampling of subject populations is clear. While nearly 50% of the studies sampled employed both males and females, meaningful and consistent sex differences remain to be found.

C. Types of Stimuli Used as Independent Variables

For the 100 studies in our sample, the following modes of stimulus presentation were used: cartoons, 52%; riddles, jokes, or stories, 23%; tapes, films, or records, 8%; others (such as comic strips, public speeches, or social situations), 17%. The 75% representation in the first two categories reflects the attitude of many researchers that a relatively noncomplex stimulus is best suited to studying humor. A simpler stimulus enhances the probability of isolating parameters bearing an important influence on the humor process. Within the usage of cartoons and jokes, the most typically controlled dimension has been stimulus content. As shown in Table III, when stimulus content was controlled, stimuli have generally been categorized as aggressive, sexual, or incongruity (nonsense), undoubtedly reflecting the impact of Freudian theory.

TABLE III

Categorization of Humor Stimuli Used as Independent Variables

Stimulus type	n
Aggressive	37
Sexual	20
Incongruity or nonsense	24
Superiority	4
Complexity	4
Other	24
Not controlled	24
Not applicable	17
Total[a]	154

[a] Total is greater than 100 because of use of multiple types of stimuli within a single study.

While a small number of studies have controlled for complexity, this dimension remains essentially unexplored. Although the significance of this dimension for adult humor is unclear, it appears to be especially important for children's humor and deserves greater attention in future research.

D. DEPENDENT VARIABLES

As suggested in earlier chapters [e.g., Chapters 2, 3, 9–11], such behaviors as laughter, smiling, and verbal statements of funniness provide valuable indices of degree of humor appreciation. However, they do not constitute the humor process itself. However, since the humor experience is an internal, empirically nonobservable process, we must be satisfied with overt behavioral measures like those given in Table IV. While two studies have related indices of arousal to humor, most have relied on some type of verbal rating or preference. Also, a small number have used overt expressions of affect. Only seven studies, however, have used both the affective-expression and rating-scale approaches. Among these seven, differential predictiveness has often been found for the two measures, suggesting that they are either influenced by different variables or simply not measuring the same event. As suggested by McGhee (*Psychological Bulletin,* 1971), methodological problems are associated with each approach, and it may be that the most fruitful approach will prove to be prediction by a combination of several weighted dependent variables.

TABLE IV
Type of Dependent Variables

Dependent variable	n
Rating scale	68
Laughter; smiling	13
Humor creation	9
Forced choice	8
Physiological measure(s)	2
Comprehension of humor	12
Other	10
Total[a]	122

[a] Total is greater than 100 because of use of multiple dependent variables in some studies.

Further research along these lines may be prerequisite for significant advances in this field. Table IV also shows that the comprehension and creative aspects of humor remain relatively unexplored. While difficult problems face the investigator attempting to define and measure comprehension, it seems clear that level of comprehension of a humor stimulus should play an important role in determining appreciation of it. Thus, future studies (especially developmental studies) would profit from increased empirical attention to this dimension.

III. An Annotated Bibliography of Published Papers on Humor in the Research Literature: 1900–1971

The following bibliography contains all published papers on humor available in the English language in the research literature. This primarily includes journals from the fields of the social, behavioral, and medical sciences. The bibliography covers the period from 1900 to August 1971. The annotation is by way of the following symbols:

D   Paper contains original data.
c   (*Subscript.*) Data are of a correlational nature. Included here are also factor and content analyses.
x   (*Subscript.*) Data are experimental. A study was categorized as D_x if at least one variable was experimentally manipulated.
T   Paper presents original theory or theoretical developments regarding humor.
F   Paper discusses the functions of humor, either in a cultural, social, personality, or physiological context.
Ch   Paper deals in some way with humor in children.
M   Paper is methodological in nature, or presents significant methodological techniques for the study of humor.
R   Review of the humor literature or some specific part of it.
G   General discussion of humor. Also included are papers which do not conveniently fit any of the above categories.
S   Studies included in the preceding methodology survey.

A number of references listed in the bibliography were, when not otherwise available, taken from secondary sources. We have not provided annotation for these papers. If any of our readers can provide us with copies of these papers—or with papers inadvertently omitted from the bibliography, we would appreciate receiving them, so that we may periodically revise the bibliography.

The nearly 400 items in the bibliography come from over 100 journals published in English. Of these, nearly 30% are dated after 1960 and less than 15% before 1930. This represents, in part, the relative unavailability of older and now-defunct publications but is largely a reflection of increasing interest in the area.

Abelson, R. P., & Levine, J. A factor analytic study of cartoon humor among psychiatric patients. *Journal of Personality,* 1958, 26, 451-466.   (D_c, M, S)
Adelson, J. Ethnocentrism and humor appreciation. *American Psychologist,* 1947, 2, 413.   (D_x)
Allin, A. On laughter. *Psychological Review,* 1903, **10**, 306-315.   (G)
Alston, J. P., & Platt, L. A. Religious humor: A longitudinal content analysis of cartoons. *Sociological Analysis,* 1969, 30, 217-222.   (D_c, S)
Andrew, R. J. Evolution of facial expression. *Science,* 1963, 142, 1034-1041.   (T)
Andrew, R. J. The origin and evolution of the calls and facial expressions of the primates. *Behavior,* 1963, 20, 1-109.   (T)

Andrew, R. J. The origins of facial expressions. *Scientific American,* 1965, 213, 88–94. (T)

Andrews, T. G. A factorial analysis of responses to the comic as a study of personality. *Journal of General Psychology,* 1943, 28, 209–224. (D$_c$)

Arieti, S. New views on the psychology of wit and the comic. *Psychiatry,* 1950, 13, 43–62. (G)

Arnez, N. L., & Anthony, C. B. Contemporary Negro humor as social satire. *Phylon,* 1968, 29, 339–346. (G)

Averill, J. R. Autonomic response patterns during sadness and mirth. *Psychophysiology,* 1969, 5, 399–414. (D$_c$, S)

Baillie, J. Laughter and tears: The sense of incongruity. *Studies in Human Nature,* 1921, 9, 254–293. (T)

Barcus, F. E. A content analysis of trends in Sunday comics, 1900–1959. *Journalism Quarterly,* 1961, 38, 171–180. (D$_c$, S)

Barron, M. L. A content analysis of intergroup humor. *American Sociological Review,* 1950, 15, 88–94. (D$_c$, S)

Barry, H., Jr. The role of subject matter in individual differences in humor. *Journal of Genetic Psychology,* 1928, 35, 112–128. (D$_c$)

Bateson, G. The role of humor in human communication. In H. von Foerster (Ed.), *Cybernetics.* New York: Macy Foundation, 1953. (T)

Berger, A. A. Authority in the comics. *Transaction,* 1966 (Dec.), 22–26. (G)

Bergler, E. A clinical contribution to the psychogenesis of humor. *Psychoanalytic Review,* 1937, 24, 34–53. (T)

Bergler, E. *Laughter and the sense of humor.* New York: Intercontinental Medical Book Corp., 1956. (T, R)

Bergson, H. *Laughter: An essay on the meaning of the comic.* New York: Macmillan, 1911. (T)

Berkowitz, L. Aggressive humor as a stimulus to aggressive responses. *Journal of Personality and Social Psychology,* 1970, 16, 710–717. (D$_x$, S)

Berlyne, D. E. *Conflict, arousal and curiosity.* New York: McGraw-Hill, 1960. (T)

Berlyne, D. E. Laughter, humor and play. In G. Lindzey & E. Aronson (Eds.), *Handbook of social psychology.* (2nd ed.), Vol. 3. Reading, Massachusetts: Addison-Wesley, 1969. (R, F)

Bird, G. E. An objective humor test for children. *Psychological Bulletin,* 1925, 22, 137–138. (M, Ch, D$_c$)

Blatz, W. E., Allen, K. D., & Millichamps, D. A. *A study of laughter in the nursery school child.* Toronto: Univ. of Toronto Press, 1936. (Ch, D$_c$)

Bliss, S. H. The origin of laughter. *American Journal of Psychology,* 1915, 26, 236–246. (T)

Bogardus, E. Sociology of the cartoon. *Sociology and Social Research,* 1945, 30, 139–147. (G)

Bogart, L. Comic strips and their adult readers. In B. Rosenbert & D. M. White (Eds.), *Mass culture.* Glencoe, Illinois: Free Press, 1957. (G)

Bowman, H. A. The humor of primitive people. In *Studies in the Science of Society.* New Haven: Yale Univ. Press, 1939.

Brackett, C. W. Laughing and crying of pre-school children. *Journal of Experimental Education,* 1933, 2, 119–126. (D$_c$, Ch)

Brackett, C. W. Laughter and crying in preschool children. *Child Development Monographs,* 1934, No. 14. (D$_c$, Ch)

Bradney, P. The joking relationship in industry. *Human Relations,* 1957, **10**, 179–187. (D_c, G)

Brandt, C. S. On joking relationships. *American Anthropologist* (New Series), 1948, **50**, 160–162. (D_c)

Brenman, M. On teasing and being teased: The problem of moral masochism. *Psychoanalytic Study of the Child,* 1952, 7, 264–285. (T)

Brill, A. A. The mechanism of wit and humor in normal and psychopathic states. *Psychiatric Quarterly,* 1940, 14, 731–749.

Brody, M. W. The meaning of laughter. *Psychoanalytic Quarterly,* 1950, 19, 192–201. (T)

Brumbaugh, F. The place of humor in the curriculum. *Journal of Experimental Education,* 1940, 8, 403–409. (F, Ch)

Brumbaugh, F., & Wilson, R. T. Children's laughter. *Journal of Genetic Psychology,* 1940, 57, 3–29. (Ch, D_c)

Burma, J. H. Humor as a technique in race conflict. *American Sociological Review,* 1946, 11, 710–715. (G)

Burrow, M. L. A content analysis of intergroup humor. *American Sociological Review,* 1950, 15, 88–89. (D_c)

Burt, C. The psychology of laughter. *Health Education Journal,* 1945, 3 (3), 101–105.

Byrne, D. The relationship between humor and the expression of hostility. *Journal of Abnormal and Social Psychology,* 1956, 53, 84–89. (D_c, S)

Byrne, D. Drive level, response to humor, and the cartoon sequence effect. *Psychological Reports,* 1958, 4, 439–442. (D_x, S)

Byrne, D. Some inconsistencies in the effect of motivation arousal on humor preferences. *Journal of Abnormal and Social Psychology,* 1961, 62, 158–160. (D_x, M, S)

Byrne, D., Terrill, J., & McReynolds, P. Incongruency as a predictor of response to humor. *Journal of Abnormal and Social Psychology,* 1961, 62, 435–438. (D_c, S)

Carpenter, R. Laughter, a glory in sanity. *American Journal of Psychology,* 1922, 33, 419–422. (T)

Carpenter, W. R. Experiments on the comic. *American Journal of Psychology,* 1925, 36, 309–310. (T)

Carritt, E. F. A theory of the ludicrous. *Hibbert Journal,* 1923, 21, 552–564. (T)

Cattell, R. B., & Luborsky, L. B. Measured response to humor as an indicator of personality structure. *American Psychologist,* 1946, 1, 257–258. (D_c, M)

Cattell, R. B., & Luborsky, L. B. Personality in response to humor. *Journal of Abnormal & Social Psychology,* 1947, 42, 402–421. (D_c, M)

Cattell, R. B., & Tollefson, D. L. *Handbook for the IPAT humor test of personality.* Champaign, Illinois: Institute for Personality & Ability Testing, 1963. (M, D_c)

Chandler, K. A. The sense of humor in children. *Century,* 1902, 42, 959–960. (Ch)

Charles, L. H. The clown's function. *Journal of American Folklore,* 1945, 58, 25–34. (F)

Chatterji, N. N. Laughter in schizophrenia and psychotic disorders. *Samiksa,* 1952, 6, 32–37. (D_c)

Clark, M. Humour and incongruity. *Philosophy: Journal of the Royal Institute of Philosophy,* 1970, 45, 20–32. (T)

Cloyd, J. S. Patterns of behavior in informal interaction. *Sociometry,* 1964, 27, 161–173. (D_c)

Collier, M. J. Popular cartoons and prevailing anxieties. *American Imago,* 1960, 17, 255–269. (G)

Coriat, I. H. Humor and hypomania. *Psychiatric Quarterly,* 1939, 13, 681–688.

Coser, R. L. Some social functions of laughter. *Human Relations,* 1959, 12, 171–182. (F)

Coser, R. L. Laughter among colleagues. *Psychiatry,* 1960, 23, 81–95. (F, D_c)

Cunningham, A. Relation of sense of humor to intelligence. *Journal of Social Psychology,* 1962, 57, 143–147. (D_c, S)

Daniels, A. K., & Daniels, R. R. The social function of the career fool. *Psychiatry,* 1964, 27, 218–229. (T, F)

Davis, J. M., & Farina, A. Humor appreciation as social communication. *Journal of Personality & Social Psychology,* 1970, 15, 175–178. (D_x, T, S)

Davison, C., & Kelman, H. Pathologic laughing and crying. *Archives of Neurology and Psychiatry,* 1939, 42, 595.

Day, H. I., & Langevin, R. Curiosity and intelligence: Two necessary conditions for a high level of creativity. *Journal of Special Education,* 1969, 3, 263–268. (D_c, S)

Dearborn, G. V. N. The nature of the smile and laugh. *Science,* 1900, 2, 851–856. (T, G, F, Ch)

Desai, M. W. Surprise: A historical and experimental study. *British Journal of Psychology* (Monograph Suppl.), 1939, No. 22. (R, D_x)

Ding, G. F., & Jersild, A. T. A study of laughing and crying in preschool children. *Journal of Genetic Psychology,* 1932, 40, 452–472. (D_c, Ch, R)

Diserens, C. M. Recent theories of laughter. *Psychological Bulletin,* 1926, 23, 247–255. (R)

Diserens, C. M., & Bonifield, M. Humor and the ludicrous. *Psychological Bulletin,* 1930, 27, 108–118. (R, F, Ch)

Dooley, L. A note on humor. *Psychoanalytic Review,* 1934, 21, 49–58. (G)

Dooley, L. Relation of humor to masochism. *Psychoanalytic Review,* 1941, 28, 37–46.

Doris, J., & Fierman, E. Humor and anxiety. *Journal of Abnormal & Social Psychology,* 1956, 53, 59–62. (D_c, S)

Druckman, R., & Chao, D. Laughter in epilepsy. *Neurology,* 1957, 7, 26–36.

Dworkin, E. S., & Efran, J. S. The angered: Their susceptibility to varieties of humor. *Journal of Personality & Social Psychology,* 1967, 6, 233–236. (D_x, S)

Eastman, M. *The sense of humor.* New York: Scribners, 1921. (T)

Eastman, M. *Enjoyment of laughter.* New York: Simon & Schuster, 1936. (T, R)

Easton, R. Humor of the American Indian. *Mankind,* 1970, 2, 37ff. (G)

Edwards, S. The function of laughter. *Psyche,* 1926, 22–32. (F)

Ehrle, R. A., & Johnson, B. G. Psychologists and cartoonists. *American Psychologist,* 1961, 16, 693–695. (D_c, S)

Eidelberg, L. A contribution to the study of wit. *Psychoanalytic Review,* 1945, 32, 33–61. (T)

Eijderveld, A. C. Jokes and their relation to social reality. *Social Research,* 1968, 35, 286–311.

Eisenbud, J. The oral side of humor. *Psychoanalytic Review,* 1964, 51, 57–73. (T)

Emerson, J. P. Negotiating the serious import of humor. *Sociometry,* 1969, 32, 169–181. (F)

Enders, A. C. A study of the laughter of the preschool child in the Merrill–Palmer nursery school. *Papers of the Michigan Academy of Science, Arts, and Letters,* 1927, 8, 341–356. (D_c, Ch)

Epstein, S., & Smith, R. Repression and insight as related to reaction to cartoons. *Journal of Consulting Psychology,* 1956, 20, 391–395. (D_x, S)

Esar, E. *The humor of humor.* New York: Horizon, 1952. (G)

Escarpit, R. Humorous attitudes and scientific creativity. *Impact of Science on Society,* 1969, 19, 253–258. (G)

Eysenck, H. J. The appreciation of humour: An experimental and theoretical study. *British Journal of Psychology,* 1942, 32, 295–309. (D_x, T)

Eysenck, H. J. An experimental analysis of five tests of "appreciation of humor." *Educational & Psychological Measurement,* 1943, 3, 191–214. (M, D$_c$)

Eysenck, H. J. National differences in "sense of humor": Three experimental and statistical studies. *Character & Personality,* 1944–1945, 13, 37–54. (D$_c$)

Feldmann, S. A supplement to Freud's theory of wit. *Psychoanalytic Review,* 1941, 28, 201–217. (T)

Feleky, A. The influence of emotions on respiration. *Journal of Experimental Psychology,* 1916, 1, 218–246. (D$_c$)

Felker, D. W., & Hunter, D. M. Sex and age differences in response to cartoons depicting subjects of different ages and sex. *Journal of Psychology,* 1970, 76, 19–21. (D$_c$, Ch, S)

Ferenczi, S. The psychoanalysis of wit and the comical. In *Further contributions to psychoanalysis.* London: Hogarth, 1911. (T)

Flugel, J. C. Humor and laughter. In G. Lindzey (Ed.), *Handbook of social psychology.* Vol. 2. *Special fields and applications.* Reading, Massachusetts: Addison-Wesley, 1954. (R)

Freud, S. Humour. In *Collected papers.* Vol. 5. New York: Basic Books, 1959. (Also: *International Journal of Psychoanalysis,* 1928, 9, 1–6.) (T)

Freud, S. *Jokes and their relation to the unconscious.* New York: Norton, 1960. (Originally: *Der Witz und seine Beziehung zum Unbewussten.* Leipzig and Vienna: Deuticke, 1905). (T)

Fry, W. F., Jr. *Sweet madness: A study of humor.* Palo Alto, California: Pacific, 1963. (T)

Fry, W. F., Jr. Humor in a physiological vein. *Beckman Instruments Newsletter,* 1969 (Aug.), 3. (D$_c$, S)

Ghosh, R. An experimental study of humour. *British Journal of Educational Psychology,* 1939, 9, 98–99. (D$_x$)

Giles, H., & Oxford, G. S. Towards a multidimensional theory of laughter causation and its social implications. *Bulletin of the British Psychological Society,* 1970, 23, 97–105. (T)

Goldstein, J. H. Humor appreciation and time to respond. *Psychological Reports,* 1970, 27, 445–446. (D$_x$, S)

Goldstein, J. H. Repetition, motive arousal, and humor appreciation. *Journal of Experimental Research in Personality,* 1970, 4, 90–94. (D$_x$, S)

Gollob, H. F., & Levine, J. Distraction as a factor in the enjoyment of aggressive humor. *Journal of Personality & Social Psychology,* 1967, 5, 368–372. (D$_x$, S)

Goodchilds, J. D. Effects of being witty on position in the social structure of a small group. *Sociometry,* 1959, 22, 261–272. (D$_c$, S)

Goodchilds, J. D., & Smith, E. E. The wit and his group. *Human Relations,* 1964, 17, 23–31. (D$_c$, S)

Goodrich, A. J., Henry, J., & Goodrich, D. W. Laughter in psychiatric staff conferences: A sociopsychiatric analysis. *American Journal of Orthopsychiatry,* 1954, 24, 175–184. (F, D$_c$)

Gopala-Swami, M. V. The genesis of the laughter instinct. *Psychological Studies,* 1926, 1, 1–25.

Graham, L. R. The maturational factor in humor. *Journal of Clinical Psychology,* 1958, 14, 326–328. (D$_c$, Ch, S)

Greenberg, B. S., & Kahn, S. Blacks in *Playboy* cartoons. *Journalism Quarterly,* 1970, 47, 557–560. (D$_c$)

Gregory, J. C. Some theories of laughter. *Mind,* 1923, 32, 328–344. (R)

Gregory, J. C. *The nature of laughter.* London: Kegan Paul, 1924. (T)

Greig, J. Y. T. *The psychology of laughter and comedy.* New York: Dodd, Mead, 1923. (T, R)

Grimes, W. H. A theory of humor for public address. *Speech Monographs,* 1955, 22, 217–226. (T)

Grimes, W. H. The mirth experience in public address. *Speech Monographs,* 1955, 22, 243–255. (G)

Grotjahn, M. Laughter in dreams. *Psychoanalytic Quarterly,* 1945, 14, 221–227. (G)

Grotjahn, M. Laughter in psychoanalysis. *Samiksa,* 1949, 3, 76–82. (G)

Grotjahn, M. The inability to remember dreams and jokes. *Psychoanalytic Quarterly,* 1951, 20, 284–286. (G)

Grotjahn, M. *Beyond laughter.* New York: McGraw-Hill, 1957. (T, R, Ch, F)

Grove, M., & Eisenman, R. Personality correlates of complexity–simplicity. *Perceptual & Motor Skills,* 1970, 31, 387–391. (D_x)

Gruner, C. R. An experimental study of the effectiveness of oral satire in modifying attitude. *Speech Monographs,* 1964, 31, 231–232. (D_x, S)

Gruner, C. R. An experimental study of satire as persuasion. *Speech Monographs,* 1965, 32, 149–154. (D_x, S)

Gruner, C. R. Is wit to humor what rhetoric is to poetic? *Central States Speech Journal,* 1965, 16, 17–22. (G)

Gruner, C. R. A further experimental study of satire as persuasion. *Speech Monographs,* 1966, 33, 184–185. (D_x, S)

Gruner, C. R. Editorial satire as persuasion. *Journalism Quarterly,* 1967, 44, 727–730. (D_x, S)

Gruner, C. R. Effect of humor on speaker ethos and audience information gain. *Journal of Communication,* 1967, 17, 228–233. (D_x, S)

Gruner, C. R. The effect on speaker ethos and audience information gain of humor in dull and interesting speeches. *Central States Speech Journal,* 1970, 21, 160. (D_x)

Gruner, C. R. Ad hominem satire as a persuader: An experiment. *Journalism Quarterly,* 1971, 48, 128–131. (D_x)

Grziwok, R. K., & Scodel, A. Some psychological correlates of humor preference. *Journal of Consulting Psychology,* 1956, 20, 42. (D_c, S)

Guthrie, W. N. A theory of the comic. *International Quarterly,* 1903, 7, 254–264. (T)

Gutman, J., & Priest, R. F. When is aggression funny? *Journal of Personality & Social Psychology,* 1969, 12, 60–65. (D_x, S)

Haggard, E. G. A projective technique using comic strip characters. *Character & Personality,* 1942, 10, 289–295. (M)

Hammes, J. A. Suggestibility and humor evaluation. *Perceptual & Motor Skills,* 1962, 15, 530. (D_c, S)

Hammes, J. A., & Wiggins, S. L. Manifest anxiety and appreciation of humor involving emotional content. *Perceptual & Motor Skills,* 1962, 14, 291–294. (D_c, S)

Hammond, P. B. Mossi joking. *Ethnology,* 1964, 3, 259–267.

Harlow, H. F. The anatomy of humor. *Impact of Science on Society,* 1969, 19, 225–240. (R, F, G)

Harms, E. The development of humor. *Journal of Abnormal & Social Psychology,* 1943, 38, 351–369. (Ch)

Harrelson, R. W., & Stroud, P. S. Observations of humor in chronic schizophrenics. *Mental Hygiene,* 1967, 51, 458. (D_c, S)

Harrower, M. R. Organization in higher mental processes. *Psychologische Forschung,* 1933, 17, 56–120. (T, D_c)

Hausdorff, D. Magazine humor and popular morality, 1929–1934. *Journalism Quarterly,* 1964, 41, 509–516. (D_c)

Hayworth, D. The social origins and functions of laughter. *Psychological Review*, 1928, 35, 367–384. (T, F)

Heim, A. An experiment on humour. *British Journal of Psychology*, 1936, 27, 148–161. (D_x)

Hellyar, R. H. Laughter and jollity. *Contemporary Review*, 1927, 132, 757–763. (T)

Hertzler, J. O. *Laughter: A socio-scientific analysis.* New York: Exposition Press, 1971. (G, T)

Hes, J. P., & Levine, J. Kibbuts humor. *Journal of Nervous & Mental Disorders*, 1962, 135, 327–331. (D_c, S)

Hetherington, E. M. Humor preferences in normal and physically handicapped children. *Journal of Abnormal & Social Psychology*, 1964, 69, 694–696. (D_c, Ch, S)

Hetherington, E. M., & Wray, N. P. Aggression, need for social approval, and humor preferences. *Journal of Abnormal & Social Psychology*, 1964, 68, 685–689. (D_x, S)

Hetherington, E. M., & Wray, N. P. Effects of need aggression, stress, and aggressive behavior on humor preferences. *Journal of Personality & Social Psychology*, 1966, 4, 229–233. (D_x, S)

Hinson, M. The assessment of children's appreciation of humorous verses. *Educational Review*, 1970, 22, 198–204. (Ch, D_c)

Hollingworth, H. L. Experimental studies in judgment: Judgment of the comic. *Psychological Review*, 1911, 18, 132–156. (D_c)

Hom, G. L. Threat of shock and anxiety in the perception of humor. *Perceptual & Motor Skills*, 1966, 23, 535–538. (D_c, S)

Horowitz, L. S. Attitudes of speech defectives toward humor based on speech defects. *Speech Monographs*, 1957, 24, 46–55. (D_c, S)

Horowitz, M. W., & Horowitz, L. S. An examination of the social psychological situation of the physically disabled as it pertains to humor. *American Psychologist*, 1949, 4, 256–257. (D_c)

Hoult, T. Comic books and juvenile delinquency. *Sociology & Social Research*, 1949, 33, 279–284. (Ch)

Jacobson, E. The child's laughter: Theoretical and clinical notes on the function of the comic. *Psychoanalytic Study of the Child*, 1946, 2, 39–60. (T, F, Ch)

Jekels, L. On the psychology of comedy. In *Selected papers*. New York: International Univ. Press, 1952. (orig. 1926) (Also: London: Imago, 1952.)

Justin, F. A genetic study of laughter provoking stimuli. *Child Development*, 1932, 3, 114–136. (D_c, Ch, F, R)

Kallen, H. M. The aesthetic principle in comedy. *American Journal of Psychology*, 1911, 22, 137–157. (T)

Kambouropoulou, P. Individual differences in the sense of humor. *American Journal of Psychology*, 1926, 37, 268–278. (D_c)

Kambouropoulou, P. Individual differences in the sense of humor and their relation to temperamental differences. *Archives of Psychology*, 1930, No. 121. (D_c)

Kant, O. Inappropriate laughter and silliness in schizophrenia. *Journal of Abnormal & Social Psychology*, 1942, 37, 398. (G)

Kanzer, M. Gogol—A study on wit and paranoia. *Journal of the American Psychoanalytic Association*, 1955, 3, 110.

Kaplan, H. B., & Boyd, I. H. The social functions of humor on an open psychiatric ward. *Psychiatric Quarterly*, 1965, 39, 502–515. (F)

Karstetter, A. B. Toward a theory of rhetorical irony. *Speech Monographs*, 1964, 31, 162–178. (T)

Kenderline, M. Laughter in the preschool child. *Child Development*, 1931, 2, 228–230. (D_c, Ch)

Kenny, D. I. The contingency of humor appreciation on the stimulus-confirmation of joke-ending expectations. *Journal of Abnormal & Social Psychology*, 1955, 51, 644–648. (D_x, T, S)

Kimmins, C. W. An investigation of the humor in children. *Reports of the British Association for the Advancement of Science*, 1921, No. 449. (Ch, D_c, R)

Kimmins, C. W. *The springs of laughter.* London: Methuen, 1928. (D_c, T)

Klapp, O. The fool as a social type. *American Journal of Sociology*, 1950, 55, 157–162. (F)

Kline, L. W. The psychology of humor. *American Journal of Psychology*, 1907, 18, 421–441. (T, F)

Koch, M. Constitutional variants of wittiness. *Psychotherapy and Medical Psychology*, 1955, 5, 203–214. (D_c)

Koestler, A. *The act of creation.* London: Hutchinson, 1964. (Also: New York: Dell, 1964.) (T)

Kolaja, J. American magazine cartoons and social control. *Journalism Quarterly*, 1953, 30, 71–74. (D_c)

Kole, T., & Henderson, H. L. Cartoon reaction scale with special reference to driving behavior. *Journal of Applied Psychology*, 1966, 50, 311–316. (M, D_c, S)

Koppel, M. A., & Sechrest, L. A multitrait–multimethod matrix analysis of sense of humor. *Educational & Psychological Measurement*, 1970, 30, 77–85. (M, D_c, S)

Kreitler, H., & Kreitler, S. Dependence of laughter on cognitive strategies. *Merrill–Palmer Quarterly*, 1970, 16, 163–177. (D_c, Ch, S)

Kris, E. Ego development and the comic. *International Journal of Psychoanalysis*, 1938, 19, 77–90. (T, F, Ch)

Kris, E. Laughter as an expressive process. *International Journal of Psychoanalysis*, 1940, 21, 314–341. (T)

Kris, E. *Psychoanalytic explorations of art.* New York: International Univ. Press, 1952. (T)

Kris, E., & Gombrich, E. The principles of caricature. *British Journal of Medical Psychology*, 1938, 17, 319–342. (T)

Kubie, L. S. The destructive potential of humor in psychotherapy. *American Journal of Psychiatry*, 1971, 127, 861–866. (F)

La Fave, L. Comment on Priest's article: Election jokes: The effects of reference group membership. *Psychological Reports*, 1967, 20, 305–306. (G)

Laffal, J., Levine, J., & Redlich, F. C. An anxiety reduction theory of humor. *American Psychologist*, 1953, 8, 383. (T)

La Gaipa, J. J. Stress, authoritarianism, and the enjoyment of different kinds of hostile humor. *Journal of Psychology*, 1968, 70, 3–8. (D_x, S)

Laing, A. The sense of humor in childhood and adolescence. *British Journal of Educational Psychology*, 1939, 9, 201. (D_c, Ch)

Lamb, C. W. Personality correlates of humor enjoyment following motivational arousal. *Journal of Personality and Social Psychology*, 1968, 9, 237–241. (D_x, S)

Landis, C., & Ross, J. Humor and its relation to other personality traits. *Journal of Social Psychology*, 1933, 4, 158–175. (D_c)

Landy, D., & Mettee, D. Evaluation of an aggressor as a function of exposure to cartoon humor. *Journal of Personality & Social Psychology*, 1969, 12, 66–71. (D_x, S)

Lauter, P. *Theories of comedy.* Garden City, New York: Doubleday, 1964. (R)

Leacock, S. B. *Humor: Its theory and technique.* New York: Dodd, Mead, 1935. (G)

Leacock, S. B. *Humour and humanity.* London: Butterworth, 1937. (G)

Lee, J. C., & Griffith, R. M. Time error in the judgment of humor. *Psychological Reports*, 1962, 11, 410. (D_c, S)

Lee, J. C., & Griffith, R. M. Forgetting jokes: A function of repression? *Journal of Individual Psychology,* 1963, **19**, 213–215. (D_x, S)

Legman, G. *Rationale of the dirty joke.* New York: Grove, 1968. (T)

Leuba, C. Tickling and laughter. *Journal of Genetic Psychology,* 1941, **58**, 201–209. (Ch, D_c)

Leventhal, H., & Mace, W. The effect of laughter on evaluation of a slapstick movie. *Journal of Personality,* 1970, **38**, 16–30. (D_x, Ch, S)

Levin, M. Wit and schizophrenic thinking. *American Journal of Psychiatry,* 1957, **113**, 917–923.

Levine, J. Responses to humor. *Scientific American,* 1956, **194**(2) 31–35. (M, G)

Levine, J. Regression in primitive clowning. *Psychoanalytic Quarterly,* 1961, **30**, 72–83. (T)

Levine, J. Humor and mental health. In A. Deutsch & H. Fishman (Eds.), *Encyclopedia of mental health,* Vol. 3. 1963. (R)

Levine, J. Humor and play in sports. In R. Slovenko & J. A. Knight (Eds.), *Motivation in play, games and sports.* Springfield, Illinois: Thomas, 1967. (F, Ch, G)

Levine, J. Humor. In D. L. Sills (Ed.), *International encyclopedia of the social sciences.* Vol. 7. New York: Macmillan, 1968. (R)

Levine, J. (Ed.) *Motivation in humor.* New York: Atherton, 1969. (R)

Levine, J., & Abelson, R. Humor as a disturbing stimulus. *Journal of General Psychology,* 1959, **60**, 191–200. (D_c, S)

Levine, J., & Rakusin, J. The sense of humor of college students and psychiatric patients. *Journal of General Psychology,* 1959, **60**, 183–190. (D_c, S)

Levine, J., & Redlich, F. C. Failure to understand humor. *Psychoanalytic Quarterly,* 1955, **24**, 560–572. (T)

Levine, J., & Redlich, F. C. Intellectual and emotional factors in the appreciation of humor. *Journal of General Psychology,* 1960, **62**, 25–35. (D_c, S)

Lindeman, H. Humor in politics and society. *Impact of Science on Society,* 1969, **19**, 269–278. (G)

Lloyd, E. L. The respiratory mechanism in laughter. *Journal of Genetic Psychology,* 1938, **10**, 179–189. (D_c)

Lloyd, J. A. T. Humour and mechanism. *Fortnightly Review,* 1922, **118**, 244–254. (T)

Lowenthal, M. M. The laughter of detachment. *Dial,* 1919, **66**, 133–135.

Luborsky, L., & Cattell, R. The validation of personality factors in humor. *Journal of Personality,* 1947, **15**, 283–291. (M, D_c)

Ludovici, A. M. *The secret of laughter.* London: Constable Press, 1932. (T, G)

Lull, P. E. The effects of humor in persuasive speech. *Speech Monographs,* 1940, **7**, 26–40. (D_x)

Lundberg, C. Person-focused joking: Pattern and function. *Human Organization,* 1969, **28**, 22–28. (D_c, F)

Maier, N. R. F. A Gestalt theory of humour. *British Journal of Psychology,* 1932, **23**, 69–74. (T)

Main, D. C., & Schillace, R. J. Aversive stimulation and the laughter response. *Psychonomic Science,* 1968, **13**, 241. (D_x, S)

Malpass, L. F., & Fitzpatrick, E. D. Social facilitation as a factor in relation to humor. *Journal of Social Psychology,* 1959, **50**, 295–303. (D_c, S)

Martin, L. J. Psychology of aesthetics: Experimental prospecting in the field of the comic. *American Journal of Psychology,* 1905, **16**, 35–116. (D_x)

Martineau, W. H. A model for a theory of the function of humor. *Research Reports in the Social Sciences,* 1967, **1**, 51–64. (F, T)

McComas, H. C. The origin of laughter. *Psychological Review,* 1923, **30**, 45–55. (T, F)

McConnell, J. Confessions of a scientific humorist. *Impact of Science on Society,* 1969, 19, 241–251.   (G)

McDougall, W. The theory of laughter. *Nature,* 1903, 67, 318–319.   (T)

McDougall, W. A new theory of laughter. *Psyche,* 1922, 2.   (T)

McDougall, W. Why do we laugh? *Scribners,* 1922, 71, 359–363.   (T)

McDougall, W. New light on laughter. *Fortnightly Review,* 1937, 148, 312–320.

McGhee, P. E. Cognitive development and children's comprehension of humor. *Child Development,* 1971, 42, 123–138.   (D_c, Ch, S)

McGhee, P. E. The development of the humor response: A review of the literature. *Psychological Bulletin,* 1971, 76, 328–348.   (R, Ch)

McGhee, P. E. The role of operational thinking in children's comprehension and appreciation of humor. *Child Development,* 1971, 42, 733–744.   (D_c, Ch, S)

Meerloo, J. A. M. The biology of laughter. *Psychoanalytic Review,* 1966, 53, 189–208.   (G)

Mendel, W. M. (Ed.) *A celebration of laughter.* Los Angeles: Mara Books, 1970.   (R, T)

Menon, V. K. *A theory of laughter.* London: Allen & Unwin, 1931.   (T)

Middleton, R. Negro and white reactions to racial humor. *Sociometry,* 1959, 22, 175–183.   (D_c, F)

Middleton, R., & Moland, J. Humor in Negro and white subcultures: A study of jokes among university students. *American Sociological Review,* 1959, 24, 61–69.   (D_c, F)

Mikes, G. *Humour in memoriam.* London: Routledge & Kegan Paul, 1970.   (G)

Miller, F. C. Humor in a Chippewa tribal council. *Ethnology,* 1967, 6, 263–271.   (F)

Mindess, H. *Laughter and Liberation.* Los Angeles: Nash, 1971.   (T, F)

Mones, L. Intelligence and a sense of humor. *Journal of Exceptional Child Psychology,* 1939, 5, 150–153.   (M, F)

Monro, D. H. *Argument of laughter,* Melbourne: Melbourne Univ. Press, 1951.   (R, T, F)

More, D. M., & Roberts, A. F. Societal variations in humor responses to cartoons. *Journal of Social Psychology,* 1957, 45, 233–243.   (D_c, S)

Morrison, J. A. A note concerning investigations on the constancy of audience laughter. *Sociometry,* 1940, 3, 179–185.   (D_c)

Mull, H. K. A study of humor in music. *American Journal of Psychology,* 1949, 62, 560–566.   (D_c)

Murray, H. A. Mirth response to aggressive jokes as a manifestation of aggressive disposition. *Journal of Abnormal & Social Psychology,* 1934, 29, 66–81.   (D_c)

Mussen, P., & Rutherford, E. Effects of aggressive cartoons on children's aggressive play. *Journal of Abnormal & Social Psychology,* 1961, 62, 461–464.   (D_x, Ch, S)

Muthayya, B. C., & Mallikarjunan, M. A measure of humour and its relation to intelligence. *Journal of Psychological Researches,* 1969, 13, 101–105.   (D_c, M)

Nerhardt, G. Humor and inclination to laugh: Emotional reactions to stimuli of different divergence from a range of expectancy. *Scandinavian Journal of Psychology,* 1970, 11, 185–195.   (D_x, T, S)

Nevo, R. Toward a theory of comedy. *Journal of Aesthetics & Art Criticism,* 1963, 21, 328ff.   (T)

Nussbaum, K., & Michaux, W. W. Response to humor in depression: A predictor and evaluator of patient change? *Psychiatric Quarterly,* 1963, 37, 527–539.   (D_c, S)

Oberndorf, C. P. Kidding. *International Journal of Psychoanalysis,* 1932, 13, 479.   (G)

Obrdlik, A. J. "Gallows humor"—A sociological phenomenon. *American Journal of Sociology,* 1942, 47, 709–716.   (F)

O'Connell, W. E. The adaptive functions of wit and humor. *Journal of Abnormal & Social Psychology,* 1960, 61, 263–270.   (D_c, F, S)

O'Connell, W. E. An item analysis of the wit and humor appreciation test. *Journal of Social Psychology*, 1962, 56, 271–276. (M, D$_c$, S)

O'Connell, W. E. Multidimensional investigation of Freudian humor. *Psychiatric Quarterly*, 1964, 38, 1–12. (D$_c$, M, S)

O'Connell, W. E. Resignation, humor and wit. *Psychoanalytic Review*, 1964, 51, 49–56. (D$_c$, S)

O'Connell, W. E. Humor of the gallows. *Omega*, 1966, 1, 32–33. (G)

O'Connell, W. E. Humor and death. *Psychological Reports*, 1968, 22, 391–402. (D$_c$, S)

O'Connell, W. E. Creativity in humor. *Journal of Social Psychology*, 1969, 78, 237–241. (D$_c$, S)

O'Connell, W. E. Humor: The therapeutic impasse. *Voices*, 1969, 5(2), 25–27. (G)

O'Connell, W. E. The social aspects of wit and humor. *Journal of Social Psychology*, 1969, 79, 183–187. (D$_c$)

O'Connell, W. E., & Covert, C. Death attitudes and humor appreciation among medical students. *Existential Psychiatry*, 1967, 6, 433–442. (D$_c$)

O'Connell, W. E., & Cowgill, S. Wit, humor, and defensiveness. *Newsletter for Research in Psychology*, 1970, 12, 32–33. (D$_c$)

O'Connell, W. E., & Peterson, P. Humor and repression. *Journal of Existential Psychiatry*, 1964, 4, 309–316. (D$_c$, S)

O'Connell, W. E., Rothaus, P., Hanson, P. G., & Moyer, R. Jest appreciation in leaderless groups. *International Journal of Group Psychotherapy*, 1969, 19, 454–462. (D$_c$, F, S)

Omwake, L. A study of sense of humor: Its relation to sex, age and personal characteristics. *Journal of Applied Psychology*, 1937, 21, 688–704. (D$_c$)

Omwake, L. Factors influencing the sense of humor. *Journal of Social Psychology*, 1939, 10, 94–104. (D$_c$)

Omwake, L. Humor in the making. *Journal of Social Psychology*, 1942, 15, 265–279.

Paskind, H. A. Effect of laughter on muscle tone. *Archives of Neurology & Psychiatry*, 1932, 28, 623–628. (D$_c$)

Perl, R. E. The influence of a social factor upon the appreciation of humor. *American Journal of Psychology*, 1933, 45, 308–312. (D$_c$, F)

Perl, R. E. A review of experiments on humor. *Psychological Bulletin*, 1933, 30, 752–763. (R, Ch)

Peto, E. Weeping and laughing. *International Journal of Psychoanalysis*, 1946, 27, 129–133. (F)

Piddington, R. *The psychology of laughter: A study in social adaptation.* London: Figurehead, 1933. (Reissued: New York: Gamut Press, 1963.) (T, R)

Pines, L. N. Laughter as an equivalent of epilepsy. *Soviet Psychology and Psychiatry*, 1964, 2, 33–38. (T)

Plessner, H. *Laughter and crying: A study of border situations of human behavior.* Arnheim, Netherlands: 1941. (G)

Pokorny, G. F., & Gruner, C. R. An experimental study of the effect of satire used as support in a persuasive speech. *Western Speech*, 1969, 33, 204–211. (D$_x$, F, S)

Priest, R. F. Election jokes: The effects of reference group membership. *Psychological Reports*, 1966, 18, 600–602. (D$_c$, F)

Priest, R. F., & Abrahams, J. Candidate preferences and hostile humor in the 1968 elections. *Psychological Reports*, 1970, 26, 779–783. (D$_c$, S)

Radcliffe-Brown, A. R. On joking relationships. *Africa*, 1940, 13, 195–210. (F)

Radcliffe-Brown, A. R. A further note on joking relationships. *Africa*, 1949, 19, 133–140. (F)

Raley, A. L., & Ballman, C. Theoretical implications for a psychology of the ludicrous. *Journal of Social Psychology*, 1957, 45, 19–23. (D$_C$, Ch, S)

Rapp, A. Towards an eclectic and multilateral theory of laughter and humor. *Journal of General Psychology*, 1947, 36, 207–219. (R, Ch, F)

Rapp, A. A phylogenetic theory of wit and humor. *Journal of Social Psychology*, 1949, 30, 81–96. (T)

Rapp, A. *The origins of wit and humor.* New York: Dutton, 1951. (R, G)

Redlich, F. C. Intellectual and emotional factors in appreciation of humor. *Journal of General Psychology*, 1960, 62, 25–35. (D$_C$)

Redlich, F. C., Levine, J., & Sohler, T. P. A mirth response test: Preliminary report on a psychodiagnostic technique utilizing dynamics of humor. *American Journal of Orthopsychiatry*, 1951, 21, 717–734. (M, D$_C$)

Reich, A. The structure of the grotesque—Comic sublimation. *Bulletin of the Menninger Clinic*, 1949, 13, 160–171. (F)

Reik, T. Freud and Jewish wit. *Psychoanalysis*, 1954, 2, 12–20. (F)

Reik, T. *Jewish wit.* New York: Gamut Press, 1962. (T, G)

Repplier, A. *In pursuit of laughter.* Boston: Houghton, 1936. (G)

Roberts, A. F., & Johnson, D. M. Some factors related to the perception of funniness in humor stimuli. *Journal of Social Psychology*, 1957, 46, 57–63. (D$_C$, S)

Roeckelein, J. E. Auditory stimulation and cartoon ratings. *Perceptual & Motor Skills*, 1969, 29, 772. (D$_X$)

Rosen, V. Varieties of comic caricature, and their relationship to obsessive compulsive phenomena. *Journal of the American Psychoanalytic Association*, 1963, 11, 704–724. (F)

Rosenwald, G. C. The relation of drive discharge to the enjoyment of humor. *Journal of Personality*, 1964, 32, 682–697. (D$_C$, S)

Roubicek, J. Laughter in epilepsy, with some general introductory notes. *Journal of Mental Science*, 1946, 92, 734–755.

Rourke, C. *American humor: A study of national character.* New York: Harcourt, 1931. (G)

Saenger, G. Male and female relations in the American comic strip. *Public Opinion Quarterly*, 1955, 19, 195–205. (D$_C$)

San Francisco Public Library. *Catalog of the Schmulowitz collection of wit and humor.* San Francisco: 1962. (R)

Schachter, S., & Wheeler, L. Epinephrine, chlorpromazine, and amusement. *Journal of Abnormal & Social Psychology*, 1962, 65, 121–128. (D$_X$, S)

Scheerer, M. An aspect of the psychology of humor. *Bulletin of the Menninger Clinic*, 1966, 30, 86–97. (T, G)

Schiller, P. A configurational theory of puzzles and jokes. *Journal of Genetic Psychology*, 1938, 18, 217–234. (T)

Senf, R., Huston, P. E., & Cohen, B. D. The use of comic cartoons for the study of social comprehension in schizophrenia. *American Journal of Psychiatry*, 1956, 113, 45–51. (D$_X$, S)

Seward, S. S., Jr. *The paradox of the ludicrous.* Stanford, California: Stanford Univ. Press, 1930. (G)

Sewell, E. *The field of nonsense.* London: Chatto & Windus, 1952. (G)

Shaffer, L. F. *Children's interpretations of cartoons.* Teachers College Contributions to Education. 1930, No. 429. (D$_C$, Ch)

Shapiro, E., Biber, B., & Minichin, P. The cartoon situations test: A semi-structured technique for assessing aspects of personality pertinent to the teaching process. *Journal of Projective Techniques*, 1957, 21, 172–184. (M, D$_C$)

Sharman, A. "Joking" in Padhola: Categorical relationships, choice and social control. *Man,* 1969, 4, 103–117. (F)

Shaw, F. J. Laughter: Paradigm of growth. *Journal of Individual Psychology,* 1960, 16, 151–157. (T)

Shurcliff, A. Judged humor, arousal, and the relief theory. *Journal of Personality & Social Psychology,* 1968, 8, 360–363. (D_X, S)

Sidis, B. *The psychology of laughter.* New York: Appleton, 1913. (G)

Simmons, D. C. Protest humor: Folkloristic reaction to prejudice. *American Journal of Psychiatry,* 1963, 120, 567–570. (G)

Singer, D. L. Aggression arousal, hostile humor, catharsis. *Journal of Personality and Social Psychology,* 1968, 8, (1, Pt. 2), 1–14. (D_X, S)

Singer, D. L., Gollob, H. F., & Levine, J. Mobilization of inhibition and the enjoyment of aggressive humor. *Journal of Personality,* 1967, 35, 562–569. (D_X, S)

Skeels, D. The function of humor in three Nez Perce Indian myths. *American Imago,* 1954, 11, 294–361. (F)

Smith, E. E., & Goodchilds, J. D. Characteristics of the witty group member: The wit as leader. *American Psychologist,* 1959, 14, 375–376. (D_C, S)

Smith, E. E., & Goodchilds, J. D. The wit in large and small established groups. *Psychological Reports,* 1963, 13, 273–274. (D_C, S)

Smith, E. E., & White, H. L. Wit, creativity and sarcasm. *Journal of Applied Psychology,* 1965, 49, 131–134. (D_X, F, S)

Smith, N. V., & Vinacke, W. E. Reactions to humorous stimuli of different generations of Japanese, Chinese, and Caucasians in Hawaii. *Journal of Social Psychology,* 1951, 34, 69–96. (D_C, F, S)

Smith, R. E., Ascough, J. C., Ettinger, R. F., & Nelson, D. A. Humor, anxiety, and task performance. *Journal of Personality & Social Psychology,* 1971, 19, 243–246. (D_X)

Sperling, S. J. On the psychodynamics of teasing. *Journal of the American Psychoanalytic Association,* 1953, 3, 458–483. (F)

Spiegel, D., Brodkin, S. G., & Keith-Spiegel, P. Unacceptable impulses, anxiety and the appreciation of cartoons. *Journal of Projective Techniques & Personality Assessment,* 1969, 33, 154–159. (D_C)

Spiegel, D., Keith-Spiegel, P., Abrahams, J., & Kranitz, L. Humor and suicide: Favorite jokes of suicidal patients. *Journal of Consulting and Clinical Psychology,* 1969, 33, 504–505. (D_C)

Spiegelman, M., Terwilliger, C., & Fearing, F. The content of comics. *Journal of Social Psychology,* 1953, 37, 189ff. (D_C, S)

Starer, E. Reactions of psychiatric patients to cartoons and verbal jokes. *Journal of General Psychology,* 1961, 65, 301–304. (D_C, F, S)

Stephenson, R. M. Conflict and control functions of humor. *American Journal of Sociology,* 1951, 56, 569–574. (F)

Strickland, J. F. The effect of motivational arousal on humor preferences. *Journal of Abnormal & Social Psychology,* 1959, 59, 278–281. (D_X, S)

Strother, G. B., Barnett, M., & Apostolakos, P. C. The use of cartoons as a projective device. *Journal of Clinical Psychology,* 1954, 10, 38–42. (M, D_C)

Stuart, I. R. Inconography of group personality dynamics: Caricatures and cartoons. *Journal of Social Psychology,* 1964, 64, 147–156. (D_C)

Stuart, I. R. Primary and secondary process as reflections of catastrophe: The political cartoon as an instrument of group emotional dynamics. *Journal of Social Psychology,* 1964, 64, 231–239. (D_C, S)

Stump, N. F. Sense of humor and its relationship to personality, scholastic aptitude, emotional maturity, height, and weight. *Journal of General Psychology*, 1939, 20, 25–32. (D$_c$)

Sully, J. Prolegomena to a theory of laughter. *Philosophical Review*, 1900, 9, 365–383. (T)

Sully, J. *Essay on laughter*. New York: Longmans, Green, 1902. (T)

Summo, A. J. Humor in review. *Journal of Social Therapy*, 1958, 4, 201–208. (R)

Swabey, M. C. *Comic laughter: A philosophical essay*. New Haven: Yale Univ. Press, 1961. (R, T, F)

Sykes, A. J. M. Joking relationships in an industrial setting. *American Anthropologist*, 1966, 68, 188–193. (D$_c$)

Sypher, W. (Ed.) *Comedy*. Garden City, New York: Doubleday, 1956. (T)

Tarachow, S. Remarks on the comic process and beauty. *Psychoanalytic Quarterly*, 1949, 18, 215–226. (T)

Taylor, P. M. The effectiveness of humor in informative speaking. *Central States Speech Journal*, 1964, 15, 295–296. (D$_x$)

Thomas, D. R., Shea, J. D., & Rigby, R. G. Conservatism and response to sexual humor. *British Journal of Social & Clinical Psychology*, 1971, 10, 185–186. (D$_c$)

Thorndike, R. L., & Stein, S. An evaluation of the attempts to measure social intelligence. *Psychological Bulletin*, 1937, 34, 275–285. (D$_c$)

Tollefson, D. L., & Cattell, R. B. *Handbook for the IPAT humor test of personality*. Champaign, Illinois: Institute for Personality and Ability Testing, 1963. (M, D$_c$)

Treadwell, Y. Bibliography of empirical studies of wit and humor. *Psychological Reports*, 1967, 20, 1079–1083. (R)

Treadwell, Y. Humor and creativity. *Psychological Reports*, 1970, 26, 55–58. (D$_c$, S)

Ullmann, L. P., & Lim, D. T. Case history material as a source of the identification of patterns of response to emotional stimuli in a study of humor. *Journal of Consulting Psychology*, 1962, 26, 221–225. (D$_c$, M, S)

Verinis, J. S. Inhibition of humor: Differential effects with traditional diagnostic categories. *Journal of General Psychology*, 1970, 82, 157–163. (D$_c$, S)

Verinis, J. S. Inhibition of humor enjoyment: Effects of sexual content and introversion–extraversion. *Psychological Reports*, 1970, 26, 167–170. (D$_c$, S)

Victoroff, D. New approaches to the psychology of humor. *Impact of Science on Society*, 1969, 19, 291–298. (G)

Walker, M. A., & Washburn, M. F. The Healy–Fernald picture completion test as a test of the perception of the comic. *American Journal of Psychology*, 1919, 30, 304–307. (D$_c$, Ch)

Wallis, W. D. Why do we laugh? *Scientific Monthly*, 1922, 15, 343–347.

Walsh, J. J. *Laughter and health*. New York: Appleton, 1928. (G)

Washburn, R. W. A study of the smiling and laughing of infants in the first year of life. *Genetic Psychology Monographs*, 1929, 6 (5, 6), 397–535. (D$_c$, Ch, R, M)

Wells, R. E. A study of tastes in humorous literature among pupils of junior and senior high schools. *Journal of Educational Research*, 1934, 28, 81–91. (D$_c$, Ch)

Williams, C., & Cole, D. L. The influence of experimentally induced inadequacy feelings upon the appreciation of humor. *Journal of Social Psychology*, 1964, 64, 113–117. (D$_x$, S)

Williams, J. M. An experimental and theoretical study of humor in children. *British Journal of Educational Psychology*, 1946, 16, 43–44. (D$_c$, Ch)

Willmann, J. M. An analysis of humor and laughter. *American Journal of Psychology*, 1940, 53, 70–85. (T)

Wilson, G. D., & Patterson, J. R. Conservatism as a predictor of humor preferences. *Journal of Consulting & Clinical Psychology*, 1969, 33, 271–274. (D$_C$)

Wilson, K. M. Sense of humor. *Contemporary Review*, 1927, 131, 628–633.

Winick, C. Space jokes as indication of attitudes toward space. *Journal of Social Issues*, 1961, 27, 43–49. (F)

Winterstein, A. Contributions to the problem of humor. *Psychoanalytic Quarterly*, 1934, 3, 303–316.

Wolfenstein, M. A phase in the development of children's sense of humor. *Psychoanalytic Study of the Child*, 1951, 7, 336–350. (Ch, F)

Wolfenstein, M. Children's understanding of jokes. *Psychoanalytic Study of the Child*, 1953, 9, 162–173. (T, D$_C$, Ch, F)

Wolfenstein, M. *Children's humor.* Glencoe, Illinois: Free Press, 1954. (T, D$_C$, Ch, F)

Wolff, H. A., Smith, C. E., & Murray, H. A. The psychology of humor. I. A study of responses to race-disparagement jokes. *Journal of Abnormal & Social Psychology*, 1934, 28, 341–365. (D$_C$)

Worthen, R., & O'Connell, W. E. Social interest and humor. *International Journal of Social Psychiatry*, 1969, 15, 179–188. (D$_C$)

Wynn-Jones, L. The appreciation of wit. *Reports of the British Association for the Advancement of Science*, 1927, 373. (D$_C$)

Yarnold, J. K., & Berkeley, M. H. An analysis of the Cattell–Luborsky humor test into homogeneous scales. *Journal of Abnormal & Social Psychology*, 1954, 49, 543–546. (M, D$_C$)

Young, P. T. Laughing and weeping, cheerfulness and depression: A study of moods among college students. *Journal of Social Psychology*, 1937, 8, 311–334. (D$_C$)

Young, R. D., & Frye, M. Some are laughing, some are not: Why? *Psychological Reports*, 1966, 18, 747–755. (D$_X$, S)

Zenner, W. Joking and ethnic stereotyping. *Anthropological Quarterly*, 1970, 43, 93–113. (D$_C$, G, S)

Zigler, E., Levine, J., & Gould, L. Cognitive processes in the development of children's appreciation of humor. *Child Development*, 1966, 37, 507–518. (D$_C$, Ch, S)

Zigler, E., Levine, J., & Gould, L. The humor response of normal, institutionalized retarded, and noninstitutionalized retarded children. *American Journal of Mental Deficiency*, 1966, 71, 472–480. (D$_C$, Ch, S)

Zigler, E., Levine, J., & Gould, L. Cognitive challenge as a factor in children's humor appreciation. *Journal of Personality and Social Psychology*, 1967, 6, 332–336. (D$_C$, Ch, S)

Ziller, R. C., Behringer, R. D., & Goodchilds, J. D. Group creativity under conditions of success or failure and variations in group stability. *Journal of Applied Psychology*, 1962, 46, 43–49. (D$_X$)

Zippin, D. Sex differences and the sense of humor. *Psychoanalytic Review*, 1966, 53, 209–219.

Zuk, G. H. A further study of laughter in family therapy. *Family Process*, 1964, 3, 77–89. (D$_C$)

Zuk, G. H. On the theory and pathology of laughter in psychotherapy. *Psychotherapy: Theory, Research and Practice*, 1966, 3, 97–101. (F)

Zuk, G. H., Boszormenyi-Nagy, I., & Heiman, E. Some dynamics of laughter during family therapy. *Family Process*, 1963, 2, 302–314. (D$_C$)

Zwerling, I. The favorite joke in diagnostic and therapeutic interviewing. *Psychoanalytic Quarterly*, 1955, 24, 104–114. (D$_C$)

Acknowledgment

We would like to thank Susan Anthony and Karen Karp Miller for their assistance on this project. Partial support for the compilation of this bibliography was provided by a grant from the National Institute of Mental Health (MH15667), T. C. Brock, Principal Investigator.

Author Index

Numbers in italics refer to the pages on which the complete references are listed.

Subject Index